CHAOS, VIOLENCE, DYNASTY

Central Eurasia in Context
Douglas Northrop, Editor

CHAOS, VIOLENCE, DYNASTY

Politics and Islam in Central Asia

ERIC McGLINCHEY

UNIVERSITY OF PITTSBURGH PRESS

Published by the University of Pittsburgh Press, Pittsburgh, Pa., 15260
Copyright © 2011, University of Pittsburgh Press
All rights reserved
Manufactured in the United States of America
Printed on acid-free paper
10 9 8 7 6 5 4 3 2 1

Some material appearing in chapters 1 and 3 and the conclusion is an expansion
of an abbreviated analysis first published as "Exploring Regime Instability and
Ethnic Violence in Kyrgyzstan" in *Asia Policy* 12 (July 2011).

Library of Congress Cataloging-in-Publication Data

McGlinchey, Eric Max, 1973-
 Chaos, violence, and dynasty : politics and Islam in Central Asia / Eric
McGlinchey.
    p. cm. — (Central Eurasia in context)
 Includes bibliographical references and index.
 ISBN 978-0-8229-6168-0 (pbk. : alk. paper)
 1. Asia, Central—Politics and government. 2. Authoritarianism—Asia,
Central. 3. Democracy—Asia, Central. 4. Islam and politics—Asia, Central. 5.
Islam and state—Asia, Central. 6. Comparative government—Case studies. I.
Title.
 JQ1080.M35 2011
 320.958—dc23   2011020878

To Carrie

Contents

Preface

MINE IS NOT the first study of post-Soviet Central Asian politics. I have benefited greatly from first-generation comparativists who blazed paths intellectually and, no less important, institutionally in their study of post-Soviet regime change. That I break from many of these scholars and, rather than focusing on transition and democratization, explore those causal factors that produce substantive variations in patronage politics does not mean that I reject the many valuable insights these scholars have offered. In chapter 1, I explore these insights in greater detail and offer my alternative approach to post-Soviet Central Asian regime change. Chapter 2 turns to the Soviet patronage model and its evolution from Lenin to Gorbachev. Here I begin with the perennial challenge confronting Central Asia's would-be rulers: establishing centralized control in distant lands. A key insight that emerges from chapter 2's analysis of governance and attempted governance in Central Asia is that attempts at transformative rule—from Stalin's attempt to create a "surrogate proletariat" through unveiling campaigns to Khrushchev's attempts to transform Central Asian agriculture through the so-called Virgin Lands program—have either failed or have been prohibitively costly. In contrast, less interventionist policies of patronage politics and proxy rule, strategies Lenin and Brezhnev pursued, met with comparative success.

This pattern of success and failure held for Gorbachev as well. His attempts to transform Central Asia during the early perestroika years brought Moscow little increased leverage. Critically important for the future of Central Asia, though,

Gorbachev's interventions—and in the case of Kyrgyzstan, noninterventions—did prompt the emergence of markedly different patterns of elite unity and disunity in Kazakhstan, Kyrgyzstan, and Uzbekistan. Perestroika unsettled state and society relations in all three Soviet republics in the late 1980s, and tragically the economic uncertainties that perestroika produced led to deadly ethnic riots in Kazakhstan (1986), Uzbekistan (1989), and Kyrgyzstan (1990). The Central Communist Party leadership cleaned up the mess it created in Kazakhstan and Uzbekistan, carefully choreographing Nursultan Nazarbaev's and Islam Karimov's replacement of perestroika figureheads and the return to indigenized Central Asian rule. Gorbachev and the Communist Party, for reasons that had little to do with Central Asia, did not step in to manage Kyrgyzstan's leadership crisis in 1990. This decision led to the fragmentation of the Kyrgyz political elite—a legacy that continues to shape governance in Kyrgyzstan today.

The Kyrgyz, Uzbek, and Kazakh case studies in chapters 3, 4, and 5 respectively explore how these inherited patterns of elite unity and disunity have fared in the post-Soviet context. Chapter 3 demonstrates how Kyrgyzstan's inherited legacy of a small and fragmented political elite has led to political chaos and executive turnover. Chapter 3 also explores why, despite the relative ease with which the Kyrgyz political elite can overthrow the executive, President Askar Akaev was able to hold on to power for fifteen years, while his successor, President Kurmanbek Bakiev, was ousted after only five years. I argue that the shifting nature of financial flows to Kyrgyzstan has played a critical role in shaping variations in executive tenure. Before 2001 the bulk of resources available to the Kyrgyz executive came from international aid. Critically, Akaev could not readily capture this aid. What he could do, though, was place his supporters in positions of power—in ministries and organizations that were the targets of international aid—so that these supporters in turn might benefit from foreign assistance. Paradoxically, this diffuse nature of economic and political reform aid to Kyrgyzstan helped Akaev maintain authoritarian rule throughout the 1990s. Following the post–September 11, 2001, opening of the U.S. air base just outside the Kyrgyz capital, however, the executive suddenly had access to readily exploitable economic rents—to lucrative fuel supply contracts that he and his family could control. Akaev, and later Bakiev, began outright expropriating these new U.S. government financial flows to Kyrgyzstan, and this brazen expropriation was met with elite revolt.

As I argue in chapters 4 and 5, Uzbek and Kazakh elites are considerably less likely to challenge executive authority than are their counterparts in Kyrgyzstan. This comparative Uzbek and Kazakh elite passivity owes directly to the fact that Karimov and Nazarbaev, in contrast to Akaev, began the post-Soviet period with large and united pro-presidential parties. Mobilizing effective collective action given the nature of these inherited Uzbek and Kazakh elite institutions is considerably more difficult than organizing effective collective action in Kyrgyzstan. That said, the Uzbek and Kazakh polities do exhibit important differences. State and society relations in Uzbekistan have proven considerably more violent than in Kazakhstan. The driving cause behind this variation in state violence, I argue, lies in the differing economic resources available to ruling executives.

Thus, although Uzbek president Karimov has enjoyed sufficient resources to maintain coercive capacity, he has struggled to provide the same degree of public goods that Uzbeks had enjoyed during the Soviet period. Other institutions, most notably local Muslim charities and businesses, now deliver the goods the Uzbek state does not. As the events in Andijan have illustrated, Karimov perceives these Muslim institutions as threats to his authority. As a result, he brutally suppresses them. Kazakh president Nazarbaev's stunning oil wealth, in contrast, has allowed him to maintain the Soviet social contract while ensuring the continued passivity of the Kazakh population. Nazarbaev does face one considerable challenge—the question of leadership succession. As I present in chapter 5, unless Nazarbaev establishes clear rules of leadership succession, growing uncertainty over who will be Kazakhstan's next president may prompt Kazakh elites to recalculate the costs and benefits of loyalty to and defection from Nazarbaev's thus far stable ruling coalition. This changing calculus of loyalty and defection could lead to the fragmentation of the now united Kazakh ruling elite and the end of Kazakh political stability.

The conclusion explores the insights this book offers not only for our understanding of Central Asia and political transition, but also for how foreign governments and international organizations might more productively engage polities struggling with the pathologies of patronage politics. Thus far, foreign engagement of Central Asian states, particularly the engagement of Central Asian states by Western governments and nongovernmental organizations (NGOs), has failed to encourage political reform. Moreover, for the local Central Asian partners of Western governments and NGOs, democracy promotion has often proven disastrous at the personal level. The journalist Alisher Saipov had funded his reporting, before his murder, with a grant from the National Endowment for Democracy. The human rights defender Umida Niyazova, now fortunately abroad after enduring prison and a Stalin-like show trial in Uzbekistan, had worked for Human Rights Watch. Ravshan Halmatov and Tulkun Karaev, two other Uzbek human rights activists now in exile, had partnered with Freedom House, and Karaev had hosted the U.S. ambassador to Uzbekistan during the ambassador's trip to Qarshi in February 2002.

Saipov, Niyazova, Halmatov, and Karaev may all have pursued their activism with or without Western financial and institutional support. Their strategies— that is, the methods they applied in pressing for political reform—very much follow the deterministic logic embedded in the democratizations and transitions literatures. These literatures, though well meaning, are poor fits for the Central Asia case. As such, I close this book with a plea for incrementalism. Most likely Uzbekistan will not become democratic in the next decade, and neither for that matter will Kyrgyzstan or Kazakhstan. These regimes, however, are not identical. If we can understand that which makes for a more peaceful and prosperous Kazakhstan and a usually peaceful if chaotic Kyrgyzstan, then perhaps Western governments and NGOs can work with local activists to push Uzbekistan away from yet another decade of fear and repression.

A Note on Case Selection, Data, and Methodology

Although I draw on research conducted in Kazakhstan, Kyrgyzstan, and Uzbekistan, compelling studies of regime change could be made using other permutations of the five Central Asian regimes. Tajikistan has wavered between civil war, tenuous political reform, and, most recently, authoritarian retrenchment. Patronage politics in Kyrgyzstan, like politics in Tajikistan, is chaotic yet thus far comparatively peaceful. Uzbekistan and Kazakhstan have remained since the early 1990s steadfastly authoritarian, yet in Uzbekistan this authoritarianism demands relentless repression. In Kazakhstan the patronage machine hums happily along much as it did during the long Brezhnev period. Turkmenistan, lastly, has moved from authoritarianism to a bizarre cult of personality and now back to authoritarianism. All of these countries are patronage-based autocracies. All share the legacy of Soviet rule. Yet each of these countries exhibits diverging patterns of patronage politics.

That I have not included Tajikistan and Turkmenistan in this comparative analysis has more to do with the nature of in-country field research in Central Asia than any concerns that these two countries are somehow inappropriate for the current comparative analysis. Indeed, I anticipate the reader will find that the causal logic I forward as driving variations in Kazakh, Kyrgyz, and Uzbek patronage politics equally applies to the chaos of Tajik politics and the comparative stability of Turkmen autocratic rule. I invite other scholars to explore the Tajik and Turkmen cases. For this book I offer findings based on a decade's work in Kazakhstan, Kyrgyzstan, and Uzbekistan.

I use a mixture of both quantitative and qualitative data in my comparative analysis of political change in Kazakhstan and Kyrgyzstan. Qualitative data come from semistructured interviews and focus groups I have conducted during several extended visits to Kazakhstan, Kyrgyzstan, and Uzbekistan beginning in 1998. Qualitative data sources also include Central Asian and Soviet archives and periodicals. Survey data come from polls from an ongoing National Science Foundation–supported study colleagues and I are conducting that explores the effects of new information communication technologies on state and society in four of the five post-Soviet Central Asian states. Survey data also come from polls conducted by the International Foundation for Electoral Systems (IFES) and the U.S. Agency for International Development (USAID). Scholars can err when applying both qualitative and quantitative research methods. Researchers unfamiliar with local contexts may be swayed by the seeming precision quantitative analysis offers and, as a result, forward findings disconnected from reality. A researcher deeply immersed in the local community he or she is researching might also fail to recognize that the community two towns over exhibits markedly differing perceptions of state and society relations. Pairing surveys with extended field research, I hope, has enabled me to avoid some of the analytical pitfalls any comparative study must confront.

But I did not avoid every pitfall. Police detained me in Bukhara, Uzbekistan, on suspicion of opiates possession. My alleged heroin possession and my fortunately brief detention remain mysteries to me. In Kara Suu, Kyrgyzstan, the local imam, reviewing those in attendance for Friday prayer, mistook me for a Chechen militant—a mistake that many in Central Asia regularly make. More troubling than these minor inconveniences, though, is the reality that colleagues with whom I have worked since the early 2000s have incurred considerable personal costs as a result of their activism. My collaboration with them was by no means the wellspring of their social activism. Nevertheless, the democratization discourse to which I and other researchers and policy makers are party has influenced the strategies Central Asian activists pursue. It is time we acknowledge that in the case of Central Asia, and likely more broadly, the democratization and transitions literatures are flawed in their imagined endpoints. Autocracy and patronage politics will remain in Central Asia for the foreseeable future. As such, rather than searching for the next revolution, scholars and policy makers might productively shift their attention from the daydream of democracy to uncovering and encouraging processes that make autocracies more tolerable and less violent.

Acknowledgments

I write these acknowledgements from Osh, Kyrgyzstan, a city divorced from central government authority, and a city whose population is struggling to recover from deadly riots. My research here and throughout Eurasia would not be possible without my Central Asian colleagues' support. Identifying many of these counterparts by name, I am acutely aware, would jeopardize their already tenuous work and family lives. In deference to these colleagues, I extend my gratitude to collectives rather than to individuals: to friends in Kazakhstan, Kyrgyzstan, and Uzbekistan as well as to mentors at Princeton, Stanford, Iowa State, and George Mason University. The Washington, D.C., area postcommunism academic and policy communities have guided me toward sharpening my analysis as have members of the Program on New Approaches to Research and Security in Eurasia. Several institutions, including the National Science Foundation (Grant #0326101), the National Council for Eurasian and East European Research, the Social Science Research Council, and the International Research and Exchanges Board, funded research leading to this book. My parents sparked my interest in Eurasia, and my partner, Carrie, helps me sustain this interest through our shared love for Central Asian "diskoteka."

CHAOS, VIOLENCE, DYNASTY

Introduction

JOURNALIST ALISHER SAIPOV left his office just before sunset. On a typical day he would be back at his laptop, drinking coffee to the ping of instant messages well into the early morning. Familiar to Western readers for his reporting with *Radio Free Europe*, the online news agency Ferghana.news, and *Voice of America*, Saipov had recently turned his attention to the local audience.[1] His new paper, *Siyosat*, was a hit among the Uzbek-speaking population in his hometown of Osh, Kyrgyzstan. News-starved residents across the border—in the nearby Uzbek cities of Andijan, Fergana, and Namangan—also patiently awaited their copies of the Friday weekly. They are still waiting. Saipov was shot on the night of October 24, 2007. His murderers remain at large. Saipov's life captures the fleeting promise and the enduring challenge post-Soviet Central Asia represents. The promise is that the Saipovs of Central Asia, along with well-intentioned Western counterparts, work tirelessly to reform autocratic rule. The challenge is that Western democracy promotion has yielded little substantive political reform; citizen activism has at best been met with government indifference and at worst with disappearances, torture, and death.

Patronage politics in Central Asia has not budged. It remains entrenched throughout the region. Autocrats—from the presidency to the village administrator—continue to rule at every level of government. Each autocrat presides over his fiefdom and in return for control over this fiefdom, economic rents (that is, licenses to exploit) flow from the top to the bottom while kickbacks flow from the bottom back to the top. Before 1991 political scientists called this system communism or Soviet socialism. Today we call it patrimonialism or neopatrimonialism—depending on whether the patrimonial state in question indeed possesses the "professional military, technocratic administrative staff, and all of the other elements of a comparatively modernized industrial society" to merit the "neo" label.[2] During the Soviet period local autocrats controlled collective farms. Today local autocrats control what are de facto collective farms as well as natural resources, local bazaars, the drug and sex trades, gambling, and construction. Despite grand democratization experiments, patronage remains unchanged. If anything, daily life for many Central Asians has gotten worse.

The fortunes of the average Central Asian autocrat have likewise not improved all that much. Today the journey from boss to bust is short; higher-level bosses regularly replace underlings, and on occasion underlings band together to unseat the alpha autocrat. The disappointing irony of Central Asian autocracy—and in part the explanation for the persistence of this autocracy—is that it is considerably safer to challenge patronage rule the old-fashioned way—by planning a putsch—than it is by publishing a newspaper. It is therefore the Saipovs of Central Asia, the human subjects of Western democratization experiments, who operate outside the patronage pack and challenge hierarchy through transparent means—through the media, through discussions following Friday prayer, through nongovernmental organizations—who find their lives and their dreams of a better future for their children cut short. Strip the Brezhnev patronage machine of centralized party control, add local activists emboldened by a newly arrived global discourse of political and religious freedom, and you have today's Central Asia. In short, you have a political mess or, as one observer put it, you have "Trashcanistan."[3]

Critically, though, and at the heart of this book, the degrees of this current political mess vary. Kyrgyzstan's political mess is one of chaos. In contrast to the heavy-handed rule in neighboring Uzbekistan, Kyrgyz presidents have tended to run from rather than steadfastly repress protesters. President Askar Akaev, facing thousands of angry demonstrators outside his "White House" in March 2005, fled to Moscow. Kyrgyzstan's so-called Tulip Revolution did not substantively alter Kyrgyz politics, however. Just the opposite: for the next five years the patronage machine in Kyrgyzstan sputtered along, enriching its mechanic of the moment, President Kurmanbek "Bucks" Bakiev. In April 2010, though, the same angry crowds, and indeed many of the same political elite that had brought Bakiev to power, crashed the gates of the White House, compelling Kyrgyzstan's second president to flee to Minsk. Perhaps this time Kyrgyzstan watchers will get it right and label these leadership convulsions for what they are: popular putsches rather than democratic revolutions.

Uzbekistan, in contrast to the chaos that exists in Kyrgyzstan, has thus far proven politically stable. This stability has been secured through horrific human cost, however. In May 2005, President Islam Karimov's troops shot and killed hundreds of protestors in the Fergana Valley city of Andijan to ensure Uzbekistan would not play host to the next post-Soviet "color revolution."[4] Karimov got his wish. The Andijan protests did not topple him from power, but they did produce an indelible color: red. "Blood was flowing on the ground," eyewitness Mahbuba Zokirava recounted, going off-script during the October 2005 show trial of the alleged Andijan protest instigators.[5] The blood of Andijan would continue to flow, and beyond the confines of Uzbekistan. In Osh, Kyrgyzstan, journalist Saipov, in addition to bearing witness to the Andijan massacre in the pages of *Siyosat*, organized a safe haven for Andijan refugees. It was this activism, many fear, that pushed the Uzbek president's agents in Kyrgyzstan to move from their steady campaign of intimidating Saipov to murder.[6]

The Kazakh state is neither as sputtering as Kyrgyzstan nor as violent as Uzbekistan. Rather, Kazakhstan's mess is contained to the presidential family. Dynasty, not demonstrators, is what keeps the Kazakh president Nursultan Nazarbaev awake at night. The president's once anticipated successor and now exiled former son-in-law, Rakhat Aliev, provided an unflattering window into the first family's dysfunction in his May 2009 tell-all, *Godfather-in-Law*. Dariga Nazarbaeva, who divorced Aliev in June 2007, has all but disappeared from the Kazakh press, a press she once controlled as director of *Khabar*, Kazakhstan's largest news outlet. Timur Kulibaev, married to Nazarbaev's second daughter of three, appears to be the president's new favorite. In May 2009, Kulibaev assumed chairmanship of the boards of Kazakhstan's most lucrative energy companies— KazMunayGaz, Kazatomprom, and Samruk-Energo.[7] Kulibaev is hedging his bets, however; Nazarbaev has yet a third son-in-law in reserve, and should Kulibaev suddenly find himself out of favor, he has a mistress and a mansion (the Duke of York's former residence) waiting for him in Berkshire, England.[8]

Kyrgyz chaos, Uzbek violence, and Kazakh dynasty—this book seeks to explain these variations. In addition to this, my categorization of Central Asian regime variation, indexes such as Freedom House's Freedom in the World and the World Bank's World Governance Indicators equally illustrate the markedly different paths the Kazakh, Kyrgyz, and Uzbek autocracies have taken since the Soviet collapse. Freedom House's Freedom in the World scores countries along a seven-point "freeness" scale. States at or above 5.5 on this scale are "not free." As such, regimes that flatline at the top of Freedom House's seven-point scale are the least free or, perhaps more appropriately, the most violent and repressive. States between 5.0 and 3.5 are "partly free." States below 3.0—terra incognita in Central

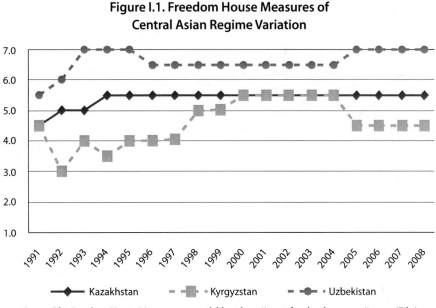

Figure I.1. Freedom House Measures of Central Asian Regime Variation

Source: The Freedom House Measures are available at http://www.freedomhouse org/images/File/
fiw/historical/FIWAllScoresCountries1973-2011.xls.

Asia—are "free." Figure I.1 provides a legend for Central Asia's post-Soviet governments, although a legend is likely not necessary for the reader to identify which line represents the chaotic Kyrgyz government, the violent Uzbek state, and the dynastic Kazakh regime.

Uzbekistan, at the line at the top of the figure, unwaveringly ranks as the most autocratic of the Central Asian states. Indeed, since the Andijan massacre, the Karimov regime has distinguished itself by winning the most autocratic score the Freedom House scale allows. Kyrgyzstan, in contrast, bounces up and down the Freedom House scale, movement reflective of the chaos that exists in Kyrgyz patronage politics. Kazakhstan is steady, neither as brutally repressive as Uzbekistan nor as jarringly unsettled as Kyrgyzstan. The ups and downs and bloody backstabbing in this polity is limited to the Nazarbaev family as the president's children jockey for his throne.

The World Bank's World Governance Indicators (WGI) are equally suggestive of Kyrgyz chaos, Uzbek violence, and Kazakh dynasty. The WGI's "voice and accountability" measure gauges "the extent to which a country's citizens are able to participate in selecting their government."[9] The measure ranges from a low of −2.5 to a high of +2.5 and here too, as figure I.2 illustrates, we find a steadily auto-

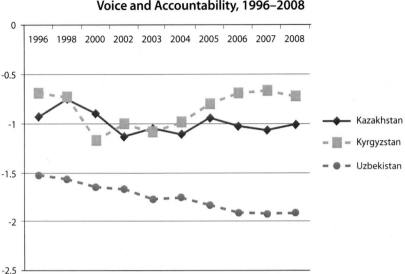

Figure I.2. World Governance Indicators—
Voice and Accountability, 1996–2008

Source: The World Bank's World Governance Indicators are available at http://info.worldbank.
org/governance/wgi/index.asp.

cratic Uzbekistan, a consistently autocratic though not excessively heavy-handed Kazakhstan, and an inconsistently autocratic Kyrgyzstan.[10]

The Karimov regime's violence exacts more than a considerable human cost. State violence has prompted an equally violent response from within Uzbek society. Uzbekistan is the only Central Asian country subject to frequent terror attacks and militant insurgency. Most notably the Islamic Movement of Uzbekistan (IMU), a militant paramilitary group that distinguished itself by landing on the U.S. Department of State terror watch list in September 2000, bombed the Uzbek capital, Tashkent, in February 1999 and July 2004. Although most in Uzbekistan do not share the IMU's Islamist agenda, the relative ease with which the IMU moves from safe havens in Afghanistan across the border into Uzbekistan suggests that a considerable portion of the Uzbek population may see armed resistance an attractive alternative to the passive acceptance of state repression. Moreover, the Andijan protests suggest that this resistance is moving beyond tacit support for the IMU. Andijan was prompted by an armed jailbreak, an effort to release twenty-three prominent Muslim leaders and businessmen whom the Karimov government had imprisoned. Andijan is by no means the only Uzbek city whose jails are filled with influential and independent Muslim businessmen. Should the

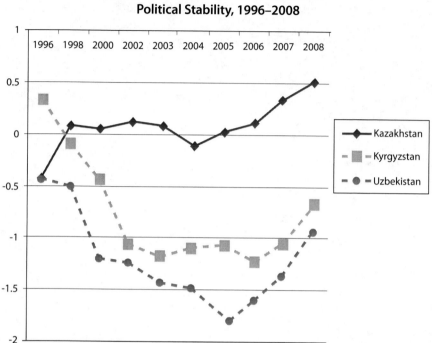

Figure I.3. World Governance Indicators— Political Stability, 1996–2008

Source: The World Bank's World Governance Indicators are available at http://info.worldbank. org/governance/wgi/index.asp.

Uzbek government continue jailing local elites for alleged Islamist leanings, Karimov will encourage the very militancy he purports to be fighting.

The "political stability" measure of the World Governance Indicators captures this potential for armed insurrection in Uzbekistan. As figure I.3 illustrates, this WGI indicator, which gauges "perceptions of the likelihood that the government will be destabilized or overthrown by unconstitutional or violent means," consistently locates the stability of the Karimov regime below that of the Kyrgyz and Kazakh states.[11] Kyrgyz patronage politics, although it may be chaotic, at least is not violent. The predictability of the Nazarbaev family, as multinationals like Chevron and ExxonMobil can attest, makes the stability of Kazakh politics attractive indeed.

This comparative equanimity in Kazakhstan stands in sharp contrast to tumultuous state-society relations in Kyrgyzstan and the often violent state-society relations in Uzbekistan. Protests specifically targeted at the Kazakh executive are rare and fleeting. The largest anti-Nazarbaev protest occurred on December 8,

1996, when approximately thirty-five hundred gathered in Almaty to demonstrate against worsening economic conditions.[12] This protest lasted three hours. Sustained large-scale protests in Kyrgyzstan, however, are regular affairs. In addition to the ten-thousand-strong March 2005 protest that ousted President Akaev, Kyrgyz citizens have gathered to protest the executive's manipulation and rewriting of the constitution (in 2007), executive manipulation of parliamentary and presidential elections (in 1995 and again in 2000), and executive embezzlement of gold reserves (in 1993). Protests likely would be frequent and sustained in Uzbekistan as well, if not for the Karimov government's harrowing coercive capacity. Given this ability to repress in Uzbekistan, dissent has assumed ephemeral and explosive forms—the Tashkent government ministry bombings in 1999 and 2004, overturned and torched police cars in Qo'qon in November 2004 following the government's imposition of new tax codes on retail sales in city bazaars, and the Adijan jailbreak in May 2005.[13]

Kyrgyz political chaos, Uzbek state violence, and Kazakh dynastic machinations within the presidential family—this is the state of Central Asian affairs two decades after the Soviet collapse. I started this book in graduate school, in the early 2000s, hoping mine would be a story of Central Asian transition. This transition has not come; rather, autocracy and patronage politics remain. Yet politics is not universally miserable in Central Asia. Kazakhstan's dynastic government can be watched with detachment by most. Kyrgyzstan's chaotic leadership convulsions can be endured. It is the steady and oppressive repression of Uzbekistan that is most worrisome. To the extent scholars can uncover the causal forces that produce chaos, violence, and dynasty—and, in so doing, assist activists in prodding the Uzbek state in the direction of its more benign neighbors—this incremental change alone will be a greater achievement than the unrealized hopes the democratization literature has thus far offered for Central Asians. At a more immediate level, if international scholars and policy makers are to further the safety of their Central Asian partners, we must concede that the transitions and democratization lenses are ill-suited for understanding post-Soviet Central Asian autocracy.

Explaining Variations in Central Asian Patronage Politics

Three factors—Moscow's engagement or lack of engagement in mediating Central Asian leadership crises during the perestroika period; differing economic resources available to the Central Asian leaders; and differing degrees of Islamic revivalism—have shaped the diverging outcomes of Kazakh, Kyrgyz, and Uzbek patronage politics. After defining what Central Asian patronage politics is, I turn to each of these causalities.

Defining Patronage Politics

Patronage politics in Central Asia closely resembles what Africanists have identified as "neopatrimonialism." Kazakhstan, Kyrgyzstan, and Uzbekistan are *neo*patrimonial in that, in contrast to the patrimonial state of the past, they exhibit, albeit in varying degrees, the characteristics of modern state bureaucracies—professional militaries, a trained and technocratic administrative staff, and industrialized economies. Like many of their African counterparts, Central Asian states are patrimonial in that executive authority is achieved through "personal patronage, rather than through ideology or law"; the relationship between executive and appointee, or patron and client, is one "of loyalty and dependence"; and money, or access to economic rents, is what encourages appointees or clients to "mobilize political support and refer all decisions upward as a mark of deference to patrons."[14] This last point of patronage politics—that it is money as well licenses to exploit—deserves particular emphasis. Patronage politics does not only entail an executive handsomely paying his appointees. Although guaranteeing high salaries certainly is one way to maintain effective rule, an executive can also provide appointees positions of authority through which they can enrich themselves.

The political scientist William Reno, drawing a parallel between Mobutu's Congo and Brezhnev's Soviet Union, has described this practice of distributing offices: "The structure of power relations, the nature of resources available to different groups and the social capital upon which they can draw also shape the options available to rulers. Even in the seemingly centralized USSR, for example, Brezhnev found that his own son-in-law had become a partner of Sharif Rashidovich Rashidov, the First Secretary of the Uzbek Communist Party, in the latter's grand scheme to fake cotton production statistics. Together they and the republic's Communist Party elite skimmed off billions of dollars from official accounts and used the money to build palaces for themselves and to enter new illicit trades."[15] Mobutu engaged in one other practice that Brezhnev, in contrast to his predecessors, avoided—mass violence. Patronage politics need not be sustained by economics alone. As the political scientists Houchang E. Chehabi and Juan J. Linz have explained, an executive can provide a "mixture of fear and rewards to his collaborators" so as to further loyalty.[16] Chehabi and Linz label these states as "sultanistic," differentiating them from neopatrimonial regimes that rely primarily on economic incentives alone. This is an important distinction and one that captures crucial variation, for example, between the Karimov regime's violence and the more benign forms of patronage politics in Kazakhstan and Kyrgyzstan.

Although my understanding of patronage politics draws heavily from the literature on neopatrimonialism, the insights I ultimately seek differ markedly from the primary thrust of this neopatrimonialism literature. Chehabi and Linz, for example, offer as their central takeaway: "The main conclusion to be drawn from a comparative analysis of sultanistic regimes is that, if overthrown, they are more likely to be replaced by a revolutionary or an authoritarian regime than by a democracy."[17] Similarly, the coauthors Michael Bratton and Nicholas Van de Walle conclude their study of neopatrimonialism in Africa as such: "Finally, if our logic is correct, the prospects for democracy are better in transitions from regime types other than neopatrimonial ones."[18] Chehabi and Linz as well as Bratton and Van de Walle are likely correct. Their singular focus on democratic transition, however, and the comparative politics literature's equally pronounced gravitation to democratization narratives, distracts our attention and subsequently our causal analysis away from substantive variations in autocratic governance.

As brash as this may sound, this book suggests our focus should not be prospects for democratization in Central Asia. The immediate prospects for this are dim. Rather, what I seek to uncover are the causal variables that produce variations in patronage politics, what I have termed the chaos, violence, and dynasty of Central Asia. I now turn to these variables—to varying patterns of Moscow's intervention in Central Asia during the perestroika period, to Central Asian states' varying economic endowments, and to these states' varying degrees of Islamic revivalism.

Variations in Moscow and Central Asian Leadership Crises

Though largely overlooked in analyses of post-Soviet Central Asian politics, General Secretary Gorbachev's decision to choreograph Kazakh and Uzbek executive change in the late 1980s and his later decision *not* to intervene in Kyrgyzstan's June 1990 leadership crisis has had profound effects on elite unity in these three countries. Gorbachev's decision to mediate crises in Kazakhstan and Uzbekistan but not in Kyrgyzstan led to the perpetuation of a united Kazakh and Uzbek political elite and to the fragmentation of Kyrgyz politics. These crises, paradoxically, were the products of Gorbachev's own attempts at political and economic reform. Thus his December 1986 replacement of the corrupt but ethnically Kazakh first secretary Dinmukhamed Kunaev with the ethnic Russian Gennady Kolbin sparked violent street protests in the republic's capital, Alma-Ata. Gorbachev's plans to decrease the strains on the Uzbek economy through family planning and outmigration to Siberia sparked violent ethnic riots between

Meskhetian Turks and Uzbeks and an immediate crisis of leadership in Tashkent in June 1989. The attempted implementation of Gorbachev's land reform policies led to deadly ethnic riots in June 1990 between Kyrgyz and Uzbeks in Osh, Kyrgyzstan, as well as a leadership crisis in Bishkek.

Despite these shared causes, the consequences of these crises differed markedly. Gorbachev and the Communist Party resolved ethnic protests and leadership crises in Kazakhstan and Uzbekistan. The general secretary quieted the 1986 Alma-Ata protests by shifting de facto control of Kazakh politics away from the disliked Kolbin to the ethnic Kazakh chairman of the Council of Ministers, Nursultan Nazarbaev. Gorbachev similarly precluded elite instability in the wake of Uzbekistan's 1989 ethnic riots by removing his Uzbek family planner, Rafiq Nishonov, from power and replacing the former first secretary with the self-proclaimed Uzbek "traditionalist" Islam Karimov.[19] Yet in June 1990, when ethnic riots in Kyrgyzstan brought down First Secretary Absamat Masaliev, Gorbachev left it to the local political elite to select their new leader. This Kyrgyz elite fractured and, absent Moscow's external choreographing of a leadership succession, settled on Askar Akaev as a compromise candidate. Akaev's winning attribute was his perceived weakness. Kyrgyz politics, in short, was unsettled even before the Soviet collapse. In Uzbekistan and Kazakhstan, in contrast, Moscow's central scripting of Karimov's and Nazarbaev's rise to power enabled these two leaders to enter the post-Soviet period with a united and executive-oriented single party.

Chapter 1 presents a simplified formal model to illustrate how these diverging perestroika legacies continue to shape executive stability and longevity in these three states. One can readily understand the insights of this formal model by imagining Central Asian presidents as pilots flying different types of planes.[20] All three presidents require the help of a copilot and a navigator. The Uzbek and Kazakh presidents, however, are in command of Boeing 747s in which the passenger cabins are filled with five hundred well-trained reserve navigators and co-pilots. The Kyrgyz president, in contrast, is flying a six-seater. Should members of Karimov's or Nazarbaev's crews become problematic, they can be tossed from the plane and easily replaced with one of the five hundred trained aviators in the passenger cabin. The Kyrgyz president enjoys no such luxury; if he throws too many from the plane, he too will perish. To make things even more challenging for him, a disgruntled copilot or navigator can readily conspire with the three passengers in the cabin. That is, it may well be the Kyrgyz president who is tossed from the plane.

The reader may recognize this stylization of Central Asian politics as an illustration of the collective action problem. I should stress that mine is not deductive reasoning divorced from comparative historical analysis. To make any sense, the microlevel insights of the collective action dynamic illustrated here must be contextualized within a historical analysis that uncovers where these differing airplanes—or differing elite institutions—come from in the first place. Chapter 2 provides further discussion of the perestroika-period ethnic riots, the concomitant leadership crises, and the elite institutions that resulted from Gorbachev's decision either to manage or not to manage executive successions in Kazakhstan, Kyrgyzstan, and Uzbekistan.

Variations in Economic Resources

The economic logic of variations in post-Soviet Central Asian patronage politics can be readily grasped. Abundant oil wealth maintains the gears of the Kazakh patronage machine. Indeed, this oil wealth is so extensive and so concentrated in the hands of the Nazarbaev family that the Kazakh state need not, in contrast to the lesser-endowed Uzbek and Kyrgyz states, appear predatory to its citizens.[21] That is, Nazarbaev can actually pay—and pay well—state employees. Take, for example, the case of teacher salaries. In Kazakhstan the average public teacher's salary in 2009 was the equivalent of three hundred dollars a month.[22] Kyrgyz teachers, according to a statement from the Kyrgyz Finance Ministry in 2008, have received no or only partial pay since 2003.[23] Uzbek teachers arguably have it even worse; in addition to poor pay, they are forced to join their students in the fields for the cotton harvest every September, an effort that ultimately serves to further the Uzbek state's repressive capacity. Repeat this pattern in other sectors of the state bureaucracy—code inspectors, village administrators, regional governors, judges, and police—and it is not difficult to imagine which civil servants will be loyal, which will defect for greener pastures, and which the state will coerce into compliance.

Coercive patronage politics, although it has thus far maintained Karimov's hold on power, forces the regime into a delicate and likely unsustainable balancing act. State control of the cotton as well as the gold industries allows Karimov, if not the ability to buy loyalty, then the ability to coerce some degree of deference to centralized authority. Uzbek bureaucrats who become dissatisfied with the rent-seeking opportunities their offices provide and, as a result, diffident to state directives, can therefore be eliminated through court trials, imprisonments, and disappearances. Coercion and the threat of coercion, however, are not always effective. Indeed, as the discussion in chapter 4 of the 1991 Namangan uprising and the 2005 Andijan protests illustrates, coercion may encourage the very challenges to centralized rule that repressive tactics are designed to prevent.

Karimov's dilemma may, from his point of view, be preferable to the Kyrgyz alternative. Here, as in Uzbekistan, patronage politics is based largely on preda-tion and rent-seeking. The average Kyrgyz teacher, for example, is not starving because he, like most state employees, receives "support" from the local popula-tion in return for services rendered. That said, should a new patron emerge who can offer incentives more attractive than the state's license to predate, bureaucrats will likely defect to this more economically powerful patron. Thus Kyrgyz State University teachers leave their departments to join the faculty of the financier and philanthropist George Soros–funded American University of Central Asia just as many local state appointees begin to work for local business elites rather than the central government. Moreover, the near complete absence of readily exploitable natural resources means that the Kyrgyz executive, in contrast to the Uzbek presi-dent, cannot as easily coerce compliance. As I demonstrate in chapter 3, ensuring that judges, prosecutors, and police reliably serve the central government requires money; this is money the Kyrgyz executive often cannot muster. In broad brush strokes this is the underlying source of political instability in Kyrgyzstan.

This book seeks to explain not only why Kyrgyzstan is politically unstable, but why the degree of this instability has increased since the early 1990s. The nature of Kyrgyzstan's economic resources, however meager, nevertheless has a profound influence on executive tenure in office. Until September 2001 the lion's share of foreign financial flows to the Kyrgyz government came in the form of political and economic aid. Foreign aid, although it may fuel rather than curtail corruption, is difficult for an executive to outright expropriate. Health aid, agri-culture aid, education aid, technical assistance—these bilateral and multilateral donor programs all have their target ministries. For example, although the minis-ter of health may give the president a kickback in return for the privilege to serve as the minister of health, the minister still oversees the distribution—both licit and illicit—of foreign donor money throughout the health administration.

Contrast this state of affairs to the new form of economic rents that began ar-riving in Kyrgyzstan in 2001—U.S. government payments for access to the Transit Center at Manas just outside of Bishkek. Manas, a critical staging point for U.S. military operations in Afghanistan, secured the sons and sons-in-law of Presi-dents Akaev and Bakiev payments in the hundreds of millions of dollars. These entrepreneurial presidential progeny, due to their monopoly control of fuel sup-plies to Manas, became the ire of the Kyrgyz political elite. U.S. government fuel payments after 2001, in contrast to foreign aid during the 1990s, were not divvied up among Kyrgyzstan's narrow political class. This slighted political class rose up first in 2005 and again in 2010 to oust the executives who were stealing rather than sharing the state.

Variations in Islamic Revivalism

Perhaps less intuitive than the resource-endowment logic of Central Asia's diverging chaos, violence, and dynasty outcomes is how differing patterns of Islamic revivalism have contributed to post-Soviet autocratic variation. Similar to the resource-endowment logic, this identity-centered causality also exhibits strong economic dynamics. This book finds that Islamic networks and shared religious norms build interpersonal trust and, as a result, provide fertile foundations for the growth of local businesses and charities. These local businesses and charities in turn provide the social welfare that the post-Soviet Central Asian state (that is, the Kyrgyz and Uzbek states) no longer provide. This shifting of social welfare provision further erodes the central state's presence.

Current variations in Central Asian Islamic revivalism are, to a considerable degree, the results of past historical legacies. Islam's roots in Uzbekistan and in Kyrgyzstan's Fergana Valley span a thousand years. In contrast, it was not until the eighteenth and nineteenth centuries that Islam saw wide adoption in what today is northern Kyrgyzstan and Kazakhstan. The ethnic and cultural reach of the Russian state was less pronounced in Uzbekistan than it was in Kazakhstan and Kyrgyzstan. Ethnic Russians, at the time of the 1989 Soviet census, constituted approximately 36 percent of the Kazakh and 20 percent of the Kyrgyz republic populations, whereas ethnic Russians constituted only 8 percent of the Uzbek citizenry in 1989. Given these societal endowments, we would anticipate that Islamic identification in the immediate post-Soviet years would be most pronounced in Uzbekistan and least prevalent in Kazakhstan. We would also expect that Islamic identification within Kyrgyz society would lie somewhere in between the high of Uzbekistan and the low of Kazakhstan.

Indeed, this is what we find. In surveys that the International Foundation for Electoral Systems (IFES) conducted in 1996, fewer than 20 percent of Kazakh respondents reported they were Muslim, whereas approximately half of Kyrgyz and 90 percent of Uzbek respondents identified as Muslim. Kazakh identification with Islam has inched up in response to Russian emigration from Kazakhstan since the mid-1990s. Still, respondent identification with Islam in Kazakhstan remains markedly less pronounced than identification with Islam is in Kyrgyzstan and Uzbekistan. In surveys colleagues and I conducted in 2008, the percentage of Kazakh respondents reporting they were Muslim remained less than 50 percent. Curiously, as figure I.4 illustrates, Islamic self-identification is now nearly pervasive among the Kyrgyz citizenry, rising from 50 percent in 1996 to slightly more

Figure I.4. Percentage of Kyrgyz, Kazakh, and Uzbek
Citizens Self-identifying as Muslim in 1996 and 2008

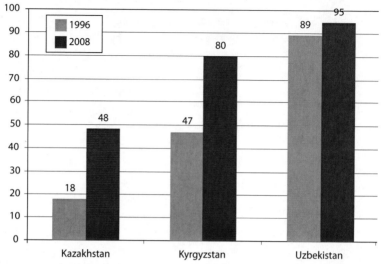

Source: For 2008, see countrywide surveys of Kyrgyz, Kazakhs, and Uzbeks (1,000 respondents
per survey), conducted in June 2008 as part of the National Science Foundation–funded project
"The Effect of the Internet on Central Asian Society." For 1996, see IFES, "Public Opinion
in Kyrgyzstan, 1996" (April 1997), available at http://www.ifes.org/Content/Publications/
Survey/1997/Public-Opinion-in-Kyrgyzstan-1996.aspx; IFES, "Public Opinion in Kazakhstan,
1996" (April 1997), available at http://www.ifes.org/Content/Publications/Survey/1997/Public-
Opinion-in-Kazakhstan-1996.aspx; and IFES, "Public Opinion in Uzbekistan, 1996" (January
1997), available at http://www.ifes.org/Content/Publications/Survey/1997/Public-Opinion-in-
Uzbekistan-1996.aspx. The IFES 1996 Kazakh survey included 1,500 respondents. The IFES 1996
Uzbek survey included 1,830 respondents.

than 80 percent today. It is all but universal in Uzbekistan, with 95 percent of
Uzbek citizens reporting they are Muslim.[24]

To a certain degree, in Kyrgyzstan as well as in Uzbekistan, Russian outmigration does account for some of this growth in Islamic self-identification. What
is most remarkable, though, is the change within the titular Kyrgyz population.
Thus, whereas 55 percent of ethnic Kyrgyz self-identified as Muslim in the 1996
IFES survey—just 8 percentage points higher than the full Kyrgyz survey sample—in our 2008 survey 98 percent of ethnic Kyrgyz self-identified as Muslim.
In short, demographics and Muslim historical legacies alone, although they can
explain much of the strong Islamic presence in Uzbekistan, cannot account for
the marked Islamic revivalism in Kyrgyzstan. What can account for this cascade
to Islam, I argue, is economics.

The Kyrgyz state has all but disappeared at the local level. Government-run enterprises are closed; public schools are shuttered for lack of heat, supplies, and teachers; and Kyrgyzstan's two largest cities, Bishkek and Osh, are in the dark four or five hours a day because of the state's inability to provide steady electricity.[25] In contrast, in Kyrgyzstan's local religious and economic communities, generators and businesses are humming. In place of the state, local organizations (most notably Islamic ones) are stepping in to meet growing welfare needs. Muslim mutual-assistance groups build schools, establish neighborhood charities, and form the core of vibrant business associations. As these organizations expand, the Kyrgyz citizens are further drawn away from the state and toward alternative Muslim elites. As long as the central state does not interfere in the everyday life of these local communities, the Kyrgyz citizens are little bothered by the accumulating failures of post-Soviet patronage politics. When the Kyrgyz executive overreaches, however, when it attempts to exert control beyond Bishkek and into the regions, it is rebuffed and, in former presidents Akaev's and Bakiev's cases, unseated by popular protest.

In Uzbekistan, Islamic charities have similarly assumed roles once fulfilled by the state. Here, and perhaps not surprisingly given demographics and the longer historical presence of Islam in Uzbekistan, these Muslim charities emerged far more rapidly than they did in Kyrgyzstan. Karimov's Muslim challenge, as I illustrate in chapter 4, did not begin with Andijan in May 2005, but rather with Muslim charities' de facto takeover of Namangan in November 1991. In further contrast to Kyrgyzstan, the state-society relations within which these Muslim charities are embedded are considerably more contentious and violent under Karimov than they were under either Akaev or Bakiev. Karimov has the coercive capacity to counter the growing influence of local Muslim charities and elites. That such coercion is in Karimov's best interest is debatable. His appointees have appeared at times to exhibit greater loyalty to local Muslim economic elites than to the central government—a reality that is understandably threatening to an autocratic ruler. At the same time, repression begets militancy. Karimov's 1991 anti-Islam campaign in Namangan gave rise to the paramilitary Islamic Movement of Uzbekistan (IMU), and his 2005 Andijan repression has reinvigorated this militant Islamist movement. Although the IMU's bombings in Tashkent in 1999 and 2004 did not hit their desired target, Karimov remains in the crosshairs of a militant movement he himself helped to foment.

How long Uzbek patronage politics will remain airborne is not clear. In May 2004, on a flight from Tashkent to Qarshi, my plane taxied past the wreckage of an Uzbek Air Yak-40. The jet had crashed three months earlier, yet the distressing jumble of engines and fuselage remained on the tarmac. Was this Karimov's way of conveying a message to his pilots? Be wary or this too will be your future. Or was this a portent of Karimov's own fate? Has he, through relentless repression and violence, depleted his reserve of copilots and navigators to the extent that his own regime is about to collapse?

Kazakhstan and Kyrgyzstan we can predict with greater certainty. Nazarbaev has had little need to reach deep into his immense reserve of political elites; few defect because the rewards of defection are so low compared with what the Nazarbaev regime itself can offer. Kyrgyzstan's elite reserve is far smaller, far more fractured, and far more likely to peel away from central government patronage in favor of local (often Muslim) business elites. This leaves the Kyrgyz executive with two alternatives: either he can do his best to maintain the peace, thereby maintaining his hand at the controls, or he can turn his back on the delicate balancing act required to secure a winning coalition among Kyrgyzstan's fractured political elite. Thus far, Kyrgyz executives have chosen the latter alternative, stripping state assets as fast as they can before they are tossed from power. This all makes for a turbulent ride, but a ride that will not end in the same political wreckage that is likely to befall Uzbekistan.

1 A Post-transitions Research Agenda for the Study of Authoritarianism

I LEFT AN October 2009 U.S. government conference on democracy assistance in Central Asia with two thoughts: policy makers and academics have developed a sophisticated conceptualization of democratization processes, and this conceptualization of democratization is largely divorced from Central Asian reality. Our conversations at the conference focused on enhancing civic engagement, promoting freedom of the press, and empowering women and youth—policies Western governments and aid organization partners have promoted in Central Asia since the Soviet collapse. These policies have had little effect. Two decades after the Soviet collapse, governments throughout Central Asia are no closer to democratization than they were in 1991. Yet the academic literature and policy conferences continue to emphasize democratization and transition, rather than variations within authoritarian rule.

One reason for our collective deficit in conceptualizing and explaining authoritarian variation, as I learned from U.S. Agency for International Development (USAID) colleagues at the conference, is domestic U.S. politics. Democracy assistance, civil society promotion, freedom of the press, youth and women empowerment—these policies "sell on the Hill." The problem, though, is these policies have no buyers among Central Asia's autocratic leaders. One would think academics would rush to point this out to lawmakers. Academics too are shaped by political pressures. U.S. Senator Tom Coburn of Oklahoma, for example, forwarded Amendment 2631 to "prohibit the National Science Foundation [NSF] from wasting federal research funding on political science projects."[1] Coburn would prefer the NSF concentrate resources on "real fields" that "can yield real improvements in the lives of everyone." The NSF political science program, if it is to withstand these criticisms, must itself demonstrate its transformative potential. Hence, following USAID's strategy, the NSF targets funding on "campaigns and elections, electoral choice, and electoral systems; and citizen support in emerging and established democracies."[2] The NSF, as with many other funding organizations, promotes the study of democratization; as such, it is understandable that this is where political scientists have placed their greatest emphasis. Our discipline offers several respected journals devoted to the study of democracy—the *Journal of Democracy, Democratization*, and *Demokratizatsiya*. We have no periodicals, however, devoted to the study of authoritarianism. Similarly, although graduate seminars on democratization can be found on most university campuses, courses on authoritarianism are few.

Another reason why there are so few seminars on authoritarianism is that there are so few instructors who could lead them. Whereas political science departments have excellent Europeanists and Latin Americanists well trained in democratic transition, the ranks of academics who focus on Africa, Asia, and the Middle East—that is, those areas where autocracies predominate—are thin. Some attribute this limited supply to the incentives political scientists face. The historian Stephen Kotkin, for one, rankled his social science colleagues when he observed in the *New York Times*: "The absence of regional experts in political science departments of many elite universities goes back to a long-running, rancorous debate over the best method for understanding the way the world works: is it using statistics and econometrics to identify universal patterns that underlie all economic and political systems, or zeroing in on a particular area, and mastering its languages, cultures and institutions?"[3]

Not lost on Kotkin is a second potential causal explanation for our inattention to authoritarianism: working in autocratic environments is not fun. A career navigating armed conflict, corrupt officials, repeated intimidation by state and nonstate actors, poor sanitation, and repeated food poisonings is one most people would avoid. "Quantitative and American studies counterparts," Kotkin points out in contrast, "can explore new material in front of their computers and still pick up the kids at 5."[4] Fortunately, tolerant families and strong stomachs have enabled several social scientists to begin exploring questions of autocratic continuity and variation. Good-natured chiding has also encouraged comparative political scientists who study the former Soviet Union to rethink their transitions models. Barbara Geddes, a Latin Americanist, ribs her transitology colleagues: "One of the reasons regime transitions have proved theoretically intractable is that different kinds of authoritarianism differ from each other as much as they differ from democracy . . . [and] comparativists have not studied these differences systematically."[5] The political scientist Frances Hagopian has explained: "The spectacular collapse of each authoritarian regime has added a new set of impatient area scholars to the ranks of comparative political scientists already committed to what Samuel Huntington has called the 'third wave' of democratization."[6] Thomas Carothers, the most vocal critic of the transitions school, has noted the dismal record of this "third wave" (twenty democratic consolidations out of approximately one hundred countries, by Carothers's count): "It is time to recognize that the transition paradigm has outlived its usefulness and to look for a better lens."[7]

This chapter builds on the strengths and identifies the limitations of the existing transitions literature in an effort to build a post-transitions research agenda for the study of authoritarianism. I begin with a formal model that provides insights into how enduring perestroika-era institutions of elite rule can either constrain or enhance executive power. Then I discuss how variations in economic resources, geopolitics, and Islamic revivalism intersect with these inherited institutional constraints to produce the violence, chaos, and dynasty existing in Central Asia today. Lastly, I turn to several leading studies of post-Soviet Central Asian politics and demonstrate how, once we move beyond the democracy-autocracy lens of the transition literature, the central causal arguments these studies highlight help us anticipate future autocratic regime change among Central Asian and other authoritarian states.

A Model for Understanding Enduring Historical Legacies in Autocratic States

One of the central shortcomings of the post-Soviet transitions literature, Hagopian has written, is the failure to anticipate that "the difficult process of political reorganization will be influenced profoundly by the legacies of authoritarian regimes."[8] Although Hagopian's focus is Latin American military states, her insight into how institutional legacies shape politics even after the regime that produced these legacies disappears holds equally for post-Soviet Central Asia. In the introduction I used the metaphor of pilots and passenger cabins as shorthand for illustrating how diverging Soviet legacies of elite rule have shaped violence, chaos, and dynasty in Central Asia. Kazakh president Nazarbaev and Uzbek president Karimov, with their oversized presidential parties, command large Boeing 747s. In these planes first officers and navigators are expendable because the Kazakh and Uzbek presidents have access to hundreds of additional well-trained airmen in the passenger cabin. The Kyrgyz executive, in contrast, sits at the helm of a six-seater and is considerably more constrained in his ability to replace his copilot and navigator. He must remain vigilant to ensure that he himself will not be tossed from the plane.

These differing elite institutions are the legacy of Gorbachev's perestroika politics—of Moscow's managing elite succession in Uzbekistan and Kazakhstan in the late 1980s and its hands-off approach to elite succession in Kyrgyzstan in 1990. Gorbachev's diverging approaches—intervention in Kazakhstan and Uzbekistan and nonintervention in Kyrgyzstan—were driven by Central Party rather than Central Asian politics. By 1990, Gorbachev had realized that if he were to achieve his vision of reform—economic revival, greater transparency, socialist democracy—he needed to eliminate the dead wood within the Communist Party who had benefitted from economic inefficiencies, corruption, and the party's monopoly hold on power. Gorbachev's challenge in achieving his transformative vision was not all that dissimilar from the challenge Stalin faced in attempting to accelerate political and economic changes during the 1930s. Stalin's solution was to kill the old elite. Gorbachev, instead, killed the party. The general secretary framed the Communist Party's February 5, 1990, death notice more as baptism than eulogy: "The party's renewal presupposes a fundamental change in its relations with state and economic bodies and the abandonment of the practice of commanding them and substituting for their functions. The party in a renewing society can exist and play its role as vanguard only as a democratically recognized force. This means that its status should not be imposed through constitutional endorsement."[9]

Four months later, imposition of discipline would be exactly what the Kyrgyz political elite needed. Deadly ethnic riots ripped through the southern Kyrgyz towns of Osh and Uzgen, tearing apart the Kyrgyz party. The Kyrgyz political elite offered up First Secretary Absamat Masaliev as atonement for the riots. In contrast to the earlier riots and elite convulsions in Kazakhstan and Uzbekistan in 1986 and 1989, however, when Moscow stepped in to restore party unity, no external enforcer told the Kyrgyz elite who their new leader would be. Kyrgyzstan's new leader did not come from within the party's upper ranks; rather, after prolonged stalemate, these now divided upper ranks selected an outsider, Askar Akaev, at the time the head of the Kyrgyz Academy of Sciences, as a compromise candidate. Akaev, these warring factions concluded, could be manipulated. They were right; for the next fifteen years President Akaev did business with anyone and everyone in an effort to cling to power.

Many scholars interpret Akaev's willingness to negotiate as a sign that he personally favored democracy. The political scientist Michael McFaul has written that Akaev used his "unchallenged authority to implement partial democratic reforms."[10] The political scientist Kathleen Collins similarly has explained that Akaev held a "democratic ideology" and "hence, Akayev [*sic*] imposed democratic reform from above."[11] And the political scientist Eugene Huskey has noted that Akaev "established an enviable reputation for Kyrgyzstan as an oasis of democracy in Central Asia."[12] Agency-oriented explanations such as these certainly have a place in social science. At the same time, these causalities are difficult, if not impossible, to falsify. In June 2007 I met with Bermet Akaeva, the daughter of Askar Akaev, and during the course of our interview I asked her about her father's political beliefs. The impression Akaeva left was not that her father was a democrat, but that he was weak. Hence, Akaeva lamented: "My father was too forgiving . . . if it were me, I would have jailed many of these criminals [the people now in office] a long time ago. Many more people should have been imprisoned . . . if he had put these criminals away, Kyrgyzstan wouldn't have had the March 2005 events."[13]

Perhaps Akaeva is correct, or perhaps Akaev was a democrat and Akaeva misreads her father's democratic inclinations as those of a "too forgiving" leader. This book offers a third hypothesis, however: that Akaev, like Nazarbaev and Karimov, was doing the best he could to hold on to power given the structural constraints he faced. In constructing this hypothesis, I draw on the work of coauthors Bruce Bueno de Mesquita, James Morrow, Randolph Siverson, and Alastair Smith and the insights of their "selectorate model."[14] I have already introduced the central insight of this model through the airplane analogy—namely that leaders who can benefit from united single parties (from large "passenger cabins") enjoy a firmer hold on power than do leaders who must balance the competing interests and potential challenges of a fragmented and small political elite. Mesquita, Morrow, Siverson, and Smith's model (hereafter the Mesquita model) sharpens this intuition and suggests how, given variations in inherited political institutions, leaders may allocate economic resources between competing state and society interests.

The Mesquita model demonstrates that leaders like Nazarbaev and Karimov—leaders who preside over large single parties—are freer to invest resources in both public goods provision and building coercive state capacity. The explanatory insights of this formal model cannot be divorced from an understanding of context-specific processes that shaped perestroika-era variations in Central Asian political institutions. Nor, moreover, can this model be separated from dynamic geopolitical, economic, and leadership succession processes that will continue to shape, even shock, Central Asian politics. Rather, what the selectorate model provides is a framework with which we can assess potential effects of complex causality, contingency, and elite agency.

Mesquita and his colleagues use the term "winning coalition" to refer to what I metaphorically identified as the Central Asian president's copilot and navigator. A winning coalition is the minimum number of individuals a leader needs to remain in power. Winning coalitions in democracies are shaped by electoral design—first past the post, proportional representation, and so on—and often represent a considerable portion of the broader population. Winning coalitions in authoritarian states, in contrast, are small and limited to the executive's inner circle of trusted elites. Mesquita and his colleagues use the term "selectorate" in the same way that I have been applying the idea of trained airmen in the plane's passenger cabin—those members of society "who have the positions (for example, military rank or party membership in a single party) to aspire to make or break leaders."[15] Just as any of the trained airmen in the passenger cabin can step in to serve as copilots and navigators, so too can anyone in the selectorate serve as a member of a leader's winning coalition. In contrast to the relatively fixed size of winning coalitions, the size of selectorates varies from one autocracy to another, just as cabin sizes vary from plane to plane.[16]

With these conceptual understandings of winning coalitions and selectorates in place, we are now in a position to explore how differences in the size of selectorates shape diverging political outcomes in Kazakhstan, Kyrgyzstan, and Uzbekistan. Central to the selectorate model is the idea of a credible threat: Does the combination of a given state's winning coalition (w) and selectorate (s) provide a credible threat to an incumbent's continued autocratic rule? When presidential parties are large and winning coalitions small—that is, when the ratio of the winning coalition to the selectorate (w / s) is small—winning coalition members rarely defect. These winning coalition members rarely defect because they know that the likelihood of landing in a new winning coalition under a new leader is remote. For purposes of illustration, I assume that Nazarbaev and Karimov each require ten supporters to rule their country (winning coalition, $w = 10$). Thanks to Gorbachev's 1980s interventions, both Nazarbaev and Karimov enjoy large executive-oriented parties from which they can construct their respective winning coalitions. To keep calculations straightforward, I set these large selectorates equal to one thousand people (selectorate, $s = 1,000$). The likelihood any one person in the presidential party is also a member of the president's winning coalition is thus w / s or 10 / 1,000 (0.01 or 1 percent).[17] Mesquita and his coauthors term this ratio w / s, the "loyalty norm." In countries like Kazakhstan and Uzbekistan, where selectorates are large and winning coalitions are small, this norm is strong; winning coalition members recognize they have only a small chance—in this case a 1 percent chance—of landing in a challenger's winning coalition.

In Kyrgyzstan, because of Gorbachev's decision not to intervene to save the party in June 1990, a large executive-oriented single party does not exist. Here the Kyrgyz elite is narrow and fragmented. As such, although the Kyrgyz president's winning coalition may be the same size as the winning coalitions of his Kazakh and Uzbek counterparts, the Kyrgyz president must form this coalition from within the strict confines of a narrow and fragmented political elite. Exactly how small is this Kyrgyz elite? I posed this question to several Kyrgyz politicians, academics, and activists in December 2006. Tursunbek Akun, the government's ombudsman for human rights, observed that although Kyrgyzstan officially has several dozen registered political parties, only four of these parties (more precisely, "a handful of personalities" within these parties) actually have a voice in Kyrgyz politics.[18] Marat Kaipov, the Kyrgyz minister of justice, sharpened Akun's assessment: Kyrgyzstan had more registered political parties than any other country in the former Soviet Union.[19]

Yet Kaipov acknowledged that few of these parties are more than shells, and the prominent Kyrgyz parties are vehicles for a handful of wealthy elites. Topchubek Turgunaliev, the leader of Erkin Kyrgyzstan, narrowed this assessment even further: there was "Beknazarov and his Asaba party, Tekebaev and his Ata Meken Party, Eshimkulov and the Social Democrats, Kulov and Ar-Namys, and of course, Turgunaliev and Erkin Kyrgyzstan."[20] In short, in contrast to the Kazakh and Uzbek selectorates, the Kyrgyz political elite is small and fragmented. The size of the Kyrgyz selectorate is not static, however. Because Kyrgyzstan did not inherit a pro-presidential single party from the Soviet era, anyone with sufficient economic resources can create a party and seek a seat at the table. Few in Kyrgyzstan possess such wealth, though. As a result, Kyrgyz politics, in contrast to the massive presidential parties in Uzbekistan and Kazakhstan, remains the realm of the privileged few. For illustrative purposes, I assign a value of twenty to this narrow political elite. The likelihood that a member of this narrow, twenty-member-strong Kyrgyz selectorate will find himself or herself in the executive's winning coalition is therefore 10 / 20 (0.50 or 50 percent).

Building on these probabilities, we can now assess how differing Kazakh, Uzbek, and Kyrgyz configurations of elite politics—again, configurations driven by enduring perestroika-era legacies—have shaped current authoritarian outcomes in Central Asia.[21] Figure 1.1 summarizes the rewards and risks a winning coalition member must assess when deciding whether or not he or she will remain loyal to the executive. The ratio w / s—that is, the size of the winning coalition relative to the broader selectorate—represents the probability of being in a new winning coalition should one defect from the president. M is the maximum pay-

Figure 1.1. Central Asian Defection Game

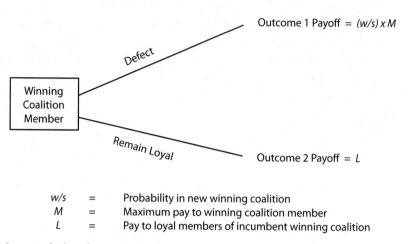

w/s = Probability in new winning coalition
M = Maximum pay to winning coalition member
L = Pay to loyal members of incumbent winning coalition

Source: Author's rendering.

off a challenger could offer to a potential defector. And L is the loyalty payoff—that is, the payment a winning coalition member receives for remaining loyal to the president.

Maximum payoffs, in the simplified selectorate model, can be calculated by dividing the amount of state resources available to a leader by the number of people in a leader's winning coalition. For now I assume that the Kazakh, Kyrgyz, and Uzbek leaders each have access to the same amount of economic resources, a wealth equivalent to a thousand dollars. Later in this chapter, I relax this resource assumption and explore the predictions of the selectorate model using actual World Bank government revenue data for Kazakhstan and Kyrgyzstan. Proceeding for now with the thousand-dollar assumption, we can calculate the maximum possible amount any Kazakh, Kyrgyz, and Uzbek head of state can pay to his ten-member winning coalition: $1,000 / 10 people = $100 per coalition member. Few leaders, however, would *want* to exhaust all resources on winning coalition payoffs. Rather, most leaders would prefer to reserve as much wealth as possible for personal enrichment and investing in projects that can secure continued passivity from the population—that is, for investing in public goods such as health care and for funding institutions of repression like the police and the judiciary. How might an executive determine what to spend on coalition member payoffs and what to spend on public goods and institutions of repression?

Imagine a scenario where a challenger emerges with nine ready supporters.[22] If this challenger can win over one member of the current leader's ten-member

Table 1.1. The Perestroika Legacy Model—Defection Payoffs for Members of the Current Winning Coalition under Conditions of Equal Government Resources

UZ Defection Payoff	=	$(w/s) \times (M)$
	=	$(10/1{,}000) \times (\$100)$
	=	$(.01) \times (\$100)$
	=	**$1**
KZ Defection Payoff	=	$(w/s) \times (M)$
	=	$(10/1{,}000) \times (\$100)$
	=	$(.01) \times (\$100)$
	=	**$1**
KG Defection Payoff	=	$(w/s) \times (M)$
	=	$(10/20) \times (\$100)$
	=	$(0.50) \times (\$100)$
	=	**$50**

winning coalition, the leader's winning coalition will collapse. This potential defector, however, will not automatically occupy the last remaining slot the challenger needs to build his own winning coalition. Any potential defector from the current ruler's winning coalition understands that the challenger may not keep his word and instead fill his remaining winning coalition spot with someone else—for example, a son or daughter, a childhood confidant, or a business partner. Indeed, any potential defector might reasonably conclude that the probability of his landing in the winning coalition of a successful challenger is no greater than the probability of any other member of the broader political elite (that is, w/s). As such, even if the challenger promises to reward a current winning coalition member with the maximum possible payoff given available state resources (in this case, a hundred dollars), any potential defector discounts this payoff by the probability of actually landing in the challenger's new winning coalition. Table 1.1 summarizes these discounted payoffs for the Kazakh, Kyrgyz, and Uzbek cases.

As table 1.1 illustrates, the payoffs for defection in this perestroika-legacy model are considerably greater in the fragmented Kyrgyz elite case than in the Uzbek and Kazakh cases, where Moscow's interventions ensured the continuity of large executive-oriented single parties. These diverging expected payoffs have

Table 1.2. The Perestroika Legacy Model—Defection Payoffs for Members of the Current Winning Coalition under Conditions of Unequal Government Resources

KZ Defection Payoff	=	$(w/s) \times (M)$
	=	$(10/1{,}000) \times (\$2{,}000)$
	=	$(.01) \times (\$2{,}000)$
	=	**$ 20**
KG Defection Payoff	=	$(w/s) \times (M)$
	=	$(10/20) \times (\$100)$
	=	$(0.50) \times (\$100)$
	=	**$ 50**

profound implications on how authoritarian rulers can allocate remaining funds. In the simplified model discussed earlier, the Uzbek and Kazakh executives need only pay winning coalition members $2 to ensure these members do not defect to a challenger. Aggregated across all ten winning coalition members, the Uzbek and Kazakh executives must pay $20 to secure continued loyalty. This leaves both executives with $980 to pursue other objectives, such as self-enrichment and investment in public goods and coercive capacity.

The Kyrgyz executive, in contrast, must offer $51 to each of the ten winning coalition members and a total of $510 of $1,000 in available resources to secure continued loyalty. This leaves the Kyrgyz executive with $490 (compared with the Uzbek and Kazakh presidents' $980) remaining for self-enrichment, public goods, and coercive capacity investments. In short, not only must the Kyrgyz executive spend more to secure elite loyalty, he has fewer resources left over to invest in public goods and coercive capacity. This dynamic between inherited elite institutions from the perestroika period and executive capacity becomes even more pronounced when figures representative of these states' actual resource endowments are used. Total Kazakh government revenues in 2007, according to World Bank data, were twenty times greater than total Kyrgyz revenues.[23] The maximum possible payoff any Kazakh executive could pay members of his winning coalition, hence, is twenty times greater than the payoff the Kyrgyz executive can extend. Instead of having only $1,000, the Kazakh president now has $20,000 in available economic resources and the maximum payoff per winning coalition member is $20,000 / 10, or $2,000 for each coalition member. The maximum payoff in the

**Table 1.3. The Perestroika Legacy Model—Kazakh and Kyrgyz
Loyalty Payoffs and Discretionary Funds under Conditions
of Identical and Diverging State Resources**

Total Wealth Available to Kyrgyz and Kazakh Autocrats Identical, $1,000

KZ Payoffs	=	$2(10)	KG Payoffs	=	$51(10)
	=	$20		=	$510
KZ Discretionary Funds	=	$1,000 - $20	KG Discretionary Funds	=	$1,000 - $510
	=	**$980**		=	**$490**

**Total Wealth Available to Kyrgyz and Kazakh Autocrats Diverging
Kazakh Wealth = $20,000
Kyrgyz Wealth = $1,000**

KZ Payoffs	=	$21(10)	KG Payoffs	=	$51(10)
	=	$210		=	$510
KZ Discretionary Funds	=	$20,000 - $210	KG Discretionary Funds	=	$1,000 - $510
	=	**$19,790**		=	**$490**

Kyrgyz case remains unchanged at $1,000 / 10, or $100 for each winning coalition member. Given the Kazakh executive's greater wealth (and given that Kazakh winning coalition members know the executive has access to greater wealth), will these coalition members now be more likely to defect to a challenger in the hopes of getting a bigger cut of the pie?

Kazakh winning coalition members, as summarized in table 1.2, will indeed demand a larger cut from the president. The maximum anticipated payoff for defection is now $20 rather than $1. Thus the Kazakh autocrat now must pay $21 rather than the previous $2 he needed to pay to ensure loyalty. Revealingly, this payoff is still considerably lower than the $50 defection payoff in Kyrgyzstan.

Moreover, as illustrated in table 1.3, although the Kazakh autocrat must pay more to ensure loyalty, this greater payout is a minor inconvenience relative to the vastly greater funds now available to the Kazakh executive for personal enrichment and for investment in capacity-enhancing public goods and coercion projects.

From the Selectorate Model to the Perestroika Legacy Model

The numbers in these examples are illustrative. Winning coalitions and selectorates are fluid and, as such, my objective in assigning numbers to these elite
institutions is not to convey a fixity to Central Asian politics that does not exist.
Rather, my aim is to illustrate the logic of Central Asian authoritarianism and how
this logic is shaped by enduring perestroika-era legacies of elite politics. More
specifically, the selectorate model suggests that we need not resort to divining the
leanings of Central Asian leaders—whether Akaev is a "democrat" or Karimov
and Nazarbaev are autocrats—but rather that with an understanding of differing
Kazakh, Kyrgyz, and Uzbek party structures before the Soviet collapse, we can
anticipate diverging patterns of authoritarian rule after the Soviet collapse. Thus
pairing historical analysis with the selectorate model, we would anticipate greater
elite loyalty to the Kazakh and Uzbek executives than to the Kyrgyz executive. In
turn, we would anticipate the greater freedom of Kazakh and Uzbek leaders to devote economic resources to capacity-enhancing projects such as providing public
goods and strengthening repressive institutions. The selectorate model points to
enduring institutional constraints—constraints frequently overlooked in transitology studies that emphasize post-1991 causalities of political change. This is not
to say that causalities of Central Asian autocratic variation that focus on the post-
Soviet period are wrong. Several of these causalities are important and act either
to amplify or dampen diverging patterns of autocratic rule that emerged during
the perestroika period.

The Intersection of Economic Endowments, Geopolitics, and Islam

Although we can attribute much of Central Asia's chaos, violence, and dynasty to enduring institutional legacies from the Soviet period, Kazakh, Kyrgyz,
and Uzbek politics are not frozen in time. These states, like all states, are buffeted
by changes coming from within and without their borders. Economic resources
available to Central Asian governments vary over time, as does the salience of
religious, regional, ethnic, and clan identities. Country demographics change as
ethnic minorities emigrate to titular homelands or migrate in search of jobs. The
geopolitics of the region, moreover, remains in flux as Russia's influence ebbs and
flows and as two new powers, China and the United States, come to see Central
Asia as important to their respective strategic interests. Lastly, new institutions
created by Central Asia's current autocrats hold the potential both to solidify and
paradoxically to undermine autocratic stability. "Pocket" parliaments housing

pro-presidential "opposition" parties can transform into real legislatures. New presidential dynasties, designed to convey an air of stability, may suddenly look vulnerable when anointed successors fall from favor. And judges and lawyers, professionalized to better serve executive interests, may gradually come to see themselves as an independent elite with a mandate to limit executive overreach.

Together, these variables form what I see as a new research agenda for understanding changes in Central Asian authoritarianism.[24] This new research agenda emphasizes the importance of inherited institutional legacies rather than an imagined tabula rasa of the immediate post-Soviet collapse. This research agenda sees interaction effects between inherited institutions and economics, geopolitics, identity, and newly created institutions as potentially transformative of authoritarian rule. I consider these interaction effects and conclude the chapter by suggesting that social scientists and policy makers can anticipate and potentially encourage new pathways to authoritarian political change by keeping "causal nets" open wide.

Economic Resources and Authoritarianism

Economic resources are central to explaining Central Asian autocratic variations. However, the resource-based argument that I outline with the help of the selectorate model diverges from the central thrust of the familiar rentier state literature. I argue that economic resources are not determinative of authoritarianism, but rather of the *kind* of authoritarianism. In short, by pairing the rentier state literature with the selectorate model, we can refine our understanding of what kind of authoritarian states are likely to emerge given variations in economic wealth. The central causal arguments offered by the rentier state literature are threefold: rents derived from economic resources (typically hydrocarbons) free governments from the need to tax and therefore be accountable to citizens; energy-rich states can spend lavishly on social welfare provision and, as such, are less likely to face a discontented public; and energy-rich states use wealth to stunt social group formation, thereby limiting social capital accumulation and concomitant demands for democracy.[25] The logic of the rentier state is compelling in that it intersects with several of the most prominent ideas of the West's own democratization discourse: the American Revolution's "no taxation without representation" protest cry; Alex de Tocqueville's discussion of polity-transforming "intellectual and moral associations"; and Barrington Moore's "no bourgeoisie, no democracy" thesis.[26] Empirically, the rentier state literature is equally compelling; it is the rare developing country that is both energy rich and democratic.

Recent studies on the Central Asian rentier state largely parallel the wider oil and autocracy literature. Coauthors Anja Franke, Andrea Gawrich, and Gurban Alakbarov have concluded about oil-rich Kazakhstan and Azerbaijan, for example: "Given our view that rents render the cementing of power to current elites an extremely attractive prospect, we cannot but answer the central question of rentier state analysis—'does oil hinder democracy?'—affirmatively."[27] Similarly, the political scientist Theresa Sabonis-Helf, writing on Turkmenistan and Kazakhstan, has found: "Early evidence suggests that the energy interests within the states are already capturing the state, and that these interests do not serve the cause of expanding democracy."[28] Just the opposite, far from expanding democracy, coauthors Pauline Jones Luong and Erika Weinthal have illustrated the Nazarbaev government is applying its oil riches, albeit with the help of foreign companies, to expand social services and thereby mitigate public discontent: "Kazakhstan's leadership not only has deliberately sold off oil and gas companies in those regions that have been hardest hit by the Soviet Union's demise but also has expected foreign companies to assume full social and economic responsibility for the well-being of these regions."[29]

The Kazakh government is behaving as oil-rich governments tend to behave—it is applying oil revenues to grease the wheels of patronage politics. This focus on social services and cash transfers has yielded results. Only 18 percent of Kazakhs live below the national poverty line, whereas 48 percent of Kyrgyz citizens and 28 percent of Uzbeks live in poverty.[30] An important question, however, is whether oil is the reason why Kazakhstan is nondemocratic. Uzbekistan's resource wealth is middling and Kyrgyzstan's resource wealth is all but nonexistent, yet both of these countries are nondemocratic as well. Perhaps the scholars cited earlier do not have the wrong causality; perhaps they have the wrong question.

Oil and economic resources more broadly are not the wellspring of Central Asian autocracy; rather, as table 1.3 has suggested, such resources amplify already existing variations within Central Asian autocracy. Even if economic resources were identical across all three Central Asian states, Uzbek and Kazakh authoritarian leaders, thanks to Gorbachev's 1980s intervention to ensure party continuity, would enjoy greater freedom than the Kyrgyz executive to spend resources on stability-enhancing projects such as public goods provision and institutions of repression. That said, when we do take into account Kazakhstan's vast oil wealth and Uzbekistan's smaller yet still substantive access to cotton, gold, and gas wealth, the import of these inherited Soviet legacies is magnified.[31] A twenty-fold increase of Kazakh resources relative to Kyrgyz economic resources therefore leads to a forty-fold increase in the discretionary funds available to the Kazakh executive relative to discretionary funds available to the Kyrgyz executive.

Variations in economic resources do not explain why Central Asian states are authoritarian rather than democratic. All Central Asian states—be they re-source poor or resource rich—are autocratic. Variations in economic resources, when placed in the context of inherited institutional legacies, do, however, help us understand diverging patterns of executive investment in capacity-enhancing projects. The Nazarbaev government, with its vast oil wealth, can invest in public goods provision to minimize societal dissatisfaction. The Karimov regime's con-trol of the cotton, gold, and small hydrocarbon industries does not provide suf-ficient resources for wide-scale public goods provision but does yield sufficient funds for building and sustaining a coercive judiciary. The Kyrgyz president, with little access to rent-yielding economic resources, is hard-pressed to sustain any stability-enhancing endeavor. Economic resources, in short, exhibit an interac-tion effect when paired with Soviet-era institutional legacies.

The presence of this interaction effect points to policy prescriptions for domestic and foreign actors hoping to encourage autocratic softening in highly repressive states like Uzbekistan. More specifically, in states where economic re-sources are sufficient to repress yet insufficient to provide public goods that would obviate the need for repression, foreign governments can erode authoritarian coercive capacity by making life unpleasant for autocrats and their supporters. Western governments can therefore deny visas, freeze foreign bank accounts, challenge the deeds to Mediterranean villas, and prevent elites' sons and daughters from studying in Western universities. Such actions serve as externally imposed costs that devalue authoritarian leaders' payoffs to winning coalition members. In contrast to broad economic embargoes, these targeted sanctions are less likely to adversely affect the already struggling broader populations in these countries. These sanctions are no guarantee that coercive rule will disappear. Such sanctions are likely to prove more effective than the failed democratization programs that continue to define the bulk of current Western government policy toward Central Asia.

Geopolitics and Autocracy

Whereas most scholars and policy makers agree that economic resources concentrated in the hands of political elites tend to solidify authoritarian rule, ac-ademics and Western government officials (particularly Western diplomats) dif-fer in their assessment of how geopolitics shapes authoritarian polities. Political scientists Jeffrey Kopstein and David Reilly, for example, have argued that neigh-borhoods matter and that Central Asia, in contrast to the post-Soviet Baltic coun-tries, has decidedly illiberal neighbors: "Geographical proximity to the West has exercised a positive influence on the transformation of communist states . . . geographical isolation in the East has hindered this transformation."[32] Central Asia is surrounded by autocratic governments, many of which boast nuclear weapons and large militaries, and all of which are eager to compete for the region's energy resources.[33] Such neighbors, Kopstein and Reilly conclude, are ideal for Central Asian autocrats who seek "to perpetuate authoritarian regimes and to gain outside support for themselves and their regional ambitions."[34]

U.S. policy makers are less pessimistic. U.S. diplomats in particular have argued that Central Asian states, despite their authoritarian neighbors, can reform and that U.S. activism in the region can assist this reform. B. Lynn Pascoe, the deputy assistant secretary of state for European and Eurasian Affairs, therefore testified before the Senate Foreign Relations Committee in June 2002, encouragingly concluding that "Uzbekistan is the most intriguing test case of our policy of enhanced engagement. . . . Uzbekistan has also taken steps to improve its human rights record. In March, for the first time ever, Uzbekistan registered an indigenous human rights organization; the government also has stated its willingness to register more of them."[35]

Similarly, George Krol, the deputy assistant secretary for South and Central Asian affairs, had been optimistic that in return for being granted the 2010 chairmanship of the Organization for Security and Cooperation in Europe (OSCE), the Nazarbaev government would implement promised reforms: "Our broader vision is for a strong, independent and democratic Kazakhstan that is a leader and anchor of stability in the region. We believe Kazakhstan's service as chairman in office for the OSCE will help serve that broader vision."[36] The OSCE chairmanship is a carrot the West extended directly to the Kazakh state leadership in return for promises of political liberalization. Thus the foreign minister, Marat Tazhin, pledged in Madrid in November 2007 that "in the context of future Chairmanship," Kazakhstan would "develop media self-regulation mechanisms . . . and liberalize the registration procedures for media outlets"; "implement ODIHR [Office for Democratic Institutions and Human Rights] recommendations in the area of elections and legislation concerning political parties in Kazakhstan"; and "further liberalization and greater openness and transparency of political-governmental processes."[37]

Not everyone shared Krol's enthusiasm that Kazakhstan would indeed make progress toward the reforms Tazhin pledged. At the same congressional hearing where Krol articulated his vision of a democratic Kazakhstan, U.S. Representative Christopher Smith noted that he had "re-read the Kazakhstan entry in the U.S. Department of State's country reports on human rights practices and it does not make for good reading. . . . It's very disturbing." Evgeny Zhovtis, the director of the Kazakh International Bureau for Human Rights and Rule of Law, echoed

Smith's misgivings and noted that the peaceful assembly petitions of "most opposition political parties and human rights groups . . . are usually rejected by the authorities."[38]

Conditionality is not the only tactic Western governments pursue in the hopes of furthering political reform in Central Asia. The United States, for example, funds extensive democratization and human rights programs in the region. The U.S. National Democratic Institute (NDI) and International Republican Institute (IRI) have worked to advance political party formation in political pluralism in Central Asia since the early 1990s. The USAID-funded nongovernmental organization Freedom House, the International Research & Exchanges Board, Radio Free Europe / Radio Liberty, and Counterpart Consortium have actively promoted civil society and media freedoms in the region since the mid-1990s. The returns on reform-oriented engagement, some analysts fear, are outweighed by Washington's pursuit of strategic interests. Following the September 11 attacks, Washington deepened its military relations with Uzbekistan and Kyrgyzstan. Such scholars as Alexander Cooley have argued that these deepened relations, particularly U.S. bases in Kyrgyzstan and Uzbekistan, have emboldened Kyrgyz and Uzbek autocratic leaderships while, at the same time, they have linked the U.S. government in the minds of the local reformists to the "undemocratic practices of new host countries."[39] Cooley's concerns are echoed by Central Asian reformers. Bakyt Beshimov, the campaign manager for opposition candidate Almazbek Atambaev in the July 2009 Kyrgyz presidential elections, told the *New York Times:* "This regime clearly understands that for the United States, democracy is not a priority, freedom of speech is not a priority. . . . They want peace, stability, air bases and regional security connected with Afghanistan."[40]

Seeming quid pro quos also appear to have shaped U.S. relations with Uzbekistan. In the summer of 2000 the CIA began using Uzbek airfields to launch Predator drone missions over Afghanistan. Immediately following the Karimov government's granting of access to Uzbek airfields, the U.S. government designated the Islamic Movement of Uzbekistan (IMU) a "foreign terror organization"—a designation Karimov subsequently used to justify dragnet police sweeps for alleged Islamist militants.[41] A State Department official would later confide that U.S. base negotiators fully understood that they needed to "throw Karimov a bone" in return for Tashkent's cooperation on the covert Predator program.[42] As U.S. engagement in Afghanistan deepened, more bones would be tossed. Between 2002 and 2005, Washington extended $480 million in aid to Uzbekistan in return for what U.S. defense secretary Donald Rumsfeld noted was President Karimov's "stalwart support in the war on terror."[43]

Perhaps even more meaningful to Karimov's continued hold on power, though, is the increasingly muscular role China is assuming in Central Asia. Indeed, the bones Washington delivers to Central Asian autocrats pale in comparison to the predictable feast China now offers. China is second only to Russia in bilateral trade with Kazakhstan and Kyrgyzstan.[44] Although reliable trade data for Uzbekistan are not available, China's growing influence in Tashkent is unmistakable. Less than two weeks after the Uzbek government's repression of the Andijan protests in May 2005, at a time when Western governments were withdrawing support to Tashkent, President Karimov was in Beijing inking a six-hundred-million-dollar agreement to develop Uzbekistan's hydrocarbon sector. During this same visit Beijing made it clear that, in contrast to its Western counterparts, China would continue to "support the efforts by the authorities of Uzbekistan to strike down the three forces of terrorism, separatism and extremism."[45]

China's new activism in the region leaves little doubt that Western strategies to link aid to Central Asian political reform will continue to struggle. Now not only the Moscow option is open to Central Asian leaders—the Beijing option is open as well. Karimov can close Western air bases and replace rent payments for these bases with financial windfalls from China. Nazarbaev can continue to orchestrate Kazakh politics and rest assured that Western states will remain reluctant to oppose Kazakh OSCE chairmanship for fear of pushing Nazarbaev further toward Russia and China. Similarly, President Bakiev, whom one high-ranking U.S. defense official labeled the "Blagojevich of Central Asia," was able to hold the U.S. air base in Kyrgyzstan—Washington's single remaining air base in Central Asia—for ransom and in return be rewarded with a three-fold increase in U.S. rent payments for the base in 2009.[46]

Although current geopolitics is not conducive to political reform in Kazakhstan, Kyrgyzstan, and Uzbekistan, neither was democracy on the march in Central Asia when in the early to mid-1990s Russia's imploding economy and China's fear of more Tiananmens left Washington free to champion liberalization policies in the region. Attention to the enduring institutions of Central Asian politics provides insights into why the West's enhanced engagement has not worked and why, on balance, geopolitics furthers rather than limits Central Asian authoritarianism. As I explore in greater detail in the conclusion, foreign governments can pursue policies to lessen the severity of authoritarian rule; they can freeze access and assets and thereby discount the payoffs Central Asian elites receive in return for loyalty to repressive presidents. These policies will not lead to democratization; these policies may, however, make presidential followers less accepting of the coercive excesses of authoritarian rule.

Islam and Autocracy

Islam, much like oil wealth and challenging geopolitics, is thought to inhibit political liberalization. The causalities scholars offer for how Islam acts as a break on political reform vary. The historian Bernard Lewis has suggested that the West and Muslims are locked in a "clash of civilizations—the perhaps irrational but surely historic reaction of an ancient rival against our Judeo-Christian heritage."[47] Exactly what about "our Judeo-Christian heritage" Muslims do not like, though, depends on which scholar you read. For Lewis, it is Western culture broadly that Muslims do not like. Muslims, he explains, are angry, indeed enraged, that the Islamic world has ceded its leading role in the arts and sciences to the West, to what was once the "outer darkness of barbarism and unbelief from which there was nothing to learn and little even to be imported, except slaves and raw materials."[48]

Lewis has been eviscerated for this sweeping thesis. The anthropologist Clifford Geertz, for one, suggests Lewis is a storyteller, albeit a good one, with "cloudscapes mighty like a whale and concocting Joycean big words that make us all afraid."[49] The literary theorist Edward Said likened Lewis's clash-of-civilizations depiction of Islam and the West to a "cartoonlike world where Popeye and Bluto bash each other mercilessly."[50] What is missing from clash-of-civilizations hypotheses, both Said and Geertz instruct, are the particulars—in Geertz's words the exact "lines of dispute"—that make Western civilization anathema to many Muslims.[51]

In an attempt to add such specificity, the political writer Ali Mazrui tells us it is the West's sex, drugs, and rock and roll that Muslims find most offensive. Thus, Mazrui writes, it is the West's toleration of "premarital sex, extramarital fornication, homosexuality and lesbianism, alcoholism and marijuana" that alienates most Muslims.[52] Values, of course, are relative; where Mazrui faults the West and the United States in particular for its moral laxity, coauthors David S. Landes and Richard A. Landes fault Muslims and Muslim men for their "oppression of women."[53] This oppression, they explain, is all but hardwired for, "according to the Hadith, Mohammad said, 'I was shown the hellfire and that the majority of its dwellers are women.'"[54]

According to these scholars and others, such are the fault lines that divide Western and Muslim civilizations. As for the chances that Popeye and Bluto will share a fist bump in Central Asia, this, the journalist Ahmed Rashid has concluded, is unlikely: "There is a palpable cultural vacuum at the heart of Central Asia, which cannot be filled by consumerism or imitations of Western culture."[55]

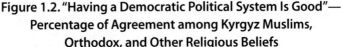

**Figure 1.2. "Having a Democratic Political System Is Good"—
Percentage of Agreement among Kyrgyz Muslims,
Orthodox, and Other Religious Beliefs**

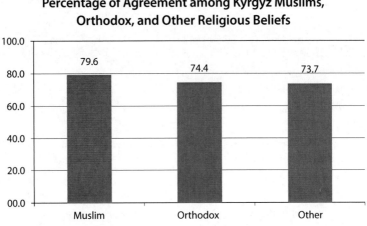

Source: World Values Survey, 2003.

How closely linked, though, are people's purported views of gender, sexuality, and consumerism and the forms of governance they are thought to prefer? The political scientist Samuel Huntington believes this link is immediate and concludes: "Western ideas of individualism, liberalism, constitutionalism, human rights, equality, liberty, the rule of law, democracy, free markets, the separation of church and state, often have little resonance in Islamic . . . cultures."[56] Recent survey research suggests, however, that Huntington's argument that Islamic cultures are adverse to democracy is tenuous. The political scientists Ronald Inglehart and Pippa Norris, for example, in their review of World Values Surveys data from 1995 through 1996 and 2000 through 2002, have found that "support for democratic institutions is just as strong among those living in Muslim societies as in Western (or other) societies."[57]

In 2003 the World Values Survey was conducted in Central Asia for the first time. Analysis of the 2003 poll, conducted in Kyrgyzstan, mirrors Inglehart and Norris's findings from the earlier World Value Surveys. Indeed, in Kyrgyzstan, Muslim respondents reported greater support for democratic institutions than did non-Muslims; 80 percent of Muslim respondents in the 2003 Kyrgyz survey agreed that "having a democratic political system is good," while 74 percent of Orthodox respondents as well as 74 percent of "other" believers and nonbelievers agreed that democratic systems were good.[58]

If the Kyrgyz case is an accurate indication, the familiar Islam as civilization explanation for nondemocratic outcomes finds little empirical support in Central Asia. This is not to say that Islam is inconsequential to Central Asian political outcomes. As discussed in the introduction, Islamic norms promote society-based capital accumulation; this capital in turn helps provide public goods that national governments, particularly the Uzbek and Kyrgyz national governments, do not provide at the local level. This finding is grounded on my own participant observation of local Islamic communities in Central Asia as well as on public opinion surveys that colleagues and I have been conducting in Kazakhstan, Kyrgyzstan, and Uzbekistan. The ensuing chapters discuss in detail the findings of my participant observation field research with these Muslim communities.[59] The survey results summarized next serve as a helpful shorthand illustrating the dynamic between Islam and local capital accumulation.

Three questions from our 2008 surveys in Kazakhstan, Kyrgyzstan, and Uzbekistan address the question of Islam and capital accumulation: religious identification; frequency of religious attendance; and donations of money or time to religious organizations. The vertical axis in figure 1.3 measures the percentage of people who donate money or time to religious organizations. The horizontal axis groups the Kyrgyz, Uzbek, and Kazakh survey samples into the following populations: the full survey sample for each country; Muslims within country survey samples who attend religious services once a month or more; and Muslims within country survey samples who attend religious services once a week or more.[60]

In all three Central Asian countries Muslims who attend religious services once a month or more are considerably more likely to donate money to religious organizations than the population as a whole. This might appear unremarkable, but when one considers what these religious organizations do—provide social as well as spiritual welfare—the potential challenge to Central Asian autocratic stability becomes readily apparent. Local religious organizations, to the extent that they provide public goods that the authoritarian state cannot, hold the potential to weaken economic incentives that help hold patronage-based regimes together. Moreover, as the historian Douglas Northrop has observed about the Stalin period, local Muslim communities present not only an economic threat to the state; they can also challenge the very legitimacy of the central state: "By looking from the perspective of the Muslim periphery, one gains new insight into the Stalinist state, seeing more clearly the character and extent of its power and its ongoing negotiations with society. This peripheral perspective illuminates the state's limits, its very real weakness in its efforts to extend cultural hegemony to other cultures."[61]

The hegemony of the secular autocratic state must not always be at odds with local religious communities. Kazakh president Nazarbaev, a leader who can provide extensive public goods, need not fear the rise of local Islamic charities and economic elites. In contrast, as figure 1.4 suggests, the Kyrgyz and Uzbek govern-

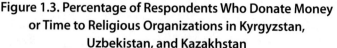

Figure 1.3. Percentage of Respondents Who Donate Money or Time to Religious Organizations in Kyrgyzstan, Uzbekistan, and Kazakhstan

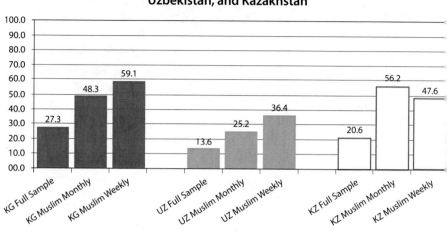

Source: Author surveys, 2008.

ments' ability to provide basic public goods is marginal. Given this limited ability, the Kyrgyz and Uzbek executives understandably are unnerved when Muslim charities and business elites emerge as alternatives to the state as economic and cultural focal points in local communities. These charities and economic elites, although they themselves rarely aspire to national power, do build through their everyday activities community networks. These networks in turn can and are mobilized against the central state when local populations feel aggrieved. The outcome of this mobilization, importantly, varies. The Uzbek president, unencumbered by worries of political elite disloyalty, can concentrate on repressing societal dissent. In contrast, the Kyrgyz president, distracted by the double challenge of a fragile winning coalition and comparatively limited economic means, is considerably more vulnerable to societal protest and unrest.

A New Authoritarian Research Agenda

Central to the preceding discussion of Kazakh, Kyrgyz, and Uzbek authoritarianism is the finding that perestroika-era institutions of autocratic rule endure. The formal model helps us understand why these institutions endure. The intersection of economic resources, geopolitics, and Islam with diverging perestroika institutional legacies helps us understand autocratic variations in ways that have

Figure 1.4. Kyrgyz and Uzbek Public Goods Provision as a Percentage of Kazakh Public Goods Provision

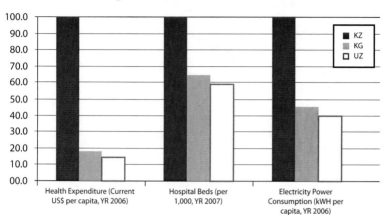

Source: World Bank World Development Indicators, available at http://data.worldbank.org/data-catalog/world-development-indicators.

largely been overlooked because of the transitions literature's focus on processes that lead to democratic outcomes. That said, this book would be incomplete without discussion of the possible, even probable, end to the perestroika institutional legacies that I have identified as driving the chaos, violence, and dynasty of Central Asian rule.

Uzbek and Kazakh authoritarian rule faces one challenge that expectantly chaotic Kyrgyz authoritarianism does not: the question of leadership succession. Nazarbaev's and Karimov's key strength—that they preside over large, executive-oriented parties—is also a potentially devastating weakness. These parties are fundamentally different from the Communist Party in that they are personality driven. Unlike the Communist Party, they may crumble should the Kazakh or Uzbek president die or suddenly fall ill. Should the party indeed crumble, as the scholar John Herz noted in his 1952 review of dictatorial regimes, "the power vacuum caused by the demise of the dictator may revive latent trends toward replacing the dictatorial regime."[62]

The existing transitions literature, because it is oriented to political change rather than institutional continuity, is particularly helpful in identifying what "latent trends" might emerge should presidential illness or death bring an end to perestroika legacies. Three of these still latent trends—the potentially divisive role of ethnic, regional, and clan identities—deserve particular emphasis in the Central Asian case.

Ethnic Identities

Ethnically heterogeneous postcolonial societies are thought to be more prone to conflict and instability than are postcolonial societies dominated by one titular nationality. Political scientists Alvin Rabushka and Kenneth Shepsle have observed, for example, that when newly independent states begin to assume the resource allocation responsibilities once performed by the colonial ruler, "internal rules of distribution become especially salient" and the potential for conflict among "citizens of different communities" grows.[63] Although Rabushka and Shepsle have focused on the postindependence period, their logic can be applied to any instance in which "internal rules of distribution" are in flux. The historian Francine Hirsch, for example, has illustrated that when Moscow delineated Central Asian republics in the 1920s and 1930s along centrally perceived nationality lines, "members of new national minorities—groups linguistically, physically, or culturally different from the titular nationalities (such as Kazakh native speakers in Uzbekistan)—faced forced discrimination, assimilation, and the loss of land and livelihood."[64] Similarly, when Gorbachev's perestroika reforms threatened long-standing patronage politics patterns of resource distribution in Central Asia, we saw ethnic riots in Kazakhstan, Kyrgyzstan, and Uzbekistan.

A reasonable hypothesis one might draw for post-Soviet Central Asia given these past instances of resource-redistribution conflict is that ethnically heterogeneous countries are likely to see conflict and instability whereas titular-dominated countries will likely prove more peaceful. Indeed, this is an outcome that Martha Brill Olcott, a Central Asia expert at the Carnegie Endowment for International Peace, fears in Kazakhstan. In contrast to the now overwhelmingly titular-dominated populations in Uzbekistan, Kazakhstan remains remarkably heterogeneous. As of the 1999 census (the results of the 2009 census are not yet available), ethnic Kazakhs were slightly more than half of the total population (53.4 percent), while Russians and Ukrainians were just over a third of the total population (33.7 percent). Because of this continued ethnic heterogeneity, Olcott has warned, "the Kazakh government's embrace of the vocabulary of postcolonialism has further divided the country into the colonized and the colonizers."[65] Olcott goes so far as to envision a future in which "state-sponsored ideological tenor of postcolonialism will continue to divide the population along ethnic lines and create the various ethnically rooted forms of radicalism that the state has identified as antithetical to its goals."[66]

Olcott's concern, importantly, is not without foundation. Fortunately, Kazakhstan's comparative wealth has thus far dampened the ethnic radicalism she fears. In poverty-stricken Kyrgyzstan, Rabushka and Shepsle's anticipation that in postcolonial environments redistribution politics can lead to interethnic violence has lamentably proven true. In June 2010 ethnic Kyrgyz and Uzbeks once again clashed in the southern Kyrgyz cities of Bazar Korgan, Jalal Abad, and Osh. Although Kyrgyzstan's June riots have been the only case of deadly ethnic conflict (approximately three hundred people, mainly Uzbeks, died in the violence), Olcott's and Rabushka and Shepsle's sober warnings nevertheless are worth heeding.

Clan and Regional Identities

The work of political scientists Kathleen Collins and Edward Schatz on clan identities suggests that even in the Kyrgyz and Uzbek cases of comparative ethnic homogeneity, autocratic polities are still vulnerable to destabilizing identity politics. Collins has defined clans as "informal organizations linked by kin and fictive kin identities."[67] These kin identities, she argues, pervade politics in Central Asia and debilitate the state from the inside out: "Authoritarian law has been strong when repressing democracy, but weak when controlling its own cadre of increasingly corrupt clan elites."[68] Schatz, moreover, has warned that a greater distribution of wealth among clans is necessary if the Kazakh government is to "transform clan politics into something less explosive."[69] Collins is cautiously more optimistic and suggests that both the Kazakh and Turkmen leaderships' access to oil wealth means these "regimes are temporarily more durable than their neighbors."[70] Yet she also has argued that this same oil wealth will "foster instability between clans and hinder democratization in the long run."[71]

These scholars are correct that clan identities are keenly perceived both among the elite and in broader Central Asian society. USAID surveys conducted in Kazakhstan and Kyrgyzstan in 1999, for example, reveal that 34 percent of Kazakh and 28 percent of Kyrgyz respondents agree with the statement: "People in your society are excluded from meaningful political, social, or economic participation on the basis of clan ties."[72] Kazakh president Nazarbaev himself has acknowledged that clans shape government and commerce: "Certain forms of kinship protectionism and clan and territorial lobbies do, at times, appear in government institutions and in the financial and commercial spheres."[73] As illustrated in figure 1.5, other identity-based cleavages are perceived as equally if not more exclusionary than clan identity. Thus survey respondents are just as, if not more likely, to cite ethnicity and region as the dividing line between favored and unfavored populations.

Collins would question my inclusion of region as an identity with any potential causal effect on political outcomes. She has criticized Pauline Jones Luong, for

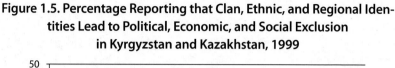

Figure 1.5. Percentage Reporting that Clan, Ethnic, and Regional Identities Lead to Political, Economic, and Social Exclusion in Kyrgyzstan and Kazakhstan, 1999

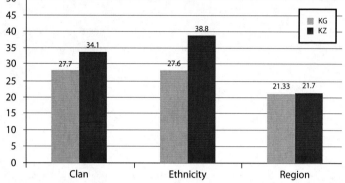

Source: Nationwide surveys commissioned by USAID and conducted by the Almaty-based Central Asian polling agency, Brif, in June 1999. The Kazakh survey includes 1,219 respondents. The Kyrgyz survey includes 1,200 respondents.

example, for "several faulty assumptions: that regions are equivalent to identities; that regions are the only salient political identities in post-Soviet Central Asia; and that the administrative-territorial institutions of the Soviet regime created regional identities."[74] Luong does not argue that regional identities are invariably salient. Rather, she suggests regional identities may become salient as a result of a "transitional bargaining game."[75] Hence, in the Kyrgyz case regional identities proved strong because President Akaev, although he "had the opportunity to decrease or at least impose greater limits on regional akims' growing authority," chose instead to support the "'spontaneous' devolution of power occurring in the republic."[76] These strong regional identities in turn have produced Kyrgyz electoral institutions that allowed for substantive contestation.

In Uzbekistan, in contrast, Luong finds that Karimov made "a concerted effort to bring decision making and implementation under the exclusive control of central authorities rather than to devolve authority to the regional leaders."[77] Karimov's hard-headedness undermined regional actors' perceived sense of strength and therefore produced Uzbekistan's highly centralized autocracy. In Kazakhstan, Luong finds a government that "allowed the media as well as independent political organizations to develop virtually uninhibited." At the same time, Luong emphasizes that the Nazarbaev government "concentrated the bulk of political authority in its own hands."[78] Nazarbaev's "mixed" policy of enabling a relatively free media yet concentrating executive power emboldened regional actors, allowing them to exert some say over electoral institutions at the local level. However, Nazarbaev's firm control over national-level electoral institutions, Luong illustrates, remained unchallenged.

Although the 1999 survey results summarized in figure 1.5 suggest that regional identities may not be as widely perceived as clan identities, Luong's depiction of Kyrgyz, Uzbek, and Kazakh executive bargaining is insightful. Luong points to variables temporarily specific to the "transitional context" of the 1990s and emphasizes how the geopolitics and economics of the post-Soviet period strengthen or weaken the bargaining power of central and regional political elites. I build on Luong's insight and illustrate that although Luong's "transitional context" is important, we can trace Central Asian executives' diverging bargaining positions during this transitional context to an earlier period: to the diverging perestroika-era institutional legacies that resulted from Moscow's intervention to preserve united elite politics in Kazakhstan and Uzbekistan and to Moscow's non-intervention during Kyrgyzstan's June 1990 crisis in elite politics.

I do not wish to suggest that identities—be they regional, clan, or ethnic—have no role in Central Asian politics. These identities, just like changes in geopolitics and economic resource wealth, do hold the potential to redefine patterns of Kyrgyz, Uzbek, and Kazakh authoritarianism. The potential influence of these variables, moreover, increases as the question of leadership succession, particularly in the Uzbek and Kazakh cases, becomes more and more pressing. Should Karimov or Nazarbaev die or weaken and the process of leadership succession appear uncertain, then political elites may well abandon presidential parties in favor of more ascriptive identities. To some degree, the Uzbek and Kazakh presidents have anticipated this likelihood and have sought to set in place mechanisms that would facilitate the transfer of power to a chosen successor. As I describe in chapters 4 and 5, Karimov and Nazarbaev have drafted new constitutions, redesigned parliaments, and empowered judiciaries—all to buttress presidential power. These constitutions, parliaments, and judiciaries contain within them mechanisms to facilitate the transfer of power to Karimov's and Nazarbaev's chosen successors.

Curiously, although Karimov and Nazarbaev (as well as Kyrgyz leaders) have promoted the growth of parliaments and judiciaries, their embrace of these institutions is often lukewarm. Building legislatures and courts so as to further authoritarian rule is a gamble; deferential parliaments and judiciaries can turn on their executive patrons, particularly when these patrons begin to look weak. John Herz noted, for example, that creating "institutions may mean conferring authority and prestige on them which may well be exploited by anti-dictatorial groups at the demise of the dictator, or even prior to it."[79] Similarly, the political scientist Joel Migdal has illustrated how the "unique perspective any state agency assumes creates in it centrifugal tendencies, pulling it from the views of other agencies and the executive state leadership."[80]

In Egypt, for example, the Supreme Constitutional Court issued a series of decisions in the 1990s that, as demonstrated by the Tamir Moustafa, allowed the political opposition as well as human rights organizations "to score impressive political victories" and thereby limit the degree of President Hosni Mubarak's authoritarian rule.[81] These decisions in turn enabled representatives from the Muslim Brotherhood, an organization long repressed by the Mubarak government, to contest and actually win seats in Egypt's 2005 parliamentary election, thereby transforming this once executive-dominated institution into a sounding board for criticizing Mubarak's limitations on political rights and civil liberties.[82]

Moustafa emphasized that there are limits on how far these institutions can pull away from Mubarak. Thus he quoted the former chief justice 'Awad al-Murr's observation that the Supreme Constitutional Court must adhere to a "red-line system" and ultimately deferred to Mubarak in cases where the president perceived strong threats.[83] As the February 2011 popular uprising demonstrates, though, Mubarak's red-line system was adequate for sounding alarms but not up to the task of eliminating all threats. Egypt's combination of an aging autocrat, an activist judiciary, an emboldened parliament, and a mobilized civil society ultimately has led to substantive political change.

I began this chapter with the observation that many in the academic and policy worlds remain focused on explaining what Central Asia is not—democratic—rather than on providing causal logics for the marked and substantive variations in Central Asian autocratic rule that do exist. I then offered an alternative lens with which to view Central Asia and authoritarian states more broadly. Central to this alternative lens is an emphasis on enduring institutions and, specifically, the elite institutions that emerged before the collapse of the ancien régime. That Presidents Karimov and Nazarbaev entered the post-Soviet period with stable, executive-oriented parties enabled these two leaders to devote their attention to capacity-enhancing activities, most notably to public goods provision in the Kazakh case and the building of coercive institutions in the Uzbek case. The Kyrgyz executive, in contrast, entered the post-Soviet period dependent on a fragmented and narrow political elite. As a result, President Akaev and his successors have had to concentrate on maintaining sufficient support from within this elite to remain in power.

The next chapter discusses the emergence of these diverging perestroika-era institutions in detail and provides further confirming evidence for the Mesquita selectorate model, a model that owes considerable intellectual debts to political scientist Mancur Olson's 1971 *Logic of Collective Action* and economist Albert Hirschman's 1970 book, *Exit, Voice, and Loyalty.*[84] The central insights of this model—that loyalty to the executive decreases as the size of the broader political elite decreases and that resource wealth enhances an executive's ability to engage in capacity-building projects increases—help us understand the considerable constraints the Kyrgyz executive faces and the considerable agency the Kazakh and Uzbek presidents enjoy.

The explanatory power of these models is itself dependent on the specifics of Central Asian history as well as the specifics of the current geopolitical, economic, and societal world in which Kazakhstan, Kyrgyzstan, and Uzbekistan are immersed. Authoritarian states are not fixed entities; rather, they are dynamic and always possess the potential for change. My research emphasizes two variables—economic resources and the increasing prominence of local Islamic communities—that motivate the diverging patterns of authoritarianism, the chaos, violence, and dynasty, detailed in the introduction. Thus, although Uzbekistan and Kazakhstan share similar elite institutions, thanks to Moscow's intervention, these countries have differing economic endowments. Extensive hydrocarbon reserves allow the Kazakh president to invest in public goods and thereby mitigate societal dissent. The Uzbek president enjoys less access to economic resources. Control of the cotton industry, gold mining, and the country's small hydrocarbon reserves does provide funds for building coercive capacity. Revenue from these industries, as illustrated in figure 1.4, has not proven sufficient for the large-scale provision of public goods.

In Kyrgyzstan the executive's challenge is even greater; not only are easily tapped economic resources scarce in Kyrgyzstan, the structure of Kyrgyz elite politics is unconducive to public goods provision. For a Kyrgyz president to remain in power, he must devote what scarce resources he does have to securing his tenuous winning coalition. For the first decade of post-Soviet Kyrgyz rule, President Akaev was successful in maintaining this coalition. Paradoxically, though, it was largely the economic resources available to the Kyrgyz executive—that is, the nature of foreign aid—that enabled Akaev to secure a stable coalition. Given the diffuse nature of foreign aid, the president was forced to share state wealth. In contrast, when presented with a windfall of U.S. dollars in return for American use of the Manas Air Base in 2001, first Akaev and next Bakiev outright stole state wealth. This stealing of state wealth (rather than use of scarce resources to maintain viable winning coalitions) compelled disgruntled Kyrgyz political elites to overthrow Akaev in 2005 and Bakiev in 2010.

Lastly, in both the Kyrgyz and the Uzbek cases, the state's inability to provide public goods has accentuated the importance of local charities and businesses,

Table 1.4. Explaining Chaos, Violence and Dynasty in Central Asia

	Perestroika Period	Economic Resources	Presence of Local Islamic Charities and Businesses	Authoritarian Outcome
Uzbekistan	Intervention, Party Maintained	Moderate	High	Repressive Authoritarianism
Kyrgyzstan	No Intervention, Party Collapse	Low	High	Chaotic Authoritarianism
Kazakhstan	Intervention, Party Maintained	High	Low	Stable Authoritarianism

particularly local Muslim charities and businesses. The shared norms of Islam, like the norms of many belief systems, facilitate community trust and capital accumulation. These charities and businesses therefore become increasingly central to public welfare. Rarely do the leaders of these charities aspire to national politics. The networks and overlapping identities—be they regional, clan, or even ethnic identities—that these Muslim charities and businesses facilitate, however, can be mobilized in response to perceived injustices of central government rule. We have seen this mobilization in both the Uzbek and Kyrgyz cases, the central governments' responses, and the chaos and violence that results. Table 1.4 illustrates these diverging Uzbek, Kyrgyz, and Kazakh outcomes and the causal variables that have driven these outcomes in Central Asia.

Table 1.4 also directs our attention to future potential regime variations. For example, current economic endowments enable the Kazakh president to provide extensive public goods and the Uzbek executive to build repressive power. A collapse in hydrocarbon prices, though, could erode the Kazakh president's ability to distribute state largesse, while boycotts of Uzbek cotton and falling gold prices could eliminate Karimov's ability to repress. Conversely, outside powers—China, Russia, or even the United States—could send financial windfalls to the Kyrgyz executive in return for desired cooperation and thereby enable the Kyrgyz president to distribute payoffs sufficiently attractive to secure what otherwise would be a tenuous winning coalition.

Such changing economic endowments in turn would alter the state-society dynamic of Islamic revivalism. Declining economic resources would further accelerate revivalism and the devolution of public goods provision to local Muslim communities in Uzbekistan and Kyrgyzstan, which might precipitate a rise of these communities in Kazakhstan. Increasing resources likely would not eliminate the importance of Islamic charities to local communities, but increasing resources may allay governments' concerns (most notably the Uzbek government's concerns) that these charities threaten the autonomy and legitimacy of the central state. Most important is the fragility of these autocrats themselves. Presidents Nazarbaev and Karimov are in their seventies. Although the presidents may not be focused on their accumulating frailties, members of their inner circles most definitely are. Change will come to Central Asia, and a clear understanding of how diverging patterns of elite rule interact with economic resources and the region's increasingly robust local Islamic communities will help us anticipate what direction this change is likely to take.

2 The Soviet Origins of Post-Soviet Autocratic Variation

CENTRAL TO UNDERSTANDING the diverging paths of Kazakh, Kyrgyz, and Uzbek authoritarianism are the differing legacies of the perestroika period. In the framing of this book's causal arguments, I suggested that Moscow's interventions to restore Communist Party discipline in Uzbekistan and Kazakhstan in the late 1980s following each of these countries' elite-destabilizing ethnic riots enabled the Karimov and Nazarbaev leaderships to emerge from the Soviet collapse with intact executive-oriented parties. Drawing on the insights of the Mesquita selectorate model, I illustrated how these large executive-oriented parties not only provide Karimov and Nazarbaev with greater elite loyalty, but also free both presidents to invest resources in such capacity-enhancing projects as public goods provision and building institutions of state coercion.

In contrast, Moscow's decision not to intervene in Kyrgyz politics after the Osh and Uzgen ethnic riots in 1990 prompted the dissolution of single-party politics and the rise of a fragmented Kyrgyz political elite. This fragmented elite forces the Kyrgyz executive to devote attention and resources to maintaining his fragile winning coalition and limits the executive's ability to invest in capacity-enhancing public goods and institutions of coercion. This shifting of the Central Asian causal narrative to the earlier perestroika period helps produce a more accurate accounting of diverging patterns of governance in the region. In emphasizing pre-transition causalities rather than the post-1991 focus that typifies much of the democratization literature, I recognize that my analysis must address the challenge of what methodologists have termed "infinite regress."[1] Moscow's interventions and noninterventions during the perestroika era themselves are outcomes in need of explanation.

This chapter explores the history of Soviet rule in Central Asia to uncover the chain of events that led to Moscow's interventions in the late 1980s in Uzbekistan and Kazakhstan and the subsequent nonintervention in 1990 in Kyrgyzstan. Three themes emerge from this historical review. First, Soviet leaders' need to differentiate their policies from those of their predecessors encouraged alternating patterns of incrementalist and radical reform policies in the USSR broadly and in Central Asia in particular. Second, the radical reform policy set available to Soviet leaders narrowed over time, as first Stalin's coercive reengineering and second Khrushchev's scientific reengineering of the Soviet polity failed to secure Communism's promise of a better future. Third, this narrowing of available reform strategies made Gorbachev's own approach to radical reform, his elimination of Communist Party monopoly power, more probable. In short, although formal models based on existing institutional endowments may help us understand diverging political outcomes when systems more or less are in equilibrium, the institutional endowments that set these parsimonious models in motion are often the result of complex causal chains that cannot be reduced to broadly generalizable theories.

This chapter examines the pre-Gorbachev history of Soviet rule in Central Asia and highlights how ideology, specifically Communism's promise for a better future, encouraged Soviet leaders to solidify their positions and build political legitimacy. They did so by pointing to the failures of their predecessors' policies while forwarding new prescriptions toward securing this better future. Lenin distinguished Soviet rule from tsarist land confiscations and forced military conscription by promising Central Asians less intervention and greater local autonomy. Stalin in turn rejected Lenin's incrementalism and, rather than tolerate Central Asian practices that were at odds with his vision of Communism (most notably Central Asian Islam and small-scale private agriculture), sought to eliminate these practices through collectivization and through the conscription of Muslim women as a "surrogate proletariat." Khrushchev too had grand visions for the region but, seeing the political gains to be had by rejecting Stalin's repression, instead turned to the promise of science and industry to transform Central Asia's deserts into the Soviet Union's new Virgin Lands. Brezhnev, who developed a firsthand understanding of Central Asia while serving as the deputy and then first secretary of the Kazakh Communist Party (from 1954 through 1956), dismissed what he saw as the folly of the Virgin Lands. Rather, he argued that a stable cohort of Communist Party cadres would guarantee Communism's advance in Central Asia.

In addition to setting in motion a causal chain leading to Gorbachev's own perestroika attempts at radical reform, this pre-Gorbachev history also contributed to the formation of many of the institutions that define Central Asia today. Lenin emphasized patronage politics as an attractive alternative to heavy-handed tsarist-ruled Central Asia. Stalin, much as Central Asia's current leaders do to varying degrees of effectiveness today, used the judiciary to hobble perceived political threats. Brezhnev returned to and deepened Lenin's strategy of patronage rule, creating an extensive network of embezzlement-based relations between Moscow and the Central Asian political elite, a network that Gorbachev would have to confront when in the mid-1980s the Soviet economy turned sour.

This chapter also addresses the worsening Soviet economy of the 1980s, Gorbachev's attempts to reform Communism to meet mounting economic challenges, and the consequences these attempts at reform had on elite politics in Central Asia. I focus on the sequencing of four perestroika-era events. Three of these were ethnic riots: riots between Kazakhs and Russians in Alma-Ata in December 1986; clashes between Uzbeks and Meskhetian Turks in Uzbekistan's Fergana Valley in 1989; and fighting between Kyrgyz and Uzbeks on the Kyrgyz side of the Fergana Valley in 1990. The causal import of these riots was not uniform. In Kazakhstan and Uzbekistan ethnic conflict paradoxically solidified patronage rule. Ethnic riots in Kyrgyzstan, however, eroded patronage politics stability. That these similar ethnic conflicts should produce dissimilar political outcomes is the product of the fourth critical event: General Secretary Gorbachev's February 1990 decision to end the Communist Party's monopoly hold on power and introduce a measure of competition in Soviet politics. Taken together, the pre-Gorbachev history of Soviet rule in Central Asia and the worsening Soviet economy of the 1980s demonstrate that, although the periodization of causality is tricky, by expanding our "time horizons" we can more accurately evaluate the causes and consequences of specific events.[2]

Transitologists have tended to view the Soviet collapse as an exogenous shock that in short order propelled post-Soviet states toward greater or lesser degrees of democratic outcomes. I too cite what some might argue is an exogenous shock—Gorbachev's diverging intervention policies in Central Asia—as a causal explanation for differing Kazakh, Kyrgyz, and Uzbek political trajectories. Yet by placing this decision within an expanded historical context, we can remove at least some of the mystery behind why Gorbachev pursued the policies he did and the diverging consequences these policies would later have on Central Asian politics. The divergence in Central Asian authoritarian rule we now see is the product of path dependency and critical junctures. Although the parsimonious and generalizable formal model developed in the preceding chapter helps us understand the mechanics of Kyrgyz chaos, Uzbek violence, and Kazakh dynasty, the model itself is predicated on an understanding of how inherited perestroika-era institutions of elite rule emerged in the first place. These institutions are products of long causal chains in which Moscow's leaders, often in response to political challenges far outside of Central Asia, repeatedly attempted to revitalize a flagging Communist system. Within Central Asia, Moscow's attempts at revitalization manifested as oscillations between purges and patronage. These waves washed across all of Central Asia. The late-perestroika period undercurrents within Central Asia meant that the residue of Soviet rule that these waves left behind varied markedly in Astana, Bishkek, and Tashkent.

Soviet Rule in Central Asia from Lenin to Brezhnev

Central Asia was not unknown territory for the Bolsheviks in 1917. To the extent that they drew lessons from the tsarist experience, the Bolsheviks had cause both for optimism and concern regarding the ability to project power from European Russia into the Central Asian borderlands. Working in Moscow's favor were the region's internal divisions and, according to some Central Asian historians, a desire within Central Asia for an external power, some form of a Leviathan, to quell these divisions. The Kazakhs were "exhausted by internecine battles between khans, sultans and elders and by the prolonged war with the Jungars," and among the Kyrgyz people "tribal divisions limited unity and consolidation."[3] The Jungars and the Kalmyks had been encroaching on Kazakh and Kyrgyz grazing lands since the early seventeenth century. Kazakhs viewed tsarist suzerainty, as the Central Asian historian Manash K. Kozybaev has explained, as a way "to protect their nation."[4] The Uzbek lands may have been less divided than the Kazakh and Kyrgyz territories, but here too the historian Adeeb Khalid has noted, tsarist power was not unwelcome; the Uzbek political and religious hierarchy (often one and the same) "were happy enough to cooperate with the Russian administration and to accept state honors and decorations."[5]

Admittedly, there may be a degree of teleology in these portrayals of Central Asian receptivity to Russian authority. For example, nineteenth-century observers of Russian–Central Asian relations did not always share their twentieth-century counterparts' certainty that Russian authority would take hold in these distant lands. The British traveler Alexander Burnes, for one, noted that although it arguably was a step forward that "the subjects of Russia have ceased to be sold into slavery in Bukhara," Saint Petersburg's effort to exert power faced daunting challenges: "Should these countries ever be subdued from that quarter, it would be found most difficult to retain them, or control the wandering tribes around. Regular troops would be useless, and irregulars could not subdue a race who had no fixed places of abode. It is not, however, to be concealed that the court of St. Petersburg have long cherished designs in this quarter of Asia."[6]

Moreover, it was not only the wandering tribes who tested Saint Petersburg's will. So too did the tsarist administration face considerable challenges in compelling its own bureaucrats to Central Asia. The sands of Central Asia did not hold the same attraction as the beaches of Sochi and, as a result, it was not Saint Petersburg's best and brightest that sought posts in these borderlands. Saint Petersburg "habitually rid itself of its worst officers by sending them to Turkestan," and these officers struggled to understand Central Asia's complex and fluid hierarchies of power and authority.[7] Tsarist authorities did attempt to divide the region into governorships, oblasts, and counties. These same authorities realized that beyond the stationing of military force to prevent the "internecine battles" that had once destabilized the region, day-to-day governance in Central Asia was best left to local elites, to the region's clans, *aksakals* (elders), *qadi* (judges), ulema, and khans.

To encourage some measure of accountability, these elites were paid directly from the tsarist budget. Elected by their villages to three-year terms, local elites were given salaries in the hope that this would provide them with some incentive to implement central directives, collect taxes, and adjudicate local disputes.[8] These qadi and aksakals ruled much as they had before—sporadically and not always effectively. The great innovation of tsarist rule, and an innovation Lenin would replicate once in power, was that these indigenous elites were now tied, if only nominally, to centralized patronage—that is, to tsarist coffers.[9] These economic ties did not run only from the tsarist administration to local elites. As the Kyrgyz historians Zhyrgal K. Baktygulov and Dzhumadil S. Mombekova have noted, Russian bureaucrats were often co-opted by local economic elites—a pattern we see among today's centrally appointed bureaucrats in post-Soviet Kazakhstan, Kyrgyzstan, and Uzbekistan.[10]

Not all went smoothly with tsarist rule. Although the passivity of the tsar's Central Asian bureaucrats proved a good trait given their underwhelming administrative capacity, passivity also gave free license for a newly arrived Russian peasantry to appropriate the best farmlands from local Central Asian populations.[11] On the few occasions tsarist administrators did assert themselves, the results were devastating. In June 1916, for example, Nicholas II, desperate for more bodies to throw at the Germans, decreed that all Central Asian males between the ages of nineteen and forty-three were to enlist and join the war effort.[12] This 1916 decree "detonated" deadly anti-tsarist protests and, in so doing, gave rise to incipient Central Asian nationalism—a process that would prove helpful to later attempts to extend Soviet rule to the region.[13]

Lenin's Proxy Rule

Lenin was quick to recognize his tsarist predecessor's mistakes. The new Bolshevik leader pointedly rejected anything that resembled Russian imperialism. He sought to limit the "tide of chauvinistic Great-Russian riffraff" in the non-Russian territories, while at the same time he championed "the full and unhindered development not only of locally peculiar characteristics, but also of local initiative, local innovation, of diversity in the means and approaches."[14] Lenin's words were matched in practice. He amnestied members of the Alash Orda, Kazakh nationalists who had fought alongside the White Army in the Russian Civil War, and extended these nationalists prominent positions in the new Bolshevik bureaucracy in Central Asia. Lenin sought the indigenization of Soviet politics in Central Asia and the equitable division of economic resources among local populations. This localization of rule, in part ideologically driven with the goal of distinguishing Communism from what Lenin believed was the more pernicious European model of imperialism, had the added advantage of making Moscow the central court of appeals for all local disputes. As the historian Francine Hirsch has demonstrated, Moscow, in dividing territories among what it perceived to be ethno-linguistically differentiated Central Asian populations, not only became the arbiter of Central Asian identities but also the distributor of wealth in Central Asia.[15] Border populations that once held fluid identities began emphasizing their Kazakh, Kyrgyz, or Uzbek heritages in an effort to lay claim to disputed land and resources. Conveniently for the Bolshevik elite, Moscow adjudicated these competing claims and in the process established itself as the authority to which Central Asian populations would turn to solve local and regional disputes.[16]

Although this role as external arbiter helped Moscow solidify authority within Central Asia, Lenin feared that Russian chauvinism would undermine Soviet power in the borderlands. He feared that "any political system" would be hard-pressed to limit the "yoke of national oppression and the striving for annexations, i.e., the violation of national independence."[17] One year before his death in January 1924, Lenin questioned whether the Soviets had been "careful enough to take measures to provide the non-Russians with a real safeguard against the truly Russian bully."[18] This unease proved well founded. As the historian Gregory

Massell has written, "Bolshevik arch-centralizers could always justify a ruthless crackdown" on Central Asian elites by claiming a need to "root out opponents of 'overall coordination' and hence harbingers of fragmentation."[19] In the Kyrgyz case local elites brought the abuses of these "arch-centralizers" to Lenin and Stalin's attention and likened them to tsarist excesses during the 1916 conscription campaign. Had Lenin not died in 1924, perhaps these abuses would have been addressed. Instead, Stalin filed away this complaint and subsequently used what has become known as the "Letter from the Kyrgyz Group of Thirty" as a who's who list for those who would be first eliminated in the 1930s party purges.[20]

Lenin, despite his lionization as the leader of the Bolshevik revolution, was anything but revolutionary in his rule of Central Asia. His indigenization and ethno-territorial delimitation policies did aid the Bolsheviks in their attempts to solidify authority in the region. Lenin did not seek to fundamentally redefine local power structures and hierarchies. If Moscow was a distant patron, the ulema, aksakals, and qadi were Central Asia's day-to-day rulers. In short, Lenin planted the flag of Soviet power in the regions but did little to alter the Central Asian status quo. Six decades later, protesters, angered by Gorbachev's appointment of an ethnic Russian as the new Kazakh first secretary, would approvingly invoke Lenin's pursuit of the Central Asian status quo. Thus the protestors took to the streets of Alma-Ata with signs reading: "We are for Leninist nationality policies," "To every people—their own leader," "We need a Kazakh leader," and "If this is perestroika, where's the democracy?"[21]

Stalin, Replacing Patronage Rule with Coercion

Lenin's legacy, as the 1986 Alma-Ata protest placards illustrate, was that of indigenization and proxy rule. Subsequent leaders, even those who pursued radical change like Stalin and Gorbachev, would never fully abandon Leninist nationality policies and patronage politics. Yet the emphasis in what strategies Soviet leaders would use in the borderlands would shift as each new leader attempted to differentiate himself from his predecessor—and his predecessor's protégés—by offering a fresh vision for achieving Communism's promise. For Stalin this meant countering the gradualist approach of Leninist torchbearers, most notably Bukharin, with a strategy of bold change. Thus, as the historian Stephen Cohen has written, Stalin's "intensification theory" was an alternative to Bukharin's emphasis on the Leninist status quo: "The warfare themes of nascent Stalinism were central to the struggle between Bukharin and Stalin. They constituted a radical counterpoint to Bukharin's fundamental arguments—class collaboration, civil peace, and evolutionary development; systematic 'extraordinary measures' were antithetical to the conciliatory, peaceful policies he called 'NEP' [New Economic Plan] methods."[22]

Central Asia was an ideal exhibit for Stalin to demonstrate how Bukharin's favored New Economic Plan was retrograde rather than revolutionary. Under the NEP the power of the Central Asian traditional elite (the ulema, aksakals, and qadi) had actually increased rather than decreased. This elite, the historian Martha Brill Olcott has written, "emerged from the Civil War period with their authority enhanced . . . [they] simply reconstructed themselves as soviets and governed their populations much as before."[23] The Soviet Union, as Central Asia painfully illustrated, was going backward, this at a time when the rest of Europe advanced its "hostile capitalist encirclement."[24] If radical measures were not taken, Stalin asserted in contrast to Bukharin's argument in favor of incrementalism, Russia would suffer "one more beating by foreigners."[25]

These radical measures would introduce two new and ultimately enduring strategies for projecting power in Central Asia: the state's instrumental politicization and attempted pacification of Islam and the use of predatory courts. Both strategies were framed as progressive policies that, by eliminating tsarist and feudal vestiges, would move Central Asia and the Soviet Union toward a brighter and more equitable future. Central Asians, however, remember this period as that of the gravest injustice of their Soviet past. Stalin's politicization of Islam was an attempt to humiliate and thereby eliminate Central Asia's Muslim elite. In late 1926 the Bolsheviks began the *hujum* (the "storm") to liberate what Stalin and his supporters defined as the unjust subjugation of Central Asian women.[26] The hujum in many ways was likely viewed in Moscow as a perfect storm. Images of Central Asian women, their faces hidden by horsehair veils, instantly resonated among the party faithful.

As the scholar Douglas Northrop has written, few seemed troubled by the Bolsheviks' new tactic, by the fact that "a Marxist revolution promising class liberation had been transfigured into a project of gender emancipation."[27] Just the opposite, as the historian Gregory Massell has illustrated, the liberation of Central Asian women provided the foundations for a new Soviet vision of Marxism: "It may be said, then, that Moslem women came to constitute, in Soviet political imagination, a structural weak point in the traditional order: a potentially deviant and hence subversive stratum susceptible to militant appeal—in effect a *surrogate proletariat* where no proletariat in the real Marxist sense existed."[28] Conveniently, the hujum served another goal: the delegitimation of Central Asia's Islamic elite. The hujum was designed to be a "'symbolic subversion' that was meant to overturn the old ways completely."[29] The hujum, so Moscow believed, would lay bare how Central Asian Islam demeaned and subjugated women. Once made aware of their oppression, Central Asian women would revolt against "traditional family structures" and this, Moscow reasoned, was "the key to undermining traditional social order."[30]

The strategies Moscow employed in undermining Central Asia's traditional Muslim elite were ruthless. Massell has recounted, for example, how one village aksakal was "forced to climb to the top of the mosque's minaret (whence the *muezzin* usually calls the faithful to prayer) and was obliged to urinate from there while the prayers were in progress."[31] Similarly, Northrop writes that "public shame also was used against Communists who refused to unveil their wives." The purpose being "to reach a large audience, these local episodes were then recounted in newspaper articles, editorials, even newsreels."[32] Such public shaming, however, failed ultimately to delegitimize Islam in Central Asian society.[33]

As Northrop has illustrated through his recounting of the so-called Chust Affair, local populations often rallied behind embattled Muslim elites rather than sit passively as hujum organizers sought to reshape local politics. On April 16, 1927, hundreds of Uzbeks gathered outside the Chust Communist Party building to protest the detention of several local imams, who the previous day had disrupted a "women's liberation meeting" convened to discuss the hujum.[34] The Chust Affair would be a harbinger of a similar event in post-Soviet Uzbekistan. This protest ended in bloodshed—the death of a police officer—which in turn precipitated further repression from the Soviet state. The Soviet secret police (the Ob'edinennoe gosudarstvennoe politicheskoe upravlenie, known as the OGPU) prepared a list of 127 "ringleaders" and mounted Soviet police frightened the Chust population into passivity.[35] Seventy-eight years later and sixty miles to the east of Chust, thousands of Uzbeks gathered in the streets of Andijan on May 13, 2005, to protest the Karimov government's imprisonment of prominent local Islamic elites. Karimov, claiming that this was an Islamist uprising, dispatched heavily armed troops to quell the protesters. Hundreds—189 according to the Uzbek government, as many as 700 according to the U.S. State Department—died in the ensuing clash.[36]

This inability to eradicate Islam presented first Stalin and now Karimov a litmus test with which to police the political elite. Hence, when Stalin sought to rid the Communist of an elite still inclined toward Bukharin's and Lenin's evolutionary policies, alleged Islamic perversions served as ready justification for the Central Asian party purges. Party members were tried and ultimately purged for having "threatened or beat women who wished to unveil; harassed Zhenotdel activists; practiced polygyny, bride price, and underage marriage; and took sexual advantage of—even raped and murdered—unveiled schoolgirls, women and activists."[37] Others party members were found guilty of "showing no inclination to break their ties with *mullahs* and *ishans* . . . [for their] being under the influence of an ideology alien to the party."[38]

These early hujum-related trials were a precursor of broader purges to come and, from the point of view of the Stalin leadership, provided a valuable lesson. Whereas the hujum's efforts to create a surrogate proletariat among Central Asian Muslim women met with at best mixed success, using the judiciary to eliminate political elites was devastatingly effective. Islam enjoyed widespread legitimacy throughout Central Asia, and Stalin could not simply wipe this legitimacy away. The institution of the judiciary, however, also enjoyed legitimacy and, as such, could be employed to transform Central Asian party structures. Thus, the scholar Kozibaev has noted of Stalin's devastating transformation of the Kazakh party elite: "Only a few had the courage to raise their voice in protest of this lawless tyranny . . . the large majority of [Kazakh] nomenklatura became hostages of the system."[39] And as the Kyrgyz historians Turar K. Koichuev, Vladimir P. Mokrynin, and Vladimir M. Ploskikh have concluded of the Kyrgyz party during the 1930s purges: "The *apparat* itself became the hostage of obedience . . . both the stick and the victim of Stalin's purges."[40]

These purges left few of Lenin's appointees or Bukharin's sympathizers in power. Just one of the seven distinct purges in Central Asia (the 1937 purge) removed "55.7 percent of the party officials in primary party organizations and 70.8 percent in district party committees."[41] In one year three of Uzbekistan's leaders—Karimov, Torabekov, and Segisbaev—"were liquidated as enemies of the people," and in Kazakhstan "every member of its first Politburo was shot."[42] Here too the former members of Alash Orda were tried and found guilty of excessive "nationalism," this despite (or likely because of) Lenin's welcoming these former White Army allies into positions of power in post–civil war Kazakhstan.[43] In Kyrgyzstan the Group of Thirty—the Kyrgyz party elite who had alerted Lenin and Stalin of Bolshevik excesses in Bishkek—were all purged and replaced with younger, more compliant cadres.[44] Perhaps most ironic and revealing of Stalin's coercive strategy, the "leading architects" of Stalin's hujum (Akmal Ikramov and Faizula Khojaev) were purged from the Uzbek Communist Party and killed in 1937.[45]

As with the hujum, Stalin's use of predatory courts would find analogues in the post-Soviet period. Indeed, Central Asian presidents' use of the courts as instruments of coercion is commonplace; whereas only Karimov has replicated the hujum's politicization of Islam, Kazakh, Kyrgyz, and Uzbek executives all enlist their judiciaries in campaigns against perceived threats. How executives have used the courts, it should be stressed, varies from country to country. The Kazakh and Kyrgyz presidents use the courts to intimidate rather than devastate elites and activists perceived to be threats. The Kazakh and Kyrgyz executives enlist the courts to disqualify opposition candidates from contesting parliamentary elections or to appropriate the property and business assets of political challengers. In some cases the Kazakh and Kyrgyz executives also enlist the courts to jail particularly outspoken or charismatic opponents. Rarely, however, do these incarcerations result in torture and death—an outcome that, as the U.S. State Department's annual review of human rights demonstrates, is lamentably widespread in Uzbekistan.[46] The Uzbek government, as one might expect, does not release comprehensive data on deaths in incarceration; as a result, the State Department's analysis, like my own, is based on reports from family members of the deceased. I found these reports to be distressingly widespread. During November 2004 field research in Andijan, Namangan, Qarshi, Quqon, and Tashkent, I met with many families who had learned of the death of their son, husband, or father only upon receiving an opaque death notice.

Given the executive's predatory use of the judiciary in all three countries, it is perhaps not surprising that the courts are the least trusted institutions in Kazakhstan, Kyrgyzstan, and Uzbekistan. Fewer than half of Kyrgyz and Kazakh respondents in our 2008 surveys reported they trusted the courts. In Uzbekistan a seemingly robust 76 percent of respondents reported trust in the courts. I should hasten to note that Uzbek respondents in the survey are consistently less critical of institutions, particularly government institutions, than are their Kyrgyz and Kazak counterparts. This constraint in criticizing the government could be the result of Uzbeks' truly being more satisfied with governance than are their Kazakh and Kyrgyz counterparts. Alternatively, this constraint could be the result of an understandable desire among Uzbek respondents not to vocalize dissent because of fears that—Western university human subjects guarantees aside—voicing such criticism to a pollster could be dangerous. Nevertheless, the relative unpopularity of the judiciary holds even in the Uzbek cases, where as demonstrated in figure 2.1, local government and the local mosque are viewed more favorably than are the courts.[47]

My point in drawing these parallels between the Stalin period and present-day Central Asian politics is not to argue that Stalin's innovations, his hujum, and use of the courts proved determinative of post-Soviet Central Asian authoritarianism. Rather, my intent is to demonstrate that authoritarian practices endure. These practices have endured in varying degrees and with varying accents depending on constraints—real and perceived—executives may face. This last point deserves particular emphasis and can productively reshape the way scholars and policy makers approach regime change. Several scholars warn we should be wary of democracy or authoritarianism "with adjectives." The political scientists David Collier and Steven Levitsky, for example, instruct scholars of regime change

Figure 2.1. Trust in the Courts, Local Government, and Local Mosque

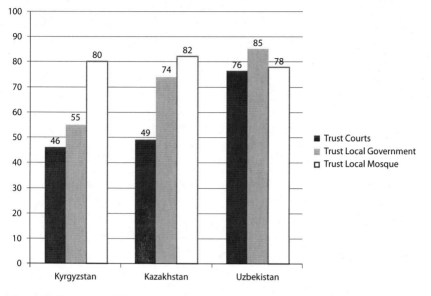

Source: Author surveys, 2008.

to "aim for parsimony and avoid excessive proliferation of new terms and concepts."[48] Similarly, Adam Przeworski and his coauthors suggest we maintain the democracy-authoritarianism dichotomous conceptualization of regime type so as not to falsely attribute liberalizing or reformist tendencies to autocratic regimes engaged in façade reform because they are secure in the knowledge that the opposition will not win power.[49] Although these scholars have offered compelling methodological arguments in favor of dichotomous conceptualizations of regime type, such conceptualizations obscure what in reality are life-and-death differences that people living in authoritarian states confront on a daily basis. Authoritarianism with adjectives is critical for conceptualizing these differences, for demonstrating that although predatory judiciaries were or remain central to the Stalin, Gorbachev, Nazarbaev, Karimov, and Bakiev leaderships, the degree to which these judiciaries were or are employed varies.

The combination of large executive-oriented parties and modest economic resources (the selectorate model discussed in chapter 1)—a combination that exists in present-day Uzbekistan and that existed in the Soviet Union during the 1920s and 1930s—encourages authoritarian leaders to invest in instruments of repression. In contrast, when resources are abundant, as they are in Kazakhstan today and as they were in the Soviet Union from the 1950s through the early 1980s, authoritarian executives can invest in public goods provision and deemphasize coercive measures.[50] When state resources are scarce and executive parties are weak, as they were at the outset of Soviet rule and as they are in Kyrgyzstan today, state repressive capacity will also be weak. Although each of these combinations of elite and economic institutions resulted in authoritarian rule, the implications of these diverging kinds of authoritarian rule (particularly the degree of repression that accompanies these diverging authoritarian outcomes) are profound.

Stalin's autocratic rule, while it provides additional support for the selectorate model, also illustrates important limitations of this model. Executive constraints change over time and indeed may vary as a direct result of an executive's own actions. Although state resources were relatively modest in the late 1920s and throughout the 1930s, by the end of Stalin's rule the resources available to Moscow were enormous. How and the degree to which Stalin effected this transformation is a question historians continue to debate. The end result of this transformation—"full employment, subsidized prices, paid vacations for workers, child care, health care, retirement pensions, educations, and the promise of advancement for oneself and one's children"—is, however, widely accepted.[51] This new economic wealth allowed subsequent leaders, Khrushchev and most notably Brezhnev, to deemphasize repression and instead build a more benign if highly corrupt social contract with Soviet society. The post-Soviet Central Asian analogue to Stalin's rule—Karimov's Uzbekistan—has yet to exhibit similar economic growth and, as such, any transition to a more peaceful Brezhnev- or Nazarbaev-like patronage politics is unlikely.

Khrushchev and the Failure of Economic and Administrative Rationalization

Khrushchev's rule in Central Asia was at once a repudiation and continuation of Stalinist practices. Khrushchev's 1956 "Secret Speech," his rejection of terror as an instrument of control, brought an end to three decades of Soviet coercion.[52] That Khrushchev was in a position to reject terror was due, however, to the economic advances Stalin's terror helped secure. Khrushchev hoped to continue these advances. Khrushchev shared Stalin's attraction to Herculean transformation and, most notably for the fortunes of Central Asia, the new Soviet leader envisioned cultivating on the Kazakh steppe fields of grain that would feed all of the USSR.[53] Khrushchev's agricultural transformation faced even greater challenges than did Stalin's political transformation of Central Asia. Not only did the so-called Virgin Lands require compliant cadres, they also required compliant weather. In the end Khrushchev was incapable of eliciting either.[54]

Like Stalin's hujum, Khrushchev's Virgin Lands proposal had decidedly Moscow-centered motivations. Just as Stalin's strategy was offered as a contrast to the more gradualist models Bukharin and Trotsky favored, so too was Khrushchev's Virgin Lands a rejection of the more gradualist policies Georgy M. Malenkov, chair of the Council of Ministers, offered. Malenkov urged the Moscow elite to cut military spending and instead focus on improving the quality and provision of agricultural and consumer goods. Khrushchev, pointing to the Kazakh steppe, argued sacrifice was unnecessary, that with Central Asia's untapped potential, Moscow could meet its grain demands without downsizing the Red Army.[55] Khrushchev's vision prevailed, and Central Asia once again became a proving ground for Moscow politics.

Khrushchev failed to heed his predecessors' learned lessons of governance in Central Asia, however. Rather than following Lenin's tactic of patronage politics or Stalin's strategy of coercion, Khruschev delivered directives to Central Asia absent sufficient positive or negative incentives. Thanks to Stalin, regional elites were now fully incorporated into the Soviet Communist Party structure and, as such, could be dismissed or demoted for failing to follow Moscow's directives. Thus were the unenthusiastic Kazakh first secretary, Zhumabai Shaiakhmetov, and his deputy, Ivan I. Afanov, replaced by Panteleimon K. Ponomarenko and, crucially for the future of Central Asia, Brezhnev.[56] Elite reshuffling proved not to be the panacea to all local Central Asian ills. Over the ten years of Khrushchev's tenure, Kazakhstan saw seven different first secretaries.[57] When leadership change failed to yield the desired results, Khrushchev attempted to improve production through administrative restructuring. Thus he removed Kazakhstan's grain-producing oblasts from republic administration and placed them directly under Moscow's control. When this administrative rationalization failed, Khrushchev resorted to public chidings. Even mountainous Kyrgyzstan, which had far less to offer than the Kazakh steppe, was faulted for not contributing enough to Khrushchev's agricultural revolution. The Kyrgyz party elite were therefore called before the Central Committee in 1963 and admonished: "Despite the government's generous aid, nearly a third of all state farms are operating at a loss due to their poorly qualified directors."[58]

Even with these chidings, cadre rotations, and administrative restructurings, the Virgin Lands continued to disappoint. Ultimately, however, the problem was not the people but the plan. As Koichuev has written, Khrushchev's policies "were doomed because they were based not on sound practices of political and economic development, but rather, on attempts at the constant strengthening of the administrative command system through the use of ideological dogmatism."[59] Ideology alone could not transform the steppe into the Soviet Union's bread basket, nor could it feed Central Asia's sheep and cows. In 1964, Khrushchev was removed in large part for the same reasons his successive appointees in Central Asia were removed—for the many failures of the Virgin Lands campaign.

Khrushchev is an outlier when it comes to the history of executive rule in Soviet and post-Soviet Central Asia. In contrast to status quo or incrementalist leaders like Lenin, Brezhnev, and the current Central Asian executives, Khrushchev shared with Stalin and Gorbachev an enthusiasm for revolutionary reform. Yet he failed to appreciate that revolutionary change in autocratic societies demands executives exert coercive capacity. To borrow from political scientist James Scott's formulation, Khrushchev shared Stalin's and Gorbachev's "high-modernist dreams" of transforming the Soviet economy, yet Khrushchev, unlike his predecessor and later successor, was unwilling to apply "coercive power to bring these high-modernist designs into being."[60] Brezhnev's answer to this challenge was not a return to Stalin's coercion, but rather to return to Lenin's incrementalism and to shelve Communism's promise of revolutionary reform.

Brezhnev and the Refinement of Patronage Politics

As deputy and then first secretary of the Kazakh Communist Party (from 1954 through 1956), Brezhnev witnessed firsthand the failure of Khrushchev's reshufflings and ideological exhortations. Rather than continue Khrushchev's attempts at administrative redesign, Brezhnev favored instead nomenklatura stability and greater devolution of power to local levels. Brezhnev and his economic point man, Aleksei Kosygin, thus explained in a June 1966 *Pravda* communiqué: "We came to the firm conviction that in the area of production it is necessary to strive for a more harmonious combination of the interests of the state, on the one hand, and the interests of the enterprise and the immediate producers, on the other."[61] This new more harmonious combination of state and local interests proved a boon for the Central Asian party leadership.

During Brezhnev's two decades in power, Kazakhstan, Kyrgyzstan, and Uzbekistan enjoyed unprecedented elite continuity. The Uzbek first secretary, Sharof Rashidov (1959–83), the Kyrgyz first secretary, Turdakun Usubaliev (1961–85), and the Kazakh first secretary, Dinmukhamed Kunaev (1964–86), remained in office. Rashidov, Kunaev, and Usubaliev's powers were more than nominal. Rather than serving as mere figureheads to Moscow's directives, the Central Asian first secretaries staffed their governments and ruled their republics largely as they wished. Kunaev, reflecting on his own appointment as Kazakh first secretary, captured this fundamental shift in how Moscow approached the Central Asian governance: "Iusupov [the outgoing, ethnic Russian first secretary of Kazakhstan] suggested that someone from the Presidium should become first secretary, but Brezhnev did not agree with this. Brezhnev said someone from among the local comrades should become first secretary."[62]

Brezhnev, though keen to let his Central Asian colleagues run the show, likely understood and accepted that proxy rule would lead to distortions of Moscow's power in Central Asia. While serving as Kazakh party second secretary during Khrushchev's more interventionist rule, Brezhnev had already noted that "leaders at various levels were often promoted on the basis of cronyism."[63] As Moscow's appointee in Alma-Ata, Brezhnev dutifully warned his Kazakh comrades that the party would not abide the "serious shortcomings and mistakes in cadre policy."[64] As general secretary, however, Brezhnev appeared little disturbed by the proliferation of Central Asian graft and excess. By most accounts, this graft began early and lasted throughout Brezhnev's rule. In Uzbekistan, for example, Yadgar Sadykovna Nasriddinova, chairwoman of the Presidium of the Uzbek Supreme Soviet, enlisted two hundred drivers and a hundred and fifty waiters to cater to the eight hundred guests at her son's wedding. Nasriddinova, according to investigative journalist Arkady Sakhnin, "contrived to pay for the wedding with state funds . . . for her, high office was a source of personal enrichment."[65]

Sakhnin's recounting of Brezhnev's response to Nasriddinova's lavish party reveals how markedly Leonid Ilyich's patronage model differed from Stalin's earlier coercive approach to the Central Asian borderlands: "The wedding affair alone should have merited Nasriddinova's expulsion from the party. But when news of the extravaganza reached Leonid Ilyich Brezhnev, his response was simply, 'You were stupid to hold a wedding like that!' To which Nasriddinova replied guiltily, 'I shall take your criticism into account, Leonid Ilyich.' That answer satisfied Brezhnev, and Nasriddinova was free to carry on, firm in the belief that she could do as she pleased with impunity."[66]

Official state funds were by no means the only resources available to Central Asia's ruling elite. Former secretary of the Uzbek Party Central Committee, Yerezhap Aitmuratov, for example, confessed in 1988 that "as a Central Committee Secretary, he had to pay bribes to several Secretaries with more seniority and, of course, to Rashidov and high-level officials in Moscow."[67] Similarly, Abdukhalik Karimov, the former party chief in Bukhara, recalled that "when Rashidov awarded him the Hero's star, he [Rashidov] whispered that such things are not dispensed free of charge."[68] One lump sum, though, was not all Karimov had to pay the Uzbek party boss. Rather, Karimov recalled: "Rashidov and his wife would tour all the provinces and collect tribute from the province party committee secretaries. . . . this was viewed as standard procedure."[69]

Patronage politics was not all that different across the borders in Kyrgyzstan and Kazakhstan. *Pravda* reported in 1987 that Brezhnev's first secretary in Kyrgyzstan, T. Usubaliyev, "surrounded himself with relatives, toadies and obsequious deputies" and, as a result, "bribe taking and favoritism flourished in this atmosphere."[70] Similarly, Kazakh first secretary Dinmukhamed Kunaev encouraged an "'anything goes' attitude, which led to the development of favoritism, abuse of office, bribe taking and corruption."[71] In short, as the journalist David Remnick has written of Brezhnev's rule in Central Asia: "These were the go-go years" during which everyone in the party was on the take.[72] Brezhnev and his aged successors in the early 1980s approved (Brezhnev died in November 1982 and his two successors, Yuri Andropov and Konstantin Chernenko, each held office for just over a year before they too died). Rashidov, Kunaev, and Usubaliev remained in power, replicating Brezhnev's model of nomenklatura stability and patronage politics in their own republics, until the markedly less convivial Mikhail Gorbachev broke up the party in the late 1980s.[73]

The Brezhnev period was not exclusively about lavish weddings, bribes, and toadyism, however. The patronage machine undeniably was keen to extract money from bottom to top, but for there to be money to extract, the system also had to provide. And this Moscow did in spades. Kazakhstan was by 1981 receiving more capital investment per capita than any other Soviet republic.[74] In Kyrgyzstan; Moscow's investment in the local economy increased by more than 120 percent during the first decade of Brezhnev's rule.[75] Uzbekistan, for its part, saw a doubling of Moscow's investment in the 1960s and, as the economist Bert van Selm has observed, this "'rich-to-poor' pattern of capital transfers continued until the late 1970s."[76]

Republic balance sheets were not the only places where Central Asians improved their numbers. Capitalizing on their autonomy from the center, Rashidov, Kunaev, and Usubaliev steadily increased the titular membership of their own administrations. Thus, for example, in Kazakhstan, although less than 40 percent of the population was Kazakh, titulars held more than half of the republic's Central Committee seats and nearly two-thirds of the Council of Minister offices by 1981.[77] Kyrgyzstan saw a similar indigenization of the party apparatus. Between 1966 and 1985 the ethnic Kyrgyz presence in the party doubled, with "familial connections" more than ideological "scrupulousness" driving the increase in numbers.[78] Uzbeks equally fared well under Brezhnev. In 1966 ethnic Uzbeks held 53 percent of the republic's Communist Party seats.[79] In 1989, even after Gorbachev's "anticorruption" campaigns designed to dismantle the Rashidov patronage machine, Uzbeks, according to Central Asia scholar James Critchlow's survey of party elites, constituted 90 percent of all *raikom* (that is, district-level seats).[80]

While Rashidov, Kunaev, and Usubaliev actively promoted their conationals, they also maintained good relations with their republic's Slavic elite. For example, Kunaev, as scholar Olcott has written, "used his loyalty to secure his own position and to reward his followers, which, unusually enough for a non-European party leader, included large numbers of Russians as well as Kazakhs."[81] Maintaining an ethnically balanced distribution of key offices, particularly if this balance included ethnic Russians and Ukrainians, proved a good strategy for securing and sustaining Moscow's favor. Importantly, however, these were not just any Russians and Ukrainians. Rather, these were *svoi* (that is, ethnic Slavs) who, like Brezhnev, had extensive experience working and living in Central Asia. These Slavic elites had risen through the ranks of the regional Kazakh, Kyrgyz, and Uzbek party structures and, as such, had extensive local knowledge. Aleksandr G. Korkin and Oleg S. Miroshkin, for example, Kunaev's last two deputy secretaries (1976–79 and 1979–87, respectively), both began their careers in Kazakhstan and were advancing up the party hierarchy several years before Brezhnev's 1954 arrival in Alma-Ata.[82] Similarly, Viacheslav A. Makarenko, Usubaliev's last deputy (1981–85), began his apprenticeship in Kyrgyz party politics in 1955.[83] Rashidov's Russian partner, First Secretary Timofei N. Osetrov, had partnered with Rashidov in the Uzbek Council of Ministers since 1970 and was a Rashidov supporter "through and through."[84]

Such cozy relations, while good for the Central Asian political elite, were of little use and potentially of considerable detriment to the broader Soviet economy. Brezhnev's stability in cadres—that is, the general secretary's sponsorship of patronage politics—was funded not by a robust manufacturing or service economy but rather by oil rents. As more Siberian oil wells came online in the mid-1970s, Brezhnev's access to oil rents skyrocketed. Between 1972 and 1977, for example, Moscow's oil revenues jumped from $23 billion to $140 billion.[85] The rest of the Soviet economy, however, floundered. Total factor productivity growth was nonexistent during the first half of the 1970s and turned negative, hovering between −0.4 and −0.5 percent from 1975 to 1985.[86] Brezhnev's patronage politics alone were not responsible for this productivity downturn. Moscow's near myopic focus on military spending, a costly war in Afghanistan, and the broader inefficiencies of the command economy all contributed to economic stagnation. Few noticed this stagnation, though, because oil revenues sustained the state's social contract. Indeed, it was not until 1986, when the oil market collapsed, that a new general secretary, Mikhail Gorbachev, began to question the wisdom of Brezhnev's patronage politics.

Gorbachev, Oil, and Central Asian Autocratic Variation

When Gorbachev took office on March 11, 1985, oil was selling at twenty-eight dollars a barrel. By January 1986 oil had slid to twenty-two dollars a barrel. Oil lost another six dollars per barrel in February, another two dollars in March, and reached twelve dollars a barrel in April. Oil sales, which brought in four-fifths of Moscow's foreign currency earnings between 1973 and 1985, suddenly evaporated and, just as suddenly, the Soviet patronage machine came under attack.[87] Brezhnev's Central Asian appointees were among the first to be targeted. On January 31, 1986, Uzbek first secretary Imanzhon B. Usmankhodzhayev warned his colleagues and foreshadowed his own demise: "Those sitting in the hall know that flagrant violations of Party norms and morality and of Soviet laws and serious shortcomings in the management of the economy have been brought to light in Uzbekistan in the past few years. Report-padding, theft and bribery have become widespread, and they have led to the corruption and degeneration of a certain number of cadres. These negative phenomena have become extremely dangerous."[88]

One month later, on March 1, 1986, the newly appointed Kyrgyz first secretary, Absamat Masaliev, denounced his predecessor, former first secretary Usubaliev, for promoting bureaucrats based on "personal loyalty, kinship and geographic origin" and for the "servility, toadying and irresponsibility [that] were engendered."[89] And three days after Masaliev's attack, a young bureaucrat in the Kazakh Republic, Nursultan Nazarbaev, turned against his mentor, First Secretary Kunaev, and condemned: "Widespread instances of window dressing, conceit, mismanagement and embezzlement of public property, the passion for 'prestigious' construction projects, violations of the principles of social justice, and violations in the selection, placement and upbringing of cadres. To call things by their right names, it should be said that, under the pretext of stability, stagnation had set in among high-ranking executives. This engendered an atmosphere of encomiums and servility and placed such executives outside criticism, while in some places the demand for a solicitous attitude toward cadres turned into a situation in which everything was permitted and everything forgiven, which led to violations of Party and state discipline."[90]

The Brezhnev machine hummed when lubricated with oil profits. With these profits now gone, the failures of the command economy and the pervasive graft within the Communist elite became painfully apparent. Gorbachev at the time did not publicly articulate this link between the oil price collapse and the need for perestroika and a purging of political elites who only added a further drag on the Soviet economy. However, the timing and nature of the Masaliev, Nazarbaev, and Usmankhodzhayev statements suggest that this link was at the forefront of Gorbachev's new thinking. Moreover, the central papers suggest this causal connection as well. For example, the economist I. Yermachenko wrote in *Izvestia* in February 1986 that "because of the constant pressure on the oil markets, the petroleum-producing countries—and especially those with large populations—have been forced even deeper into debt."[91] Although Yermachenko was referring to oil exporters like Nigeria and Venezuela, the Moscow party leadership undoubtedly understood that the Soviet system too was at risk. Gorbachev would later confirm this in his 2000 memoirs, writing that "in the final years before perestroika [our country] was able to exist only by virtue of oil and gas exports."[92]

Gorbachev's response to the 1986 crisis would fundamentally alter Central Asian politics. In Kazakhstan, Kyrgyzstan, and Uzbekistan perestroika reforms destabilized the Brezhnev-era political and economic status quo. What proved most fateful to the future of Central Asian politics, though, was the differing ways in which these perestroika reforms destabilized the Central Asian status quo. In Kazakhstan and Uzbekistan this destabilization was temporary. In Kyrgyzstan instability itself became the new status quo. The sequencing of perestroika reforms in Kazakhstan, Kyrgyzstan, and Uzbekistan proved critical to these diverging political outcomes. Perestroika and the sense of economic and political uncertainty that perestroika engendered sparked ethnic protests in all three republics. Following the Kazakh protests in 1986 and the Uzbek protests in 1989, Moscow intervened to restore both societal and political order. Moscow did not intervene, however, to restore party order after Kyrgyzstan's June 1990 ethnic riots. In February 1990 Gorbachev, frustrated that the party purges of the second half of the 1980s had failed to yield substantive reform, declared the end to Communist Party monopoly power. The Kyrgyz Communist Party, as far as he was concerned, could solve its own problems and, moreover, benefit from the cleansing effect competition might bring to the republic's leadership. Neither proved to be the case, however. Absent Moscow's guidance, the Kyrgyz elite fragmented and the Kyrgyz executive has faced the unenviable and ultimately untenable task ever since of balancing these divided elite interests.

Kazakhstan and Operation Blizzard

Brezhnev protégé and just ousted former first secretary Dinmukhamed Kunaev likely took some satisfaction with what he saw unfolding on Alma-Ata's streets on December 17, 1986. Ten thousand Kazakh protesters were out on Brezhnev Square demanding the immediate resignation of the republic's new first secretary, Gennady Kolbin, an ethnic Russian. It was not Kolbin, though, who initiated Kunaev's fall. Six months earlier, Nursultan Nazarbaev had taken the podium and publicly faulted Kunaev for fostering an atmosphere of "servility" and "stagnation."[93] Although quick to criticize his patron, Nazarbaev in March 1986 was slow to detect the irony of his criticism. As Kazakh Council of Ministers chairman, Nazarbaev himself clearly benefited from Kunaev's "violations in the selection, placement and upbringing of cadres." As such, Nazarbaev might have anticipated that his swinging of Moscow's hatchet might not immediately lead him to the seat of party power in Kazakhstan. Nazarbaev was suspect and Gorbachev, hoping to break decades of Kazakh patronage politics, appointed the outsider Kolbin because as an ethnic Russian he "was not linked with any of the local clans."[94]

Still, Nazarbaev had good reason to believe he, and certainly not the unknown Kolbin, would be Gorbachev's new man in Alma-Ata. By 1986, Nazarbaev had spent a quarter century advancing through the ranks of the Kazakh Communist Party. Nazarbaev initially had hoped to become a scientist, not a bureaucrat. His academic ambition was dashed when he had failed to pass the university entrance exam. Nazarbaev would later attribute this setback to his family pedigree, explaining in his memoirs that less talented schoolmates, "children of the [party] leadership all passed the exam and were admitted."[95] Nazarbaev has since established his intellectual bona fides; the Kazakh National Library lists seventeen volumes under the president's name. Nazarbaev took his university admissions setback to focus on what his parents did not—the importance of the single party.

Nazarbaev joined the party in 1962, at the age of twenty-two. In 1972, having risen through a series of minor party posts, Nazarbaev took leadership of the Karaganda Metallurgical Kombinat. The kombinat, home to more than thirty thousand workers, was as much a city as it was a factory.[96] Shortly after his appointment as secretary of the kombinat, Nazarbaev found himself paying court to the Moscow political elite, explaining to the Communist Party Central Committee the details of a letter he had written earlier in which he had described the poor living and working conditions at the Karaganda factory.[97] Although Nazarbaev recalls that at the time he feared his brazenness in appealing directly to Moscow rather than to his immediate superiors would land him in a smelter's frock back before the factory's blast furnaces, the opposite proved the case.[98] Nazarbaev's candid speech before the Central Committee, his Kazakh mentor Kunaev would later inform him, won Nazarbaev well-placed admirers in Moscow. Most prominent of these admirers was Mikhail Suslov, the secretary for Communist ideology and the number two in the party until his death in 1982.[99] In retrospect, it is clear that Kunaev should not have been so encouraging of his young protégé, for the older Kazakh statesman himself later became the target of Nazarbaev's irreverence for political superiors.

Although he certainly did not welcome Nazarbaev's 1986 rebuke, Kunaev may well have wished to pass the reins of power directly to Nazarbaev. Kunaev would later write that "everyone must plan for his replacement" and that, in this regard, he paid particular attention to the "young and energetic" Nazarbaev.[100] Nazarbaev, for his part, has acknowledged that he would not have been appointed secretary of industry or subsequently in 1984 chairman of Kazakhstan's Council of Ministers had it not been for Kunaev's tutelage.[101] Kunaev paved the way to Suslov and when Suslov died, Kunaev (more specifically Kunaev's cronyism) was Nazarbaev's ticket to Gorbachev. At the same time Nazarbaev was benefiting from Kunaev's patronage, the chairman of the Kazakh Council of Ministers was plotting with Gorbachev to overthrow the long-serving Kazakh first secretary. Have a strong "backbone," Gorbachev told Nazarbaev: "Hard times are ahead . . . there will be an onslaught, a battle; it won't be easy."[102]

The onslaught did not unfold to either Gorbachev or Nazarbaev's initial liking. Indeed, for a brief time Gorbachev and Nazarbaev found themselves on opposite sides of the battle. Although we likely will never know if Nazarbaev's reaction to Kolbin's appointment was impulsive or premeditated, the future Kazakh president's response could not have been better choreographed. In his 1991 memoirs Nazarbaev wrote of his role in the anti-Kolbin protests: "When the protestors on the square began to surge toward the city, I realized I had to make one of two choices: either I would have to take action or I would have to [leave the square and] return to the Central Committee building. The second alternative seemed to me to be an unforgivable treason to my people—they were right! I set off with them at the head of the column."[103]

Gorbachev, more tersely, noted of the Kolbin appointment: "It was a blunder . . . a sign of disrespect and distrust of the Kazakh people."[104] It may have been a blunder, but it was one Nazarbaev quickly capitalized on and one Gorbachev was keen just as quickly to move past. Ensuring that his new appointee would be a lame duck, Gorbachev ordered Kolbin to mobilize fifty thousand army troops and special forces along with twenty thousand police to disperse the crowds from Brezhnev Square. Dubbed Operation Blizzard, Kolbin's actions brought calm to the Alma-Ata's streets. For Kolbin, as an ethnic Russian and, even more damning, as an outsider to Kazakh politics, this calm came at a dear cost. Kolbin's reputation and authority were ruined. If Nazarbaev indeed was the architect of the protests, then Operation Blizzard was a snow job that left Nazarbaev as the de facto leader in Kazakhstan.

As Kolbin languished in Kazakhstan for two more years, it became increasingly clear to the Moscow and Kazakh political elite, as well as to Kazakh society more broadly, that Nazarbaev had free reign in managing the day-to-day affairs in the republic. That many current and former elites were enraged by the tactics Nazarbaev used to secure power was of little consequence to the man now pulling Kolbin's strings. Gorbachev refused to side with Nazarbaev's detractors. In June 1987 the now deposed Kolbin delivered a swan song Moscow Central Committee speech in which he damned Nazarbaev for organizing the December 1986 protests.[105] Others at the meeting, most notably Yegor Ligachev, the party's secretary of ideology and Gorbachev's second-in-command, backed up Kunaev's assertion.[106] These criticisms served neither Kunaev nor Ligachev well and did little to detract from Nazarbaev's growing power. Kunaev's next stop after the June 1987 Central Committee meeting was the *pansionat*. Ligachev, though he did not know it at the time, would soon see his portfolio change from Marxism-Leninism to farming. In May 1989, Gorbachev demoted Ligachev from secretary for Communist Party ideology to minister of agriculture. That same month Gorbachev dismissed the lame-duck Kolbin and appointed Nazarbaev as Kazakh first secretary, an appointment approved by the unanimous vote of the Kazakh Republic Central Committee.[107] Moscow's formal sanctioning of what by now was widely recognized as Nazarbaev's de facto leadership marked the final step in the full restoration of political order in Kazakhstan—a restoration that came just in time to deal with the conflagration that was about to engulf Uzbekistan.

Kokand, Uzbekistan, in Flames

In early June 1989 thousands of young and, according to First Secretary Rafiq Nishanov, intoxicated Uzbeks set fire to the homes of Meskhetian Turks in Kokand, Uzbekistan.[108] Homes were not the only things this minority lost; an estimated one hundred Meskhetians died in the ethnic clashes. Nishanov, pressed by his Supreme Soviet colleagues to explain how, under his watch, such interethnic violence could emerge, dismissed the events as an unfortunate misunderstanding. A Meskhetian Turk, believing that a female Uzbek vendor was attempting to swindle him, overturned the vendor's display plate of carefully stacked homegrown strawberries. This insult to the female vendor in turn led to the disproportionate retaliation against the Meskhetian Turks.

Nishanov's explanation, Fergana KGB chief N. Leskov suggested in an interview with *Pravda*, was naïve. The dispute between the Turks and the Uzbeks began not with strawberries, but rather with local brothels. In August 1988 the "Boss," a Meskhetian who was the "proprietor of amusement establishments" in the neighboring Fergana Valley town of Kuvasay, had died in a car wreck. The

Boss's sudden departure sparked a turf war between his would-be Meskhetian successors and their local Uzbek challengers.[109] His offices did what was necessary, Leskov pointedly noted in the interview: "We reported the information we received to party bodies in good time."[110] And, according to Nishanov's soon-to-be successor, Islam Karimov, that these party bodies did not respond in good time was exactly the reason why Moscow had appointed him to reassert party power in Fergana: "Before the June 1989 Fergana events we had no open opposition. In June 1989 a tragedy befell the people of Uzbekistan. The Republic's leadership at the time was petrified and at first tried to hide and later distort what happened. This gave rise to a political vacuum that various movements and organizations attempted to fill. [My response . . .] I raised the price of cotton 2.5 times, increased the size of personal farming plots, expanded social security, raised teacher salaries, and encouraged a return to our traditions. The result—most everyone has left this opposition and returned to the party."[111]

Karimov's appointment, like Nazarbaev's rise to the first secretary position in Kazakhstan, signaled the end of Moscow's attempt to dismantle Brezhnev-era patronage rule in Uzbekistan. In many respects Uzbekistan's patronage machine suffered even greater indignities than had Kazakh patrimonialism. Replacing Kunaev with an ethnic Russian first secretary was certainly an affront to Kazakhs, but far less an insult than the Soviet Union–wide humiliation that many within the Uzbek political elite suffered as a result of Gorbachev's much publicized anticorruption campaign. For Brezhnev's close partner, Uzbek first secretary Rashidov, this humiliation was posthumous. *Komsomolskaia pravda*, for example, portrayed Rashidov in 1988, five years after his death, as presiding over a republicwide fraud in which "tens of thousands of people were forced to pad cotton-production figures," "corrupt officials pocketed millions of rubles the state paid for nonexistent cotton," and "criminal millionaires often gave their riches to distant relatives in remote villages for safekeeping."[112]

Not all corrupt Uzbek officials, however, were sufficiently wise to stash their wealth in the villages. Moscow investigators found "gold coins, timepieces, jewels, and briefcases stuffed with cash" beneath the floorboards of Bukhara Party First Secretary Abduvakhid Karimov's house.[113] A. Karimov was found guilty and handed a death sentence. Close Rashidov confidant, Brezhnev son-in-law, and USSR deputy minister of internal affairs Yuri Churbanov was sentenced to twelve years imprisonment for accepting ninety thousand rubles in bribes.[114] Churbanov's counterparts in the Uzbek Interior Ministry, Khaydar Yakhyayev and Petr Begelman, were similarly found guilty of bribe taking, although each received more lenient sentences.[115] Neither, however, escaped public ridicule. *Pravda* described the defendants in the so-called Uzbek Affair as follows: "The people in the defendants' dock seem pitiful. Churbanov, pale and with a vacant stare, who has difficulty managing anything like a militarily clear answer to the questions put by the court's chairman; Yakhyayev, who came into court wearing a national Uzbek skullcap, seeming far older than his years without the tunic and shoulder boards of a lieutenant general; and Begelman with his red, inflamed eyes, now and then lowering his head in shame. Not present are Ergashev, Uzbekistan's former Minister of Internal Affairs, or Davydov, the republic's former First Deputy Minister of Internal Affairs. They committed suicide."[116]

Attacking the Uzbek patronage machine ultimately proved more a headache than it was worth for Gorbachev. Gorbachev, just as he had in Kazakhstan, had chosen a pliant Uzbek first secretary in the hopes that this would afford Moscow greater leverage in transforming the Uzbek state and society. Curiously, Gorbachev's approach to Uzbekistan echoed in design—though certainly not in bloody intensity—the policies of an earlier period. Much as Stalin had done with his appointees during the hujum, so too did Gorbachev task Nishanov with "strengthening of the Uzbek family . . . on a new basis, along new, socialist lines."[117] Gorbachev's strategy, it should be noted, was not to create Stalin's "surrogate proletariat." Rather, the new general secretary was motivated by economic reasoning—the growing Uzbek population was placing a strain on the republic's economy and accentuating already low productivity levels. Despite this clear-headed and ultimately well-intentioned logic, Gorbachev's efforts at family planning were no more welcome than Stalin's hujum was a half century earlier. The difference between Gorbachev and Stalin, though, was that the latter was willing to apply massive repression to achieve his goals while the former, as the following interchange between Gorbachev and collective farmers illustrates, was ridiculed when he attempted to bring the wisdom of modern family planning to Uzbekistan:

> Gorbachev: In family relationships there still remain survivals from the past which lead to a situation in which girls, women and the family also suffer.
> Society too suffers. But here, probably, the men have their part to play, so that when we talk, everyone says that this has to be resisted, then they go home. . . .
> Man [interrupting]: And they're at it again! [laughter].
> Gorbachev: They're laughing! [addressing man in crowd] What sort of family have you got?
> Man: We're all fine.
> Gorbachev: But how big is the family?
> Man: Oh, five now.

Gorbachev: Five?

Man: Five now. [laughter in which Gorbachev and Shevardnadze join]

Gorbachev: You haven't finished yet?

Man in the crowd: He's still working on it! [Raisa Gorbacheva smiles][118]

If this gentle ribbing in the *mahalla* (state-controlled neighborhood committee) did not bring home the point, the severity of the 1989 riots certainly did. Family planning may have been a joke to Uzbeks. For Meskhetian Turks, though, Gorbachev's discussion of population reduction—a reduction that, the general secretary suggested, could also be attained through outmigration to Siberia—was frightening. In 1943, Stalin shipped the Turks from Georgia to Uzbekistan. Stalin's logic for the forced deportation was that Turkey might side with the Germans and find in Georgia's Meskhetian population a ready ally against Moscow.[119] Although outsiders in Uzbekistan, the Meskhetians were in no mood to swap the sunny Fergana Valley for snow-bound Siberia. As such, although First Secretary Nishanov perhaps was correct in noting a dispute at the bazaar preceded the riots and although the local KGB chief was perhaps correct in noting that Kokand was home to mafia turf wars between rival Meskhetian and Uzbek gangs, it was this greater environment of uncertainty, an environment precipitated by perestroika reforms, that had raised tensions between the Uzbeks and the Turks to new heights. Indeed, in the weeks after the riots, commentators in the Uzbek press laid the blame squarely on Moscow's doorstep, arguing that it was Gorbachev's hired hands who had artificially stoked Uzbek-Meskhetian animosity to goad the Turks into moving to Russia.[120]

The Kokand riots, along with the subsequent negative press and the clear disdain Uzbeks had for family planning, prompted the general secretary to rethink his perestroika efforts in Uzbekistan. Fortuitously, First Secretary Nishanov was "elected" to chair the USSR Supreme Soviet Council of Nationalities in late June. Karimov, who had been serving as Kashkadarya province first secretary, was appointed as the Uzbek Republic's new chief executive. This careful orchestration of Nishanov's promotion was no doubt a way for Gorbachev to save face in light of his failed Uzbek policies. That the party selected Karimov as Nishanov's replacement also suggests Moscow's desire to return to the predictable status quo of proxy rule rather than to continue the bid to rid Uzbekistan of patronage politics and corruption. Karimov, as his April 1991 contrasting of himself to the "petrified" Nishanov makes clear, was bent on reasserting local Uzbek Communist Party authority throughout the republic. Moreover, as his equal emphasis on entitlements—expanding personal farm plots, social welfare provision, and salaries—also makes clear, Karimov understood that the road to peace and prosperity lay not in corruption trials nor in outlandish suggestions that Uzbeks have fewer children, but rather in restoring the money flow from Moscow to the mahalla.

That Karimov would quickly denounce his immediate predecessor and return to Rashidov's patronage practices likely did not come as a surprise to Gorbachev.[121] Under Rashidov's tutelage Karimov advanced from chief specialist in the Uzbek Ministry of Finance (1966) to minister of finance (April 1983). Karimov bluntly noted to an *Izvestia* reporter in January 1991 that Moscow's attacks on his mentor were unjust and "undermined people's faith in justice. . . . our leaders [Nishanov] made regular reports in Moscow as if they were reporting on fulfillment of the plan for cotton: so-and-so many thousands arrested, so-and-so many expelled from the Party, etc."[122] Perhaps even more revealing of Karimov's approach to his mentor's legacy, though, was the new first secretary's response to the *Izvestia* reporter's final query:

> Reporter: Pardon me if this question seems tactless, but some of your opponents see a connection between your well-known restraint on the subject of Rashidov and the fact that you yourself have concentrated a great many functions of power in your own hands: President, head of the republic cabinet, first secretary of the republic Communist Party Central Committee.
>
> Karimov: The main explanation for this, in my view, is that the transition period and the explosive situation that has developed in the country and here in our republic demand it.[123]

Gorbachev's purges in 1986 and the subsequent perestroika reforms, in Karimov's assessment, had failed. The solution—a solution that the general secretary himself approved—was to return Uzbekistan to the Brezhnev status quo.

Kyrgyzstan, Riots in Fergana and Chaos in Bishkek

Gorbachev appointed Karimov to power on June 24, 1989, two days after Nazarbaev had been appointed to the same post in the Kazakh republic. With Karimov and Nazarbaev in office, Gorbachev's Kazakh and Uzbek perestroika experiments were effectively shelved. In Kyrgyzstan, however, Gorbachev's reformist appointee labored on even as many of the same societal strains that had precipitated the 1989 Uzbek riots in Kokand began to emerge in the nearby southern Kyrgyz cities of Osh and Uzgen. Similar to what happened in Uzbekistan, here too these tensions would erupt into deadly ethnic conflict. In contrast to the Uzbek case, though, Moscow would not intervene to restore Kyrgyz Communist Party order after the Osh and Uzgen riots.

On February 5, 1990, Gorbachev informed his Central Committee colleagues: "In a society that is renewing itself, the Party can exist and perform its vanguard role only as a democratically recognized force. This means that its position must not be imposed through constitutional legitimation."[124] Gorbachev would later explain that his February 1990 decision to end the party's monopoly control was necessary because, despite attempts at "democratizing it internally," the party was too "thoroughly installed with old habits" and, as such, "never truly became a party of reform."[125] Gorbachev gambled that subjecting the party to competition would force the political elite to work "in the thick of the masses, living by their interests and needs" rather than pretending that the USSR, and with it the lifestyle of party privilege, could endure when the only exports of value the country produced were guns and oil.

The February 1990 announcement was also tacit recognition that absent reform, the union itself might collapse. The Lithuanian Communist Party had broken from the USSR party in December 1989, and by February 1990 the republic's politicians were readying for a vote of secession from the USSR. Similar parliamentary procedures were also under way in Latvia and Estonia, while in Georgia, Moldova, and Ukraine nationalist movements were openly advocating for secession. Gorbachev's own allies within the party, moreover, had brought the demand directly to the general secretary's doorstep. In January more than fifty thousand party members gathered in Moscow to create a "democratic platform."[126] If Gorbachev did not liberalize the party, these platform members warned, they would break from and actively oppose the CPSU. Forced to choose between reform or retrenchment, Gorbachev chose the latter; political pluralism and "various forms of federal ties," Gorbachev explained in his February 1990 CPSU address, were critical to the Soviet Union's future.

What Gorbachev and his CPSU colleagues did not anticipate was that centrally initiated reform designed to meet separatist challenges in the Baltic republics and liberalization demands in Moscow might lead to political instability in Central Asia. Moscow's intervention following the ethnic protests in Kazakhstan (in 1986) and in Uzbekistan (in 1989) proved critical in restoring political order in these two republics. His February 1990 reforms, however, precluded further such interventions. Political pluralism and the devolution of power, not centralized political order, was now Moscow's stated policy. For Uzbekistan and Kazakhstan, Moscow's new stance was no great threat. By February 1990, Karimov and Nazarbaev had already replaced Gorbachev's failed perestroika appointees and returned Uzbekistan and Kazakhstan to status quo patronage politics. In contrast, Kyrgyz First Secretary Masaliev, who had promised upon his appointment in the early days of Gorbachev's 1986 political purge to end the Brezhnev-era practices of "toadyism" and rewarding "kinship and geographic origin" networks, was only now beginning to realize the dangers that inattention to Central Asian kinship and geographic networks yields.

Kyrgyzstan's flashpoint proved to be in the south, where an ethnically, economically, and spatially segmented population had lived in relative harmony during the USSR's oil boom years but had become increasingly divided during the economic shortages of the late perestroika period. Here ethnic Uzbeks, employed largely in the retail economy, concentrated in urban areas like the cities of Osh and Uzgen.[127] Kyrgyz, in contrast, historically concentrated in the more rural, agricultural regions of the Osh oblast. Despite these demographic patterns, however, Kyrgyz in the late 1980s controlled a disproportionate share of city administrations. This led to a combustible situation in which the economically powerful Uzbek minority (a quarter of the oblast's population, according to the 1989 census) controlled 84 percent of all retail sales in the region while the titular majority controlled 96 percent of first and second secretary positions within the oblast party hierarchy.[128] The spark that ignited this precarious balance between state and economic power was the immigration of Kyrgyz from struggling rural villages to Osh's and Uzgen's comparatively more prosperous urban centers.

Osh and Uzgen were not without their own economic challenges. Housing stock in both cities was already in short supply and was only further strained with the arrival of the new Kyrgyz migrants. Some of these migrants were able to find apartments through the informal economy, an informal economy controlled by ethnically Uzbek landlords.[129] Other migrants sought what they hoped would be a more permanent solution; emboldened by new perestroika guarantees of freedom of organization, Kyrgyz labor migrants formed the interest group Osh-aimagy (Osh-land) to lobby the local administration for new Kyrgyz-specific housing. Osh's Uzbeks, fearing that city housing stock might be redistributed in favor of the titular population, formed their own organization, Adolat (Justice), as a counterbalance to Osh-aimagy. The local administration attempted to accommodate both groups, first by promising Kyrgyz migrants land allotments and then, once realizing these allotments were on the land of a largely Uzbek collective farm, by assuring Adolat's leaders that the migrants would be settled elsewhere.

This backpedaling infuriated Kyrgyz housing activists. On June 4, 1990, these activists rallied dozens of supporters to gather on the promised and now withdrawn land allotments. The Kyrgyz were met by Uzbek Adolat activists and a skittish Osh police force. The outcome of this meeting was disastrous and not contained to Osh. As accounts of ethnic fighting in Osh radiated out, riots spread to other cities in the south. In a few cases—for example, in southern Kyrgyzstan's second largest southern city, Jalal Abad—local militia, KGB, and Soviet army troops were able to block rural Kyrgyz from marching on Uzbek towns and thus limit the violence. In other cities, however, the Uzbek-Kyrgyz clashes proved even more deadly than those in Osh. In Uzgen, 247 died in interethnic fighting and more than 300 homes were razed.[130]

The Osh riots and First Secretary Masaliev's subsequent reluctance either to address the causes of or to accept some measure of responsibility for the riots polarized Kyrgyzstan's newly elected parliamentary elite. Before the deadly June 1990 events the members of parliament, 90 percent of whom were Communist Party members, had maintained stable ranks—this despite the differing views of Gorbachev allies like Masaliev and the growing number of even more reform-oriented deputies who favored further political liberalization.[131] For example, recalling a pre-June 1990 session of parliament, Abdygany Erkebaev, a newly elected deputy, wrote: "What happened during the first session? Nothing special.... Everything moved along calmly and according to tradition like in the pre-perestroika times."[132]

The same could not be said of the parliament's second session in October 1990, three months after the Osh riots. The Kyrgyz elite, which had never before questioned Kyrgyz executives, were politicized and divided by the bloodshed in the south. And Gorbachev's February decree ending the Communist monopoly on power meant that Moscow would not intervene to restore order to the Kyrgyz party. Although First Secretary Masaliev implored the deputies to observe a "good tone and discipline, display reason and reserve, and complete all work in three to four days," the deputies, pliant and deferential only a few months earlier, now proved anything but disciplined and reserved.[133]

Headlining the issues before the parliament was the question of who would become Kyrgyzstan's next executive and first president. From the outset it was clear that this question would not be resolved in an atmosphere similar to that of party politics of the past. Simply to enter the parliament building, the Kyrgyz deputies were forced to pass through a phalanx of hunger strikers and protesters holding placards demanding Masaliev's resignation, investigations into the Osh events, and the separation of party and state power. Protests, moreover, were not limited to the parliament. Indeed, the entire capital city was declared in a state of emergency as mass demonstrations spread to the universities and the central squares.[134]

It was in this environment of upheaval that the parliamentary deputies thus presented their nominations for the presidency. In a first for Kyrgyz succession politics, three candidates rather than one were forwarded from the floor. Masaliev was nominated by his assistant, the chairman of the Council of Ministers, Alas Dzhumagulov. Next, Dzhumagulov himself was nominated along with the pro-reform deputy Dzhmgalbek Amanbaev. Askar Akaev's candidacy was also suggested but quickly dismissed. Akaev was "still young and soft in character," the reform faction decided, and the deputies instead divided their votes between Amanbaev and Dzhumagulov.[135] The Kyrgyz 1990 election law stipulated that an absolute majority rather than a plurality of the parliament's 350 votes were required to win the presidency. In the event that no candidate received a majority in the first round, the leading two contenders were to compete in a runoff. Lastly, the law directed, should neither candidate receive a majority in the runoff, both were required to withdraw from contention. In the first round Masaliev received 154 votes to Dzhumagulov's 96 and Amanbaev's 83. In the second round Masaliev maintained his lead with 171 votes to Dzhumagulov's 160. Masaliev's tally, however, was still short of the required minimum of 176.[136] The Kyrgyz deputies, although they had yet to elect a president, had effectively deposed a first secretary.

Akaev's rise to power was as sudden as Masaliev's fall. As was the case in the first round of voting, neither in this second round was Akaev the first choice of the reform deputies. Rather, the reform faction asked Chingiz Aitmatov—one of the Soviet Union's most prominent novelists, a Gorbachev adviser, and Kyrgyzstan's most famous native son—if he would accept their nomination. Aitmatov, though living in Moscow and only months away from assuming the Soviet ambassadorship to Luxemburg, was not inclined to trade the Benelux for Bishkek. The novelist did, however, suggest an alternative: his fellow academic Askar Akaev.[137] After yet another two rounds of voting, Akaev was narrowly elected with 179 votes, three votes more than the minimum required and only 8 votes more than Masaliev's losing tally of 171. Akaev was Kyrgyzstan's new leader, but in contrast to his Uzbek and Kazakh colleagues' appointments by universal acclimation, 49 percent of the Kyrgyz parliament had voted against electing Akaev to the presidency.

Contingency, Path Dependency, and Formal Modeling

Chapter 1 illustrated how, using formal modeling, much of the autocratic variation we see in post-Soviet Central Asia today could be anticipated given sufficient knowledge of the Central Asian republics' perestroika-era institutions of elite politics. In contrast to other scholars who emphasize causalities that are decidedly post-Soviet in periodization, I argue that pre-1991 institutions of elite politics were responsible in large part for the chaos, violence, and dynasty that define current Kazakh, Kyrgyz, and Uzbek politics. More specifically, Kyrgyzstan's Soviet legacy of a fragmented political elite greatly increases the likelihood of chaos and instability in today's post-Soviet period. Conversely, Kazakhstan's and Uzbekistan's united executive-oriented parties afford the Nazarbaev and Karimov governments greater elite loyalty and, as a result, greater freedom to invest in capacity-enhancing measures such as public goods provisions and institutions of coercion. A central challenge of formal modeling, however, is that although models can help explain and even predict diverging political outcomes given known institutional configurations, formal models do not explain how these institutional configurations emerge in the first place.

Comparative historical analysis fills this lacuna. Historical analysis helps us understand how Gorbachev's reforms were an attempt to redress the corruption that was endemic in the Brezhnev patronage model. This patronage model in turn emerged as a response to the failures of Khrushchev's attempted agricultural transformation of Central Asia and the untold human costs of Stalin's coercion. Stalin's coercive policies were an effort to transform the Soviet polity from the gradualist policies Lenin, Bukharin, and Trotsky had favored. In addition to the importance of sequencing, comparative historical analysis also points our attention to the role contingency plays in effecting political outcomes. Such contingent effects, while their timing is difficult to predict, can be anticipated and, as such, can productively inform social scientists' implementation of formal models in causal analysis. This chapter's overview of Soviet Central Asian history points to three "contingent" processes that have repeatedly transformed periods of Central Asian political stasis: unplanned leadership succession, sudden political protests, and economic shocks.

In short, while I employ a formal model to explain the substantive variations in Kazakh, Kyrgyz, and Uzbek authoritarian rule that we now see, this chapter reveals that both the institutional "inputs" to this formal model and the potential contingent shocks that can transform these inputs are themselves the product of complex causal processes that are not always easily reduced to parsimonious causal explanations. I return to this observation repeatedly in the following chapters. Although the selectorate model effectively explains Uzbekistan's repression, Kyrgyzstan's chaos, and Kazakhstan's relative stability, the potential remains high for "acts of god," acts of activists, and acts of the economy to fundamentally reshape the institutional and economic constraints currently patterning Central Asian patronage politics. This potential for structural change does not mean we must jettison formal models. It does mean, however, that we must explore how potential changes in institutional and economic constraints might alter the outcomes these formal models predict.

3 Kyrgyz Chaos

FAMILIARITY WITH DIVERGING Kazakh, Kyrgyz, and Uzbek elite institutions and the perestroika legacy model should have proved sufficient for anyone assessing the Central Asian political landscape in December 1991 to anticipate that politics in Kyrgyzstan would be far more chaotic than anywhere else in Central Asia. The formal model and institutional legacies presented in chapters 1 and 2 allow the social scientist to predict, a priori, the chaos, violence, and dynasty variations in Central Asia today. Closer examination of the Kyrgyz case, though, raises further complications. Kyrgyzstan's first president, Askar Akaev, ruled from 1990 to 2005. Kyrgyzstan's second president, Kurmanbek Bakiev, ruled from 2005 to 2010. The perestroika legacy model helps us understand how Kyrgyzstan's narrow political elite banded together to overthrow both presidents. What the model does not answer, however, is variation in the two presidents' duration of rule. Why was Akaev able to hold on to power for fifteen years, while Bakiev was deposed after only five?

Kyrgyzstan's divergence from Uzbekistan's steady repression and Kazakhstan's political stability and the variation in Akaev's and Bakiev's tenures in office make the Kyrgyz case the most challenging. Yet in many ways it is the most fecund (with respect to social science theory generation) of the Central Asian cases I review. To address these challenges, I divide them in the discussion below. I begin by examining what I call the "first presidency," Akaev's fifteen-year tenure, and the Kyrgyz executive's transition from foreign-aid wealth redistribution to rent-seeking behavior. Then there is the "second presidency," Bakiev's five-year tenure and the executive rent-seeking and asset-stripping that so enraged Kyrgyzstan's political elite and everyday society. Lastly, I turn to Kyrgyzstan's "third presidency," to the country's new government and its prospects.

My analysis of these presidencies shows how executive access to markedly differing kinds of economic resources directly shapes the durability of Kyrgyz presidential rule. Throughout the 1990s Akaev benefitted from growing levels of multilateral and bilateral foreign aid. As figure 3.1 illustrates, Kyrgyzstan has received more foreign aid per capita than any other Central Asian country. This aid, extended in the hopes of furthering Kyrgyz political reform, paradoxically had the opposite effect; foreign aid to Kyrgyzstan helped sustain Akaev's fragile winning coalition for much of the 1990s. In 2001, however, the nature of foreign financial flows to Kyrgyzstan began to change. Kyrgyzstan, once of minimal importance to U.S. geopolitics, suddenly became a strategic partner in the post-9/11 "War on Terror." In December 2001 the Akaev government agreed to President George W. Bush's request for an air base at the Manas airport outside the capital Bishkek. Economic rents—both literal rents for the air base and rents from logistics and supply contracts for the base—began accruing directly to Akaev and his family. Whereas previously Akaev had to work directly with USAID's and the World Bank's Kyrgyz partners—government ministries, the parliament, nonprofits—to secure aid, now Akaev could cut out the middlemen, the members of Kyrgyzstan's narrow political elite. This was a financial boon to Akaev and his family. Politically, though, it was a disaster. Knowledge that Akaev was embezzling rather than sharing the Manas base rents encouraged challengers—as the perestroika legacy model predicts—to band together and hijack the state, as they did in March 2005.

The Manas dynamic did not disappear under the new Bakiev leadership. Just the opposite, in fact, as a new player—Russia—sought a military foothold in Kyrgyzstan and in the process promised even more rents to the Kyrgyz executive. The Bakiev government from day one was a rent-seeking endeavor. Elite pacts and compromises similar to the ones Akaev had built throughout the 1990s using diffuse political liberalization foreign aid were all but absent under Bakiev. Bakiev's appointees were constantly defecting in anticipation of the new president's downfall. Bakiev himself likely anticipated this downfall. It was as if the motto of this new government was "take the money and run." This Bakiev did in April 2010, when Kyrgyz protesters stormed the presidential administration building.

A second dynamic also contributed to Bakiev's comparatively short tenure in power: the Kyrgyz political elites' learning the art of mass mobilization. Protests, as seen in chapter 2, were instrumental in bringing down Abasamat Masaliev's government in 1990. For many within the Kyrgyz political elite and Kyrgyz so-

Figure 3.1. Aid per Capita—World Development Indicators

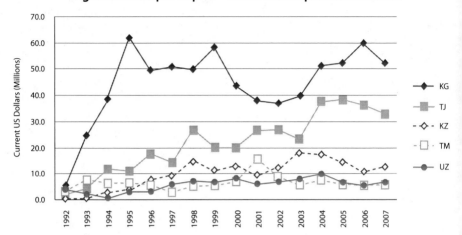

Source: World Bank World Development Indicators, available at http://data.worldbank.org/
data-catalog/world-development-indicators.

ciety in general, Masaliev's departure likely came as a surprise. The 2005 protests were more purposive, but few anticipated that President Akaev would so quickly pack his bags and vacate the Kyrgyz White House. By 2010, both Kyrgyzstan's political elite and the street protestors understood their power and the coup d'état playbook: take over central administration buildings, broadcast videos and pictures of gleeful demonstrators occupying the presidential suite, and declare a successful end to the "revolution" and convene an interim government. Considerably greater challenges lay just ahead for this new government.

Kyrgyzstan need not be forever destined to political chaos, however. Michael McFaul, a senior adviser to President Obama on Russian and Eurasian affairs, compellingly noted during his May 2010 visit to Bishkek that the U.S. administration believes Kyrgyz society and not the Kyrgyz government is best positioned to change Bishkek's political fortunes. Should a consensus emerge around McFaul's observation and international donors begin to move away from directly engaging the Kyrgyz state, then there indeed are considerable grounds for optimism for Kyrgyzstan's political future. Engaging Kyrgyz NGOs and the civil society sector will reduce executive rent-seeking behavior while compelling greater coalition building and political stability. Empowering society will encourage the provision of two critical services the Kyrgyz government currently does not provide: checks on executive corruption and enhanced local-level social welfare provision. Independent Kyrgyz media and society-based watchdog groups have already demonstrated an ability to expose government corruption. As such, the international community would do well to support these critical institutions. Locally based charities, most prominently Muslim charities, have equally demonstrated an ability to provide needed public goods that the Kyrgyz state has been woefully incapable of providing. A new policy where international donors limit funding to the Kyrgyz state while increasing assistance to community-based charities and support to independent media and watchdog organizations, although it may be a politically difficult sell in Bishkek, may ultimately better serve the interests of the Kyrgyz state and society.

The First Presidency

Although Akaev held power for fifteen years, his presidency, as we would expect from the perestroika legacy model, was precarious and repeatedly shaken by elite defection and conflict. That said, Akaev did enjoy a period of relative calm from 1994 to 2000 in between the immediate post-Soviet and post-9/11 periods of unrest. These three periods closely align with changes in economic resources available to the Kyrgyz executive. Before 1994, as figure 3.1 illustrates, foreign aid to Kyrgyzstan was all but nonexistent. From 1994 to 2000 foreign aid to Kyrgyzstan skyrocketed. And from 2001 to 2005 reform aid decreased while the Kyrgyz executive and his family began receiving direct rents in return for U.S. access to the air base at Manas. Both the absence of economic resources between 1990 and 1993 and the executive's disproportionate capture of economic resources between 2001 and 2005 undermined Akaev's ability to maintain stable winning coalitions. In contrast, the diffuse nature of foreign reform aid, the primary source of Kyrgyz state economic resources between 1994 and 2000, as shown in figure 3.2, forced the Kyrgyz executive to share the wealth—an outcome that temporarily dampened elite challenges to executive rule.

Executive-Legislative Conflict, 1990–1993

In November 1993 *Pravda* ran an article titled "The Three Lost Years—An Anniversary Askar Akaev Would Rather Forget."[1] The article began with Akaev's 1990 promise to hasten Kyrgyzstan's economic recovery and concluded that what he had achieved "was the exact opposite of what [the president] had promised."[2] Akaev tried to sidestep this criticism by blaming the Kyrgyz political elite. "They have accused me of trying to establish a personal dictatorship," Akaev fumed at the Kyrgyz parliamentary deputies in an interview on the Russian television show *Utro*.[3] "Their goal is clear," he continued, "they would like to deprive the president of certain powers and turn him into the likes of the British queen."[4]

**Figure 3.2. Aid as a Percentage of Central Government
Expenditures—World Development Indicators[1]**

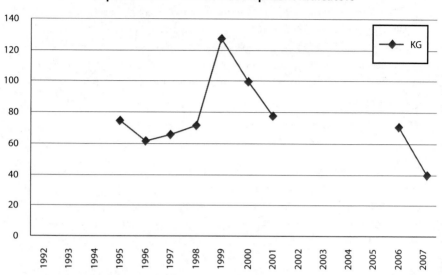

[1] The gaps indicate missing data in the World Development Indicators database.

Source: World Bank World Development Indicators, available at http://data.worldbank.org/
data-catalog/world-development-indicators.

Although ribbon cutting was not the role Kyrgyzstan's members of parliament had in mind for their chief executive, neither did they want Akaev to amass
the growing powers other presidents of Central Asia had quickly gathered. With
institutional jurisdictions neither guaranteed by a constitution nor established by
legitimizing behavioral norms, relations between the parliament and the president quickly devolved into a zero-sum game in which compromise was equated
with concession.[5] The president attempted to take an early lead in the race to popular legitimacy, submitting his office to popular vote in October 1991. Although
Akaev won with a resounding 95 percent of the vote, the parliamentary opposition was quick to retort that "it's difficult to have a democratic election when
there is only one candidate."[6] Kyrgyzstan's deputies could equally play the role of
populists.

Impasse quickly led to accusation. In late 1992 reports noting an unusually close relationship between the Swiss-based trading company Seabeco and
the Akaev leadership emerged in the Kyrgyz press.[7] Throughout 1992, Kyrgyz
reporters had observed several changes in the president and his entourage. Perhaps most noticeable, the president and the prime minister had traded in their

Soviet-made limousines for sleek new Volvos. Less visible but equally reported in the press, presidential bodyguards had added an assortment of Western-made weaponry to their standard-issue Kalashnikovs. Akaev, his fleet of Volvos, and his bodyguards could often be seen traveling to Kyrgyzstan's Manas international airport, where he would board not a tired Soviet Tupolev, but rather Seabeco's corporate jet for his state missions abroad. It ultimately would be discovered that it was not only the president the Seabeco jet was ferrying, but also large quantities of Kyrgyz gold.[8]

A parliamentary investigation would later uncover that Akaev had secured a $13.8 million line of credit from a Swiss bank in return for a 1.6-ton collateral in Kyrgyz gold. The loan was arranged by Boris Birshtein, the chief executive officer of Seabeco and a Soviet émigré with unusually close ties with several post-Soviet leaders. Birshtein, for his help, was appointed special adviser to the president, was given an office one floor below the presidential suite in the Kyrgyz White House, and was paid $2 million in consultation fees. As for the remainder of the $13.8 million, this, Akaev explained, was applied to administrative expenses—to the purchase of the Volvos, armaments, and consultation fees. Still, the numbers did not add up, and Akaev was later forced to concede that after all expenses were tallied, $4 million remained unaccounted for.[9]

That the executive office squandered $14 million—although an astounding sum for Kyrgyzstan's poverty-stricken 4.5 million people—was not Akaev's most pressing problem. Even more damaging to his image were the spin-off investigations the gold scandal inspired. Before the Kyrgyz parliament disbanded in September 1994, several close Akaev associates were implicated in corruption: Prime Minister Turgunbek Chyngyshev; Zhumagul Saadanbekov, the akim of Issyk-Kol oblast (the center of Kyrgyzstan's gold mining); Bekamat Osmonov, the akim of the politically sensitive Jalal Abad oblast; and Tologon Kasymbekov, Akaev confidant and prominent Kyrgyz novelist.[10]

Akaev himself survived the parliament's investigations, although his image and his popularity were severely damaged. Akaev's own prime minister, Chyngyshev, confessed just before his resignation that "today, only fools and loafers don't take bribes."[11] Such statements did not sit well with many within the Kyrgyz elite who, unlike Akaev, did not have direct access to multinational corporations like Seabeco, who were not chauffeured around the capital in Volvos, and who did not have jets to spirit them away to Switzerland. Akaev was not sharing the wealth, and for this Kyrgyzstan's political elite attempted to bring him down. Indeed, at every turn Kyrgyz parliamentarians attempted to stymie Akaev's initiatives. Akaev and the Supreme Soviet clashed over language law—Akaev pressed for and the parliament resisted giving Russian status as an official state language.[12] The two branches conflicted over the direction and the pace of land reform.[13] Most critically, Akaev and the Supreme Soviet clashed over constitutional design. In short, Kyrgyz executive-legislative relations, in contrast to that in Uzbekistan and Kazakhstan, were decidedly not placid. The Kyrgyz deputies to whom Akaev ultimately was beholden for his chance victory in October 1990 perceived few limits to what they considered appropriate legislative oversight.

Perhaps nowhere was this contested relationship more in evidence than in the debates surrounding the adoption of a new post-Soviet Kyrgyz constitution.[14] Kyrgyzstan's adoption of a new constitution, in stark contrast to the executive-dominated process in Uzbekistan and Kazakhstan, was a multi-actor affair. Moreover, the constitution that was ultimately passed in May 1993 provided an admirable and balanced distribution of powers between the president and the parliament. For example, the new 105-member parliament, renamed the Zhogorku Kenesh from the Russian "soviet," had both on paper and at least initially in reality substantial authority to check executive rule. The parliament could vote for the removal of the president in the case of executive abuses of power; it could override presidential vetoes of legislation; it could approve or reject presidential appointments to the government (the posts of the prime minister and his cabinet); it could initiate changes in the constitution; it could reject international treaties signed by the president and reject presidential imposition of states of emergency and executive declarations of war; and it was delegated oversight over the executive's implementation of the national budget.[15] Most important, the parliament was empowered to be a truly independent legislative body. That is, in contrast to what would be established in Uzbekistan and Kazakhstan, all Kyrgyz deputies were to be elected by popular vote, not as strangely was the case for a considerable portion of deputies in the Uzbek and Kazakh parliaments, who were directly appointed by the president.[16]

Most heartening for local reformists and international observers alike, Kyrgyz constitutional and electoral design was conducted in an atmosphere of impassioned, if not always congenial, debate among the executive, the legislature, and the country's many officially registered political parties. Representing the pro-parliament side of this debate, Tursunbai Bakir uulu, Osh oblast regional head of the newly formed Erkin-Kyrgyzstan (Free Kyrgyzstan) party, argued: "We must be vigilant in supporting the right and progressive actions of the president, the prime minister and the parliament. And if the [executive] power makes gross errors, we must candidly point them out, suggest our own variant and, where necessary, insist upon a proper resolution."[17]

Akaev retorted, and not without cause given the multiple parliamentary investigations he had endured: "The most vulnerable elements of the new Kyrgyz government are the president and his cabinet."[18] Bargaining tactics, moreover, went beyond claims and counterclaims. Thus, for example, when drafts of potential constitutions were submitted to the Supreme Soviet in July 1992, the deputies, rather than beginning debate, chose instead to adjourn and reexamine the proposals in the fall.[19] A sympathetic interpretation of the deputies' action would be that they wanted time to review the proposals and consult with their constituencies before beginning debate in session. The pro-Akaev government newspaper *Slovo Kyrgyzstana* argued, however, that the Supreme Soviet adjournment was a procedural tactic, undertaken to torpedo the president's proposal in the national media.[20] Perhaps, Akaev wondered out loud in response to the deputies' stalling, the parliament was incapable of reasonable debate—perhaps the question of the constitution might more expediently be resolved by a less impassioned, specially formed constitutional assembly.[21]

Ultimately, the president and the parliament would pass a constitution in May 1993 that was mutually acceptable. That the Kyrgyz legislature and executive were able to achieve institutional compromise, it should be emphasized in light of Kyrgyzstan's executive-dominated neighbors, was a remarkable achievement. In Tajikistan similar debates quickly devolved into civil war. In Kazakhstan, Turkmenistan, and Uzbekistan such debates were universally resolved in favor of the executive. And in Russia, where a measure of executive-legislative balance was achieved, the executive was not beyond the occasional use of tanks to make his demands heard. Kyrgyzstan, it appeared, was an outpost of pluralism and compromise in post-Soviet Eurasia—a model not just for Central Asian but for all post-Soviet political reform. Kyrgyzstan's outlier status, in the eyes of many Western observers, was due in large part to Akaev himself. In the words of Strobe Talbott, the U.S. envoy to the former Soviet Union, Akaev was a "true Jeffersonian democrat," magnanimously presiding over a political system that seemed more and more bent on ejecting him from power.[22]

A significant factor behind Kyrgyzstan's executive-legislative conflict and compromise, and a direct reason why Western diplomats like Ambassador Talbott could point to what appeared at the time to be inchoate democratic processes, was Kyrgyzstan's extensive press freedoms. Throughout the tenure of Kyrgyzstan's first parliament, the press gave wide coverage to the constant struggles between the president and the parliament. Papers like *Res publica*, *Politika*, and the parliament's own paper, *Svobodnye gori*, bore witness to these political developments: the Supreme Soviet's growing legislative oversight; the heated debates between the president and the legislature over constitutional and electoral design; the challenges of post-Soviet economic reform; and the country's growing political pluralism. Reading articles written during this initial period of post-Soviet transition, one sees a Kyrgyzstan most unlike the country we see today—a Kyrgyzstan where democracy indeed seemed a possibility, where one could be a member of the political opposition or an objective journalist and not be fearful of arbitrary imprisonment.[23] For example, Kyrgyzstan, the Central Asia analyst Martha Brill Olcott has observed, had a "virtually untrammeled and decidedly raucous press," a press markedly different from the executive-managed press in Kazakhstan and a world apart from the Stalin-like control President Karimov exerted over the press in Uzbekistan.[24] In 1994, however, Kyrgyzstan's seemingly comparative liberalism came to a sudden halt. Political elites whom the Kyrgyz electorate and the outside world had assumed were part of the "opposition" of the early 1990s suddenly switched sides and began supporting Akaev. Those elites who did not defect to the executive, the prominent journalist Zamira Sydykova has observed, found themselves before the Kyrgyz courts being tried for "God only knows what."[25]

Securing a Stable Winning Coalition, 1994–2000

In 1994 executive-legislative relations in Kyrgyzstan dramatically changed. In September of that year half of Kyrgyzstan's parliamentarians—curiously a proportion identical to the number of deputies who were simultaneously serving as state appointees either in the regions or in the central administration—declared a parliamentary boycott.[26] The reason for this boycott, the members of parliament explained, was that they could no longer "participate in a Zhogorku Kenesh [parliament] that had lost its authority in the eyes of the people."[27] Akaev in response—arguing that "the refusal of the majority of deputies . . . to participate in the parliament has made it impossible for the legislature to carry out its functions"—used the boycott as justification for summarily dismissing the legislature.[28]

Akaev's dismissal of the parliament was not met with international criticism but rather with quiet approval. One year earlier, President Boris Yeltsin had similarly disbanded the holdover Soviet-era parliament in Russia, only Yeltsin had been forced to supplement his presidential decree with artillery fire to convince members of parliament to vacate their offices. At the time, President Bill Clinton responded to Yeltsin's actions with the muted observation: "I would say that, given the circumstances that he [Yeltsin] confronted, he responded with real restraint."[29] That Akaev was able to accomplish what Yeltsin had and dismiss Kyrgyzstan's Soviet-era parliament without firing a shot was likely viewed with relief in Bishkek and Western capitals. How, though, was Akaev able to so readily disband a parliament that had before September 1994 so vociferously protested executive excesses? A partial answer to this question lies in the data summarized

**Figure 3.3. Total Foreign Aid to Kyrgyzstan—
World Development Indicators**

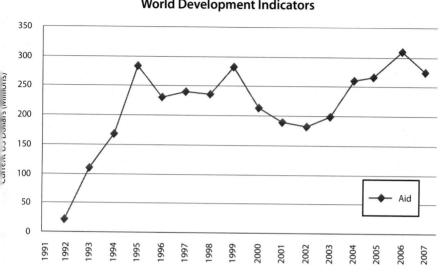

Source: World Bank World Development Indicators, available at http://data.worldbank.org/
data-catalog/world-development-indicators.

in figure 3.3. In 1994 Akaev, thanks to the international donor community, suddenly had access to economic resources.

Equally important was Akaev's astute rebuilding of patronage networks within the Kyrgyz political elite. By September 1994 Akaev had managed to appoint half of the Soviet-era elected members of parliament to positions within the presidential administration. As such, he had institutionalized mechanisms through which foreign aid could be channeled to supporters. This overlap of executive and legislative jurisdictions was critical and, moreover, it was one that the new constitution adopted in 1993 threatened to eliminate. Perhaps not surprisingly then, with the Soviet parliament now disbanded, Akaev immediately set out to change Kyrgyzstan's electoral law to maintain his ability to appoint members of parliament to serve simultaneously in the executive administration.

Before the parliamentary boycott, Akaev, national members of parliament, and regional elites (the latter two were often one and the same) agreed that the next parliament was to be smaller (105 seats instead of 350) and bicameral. Kyrgyzstan's new parliament was to be divided into two houses—a lower regularly convening Legislative Assembly with 56 seats and an upper intermittently convening chamber, the Assembly of People's Representatives, with 49 seats. The

Legislative Assembly was to be a "professional parliament"—that is, unlike the old Kyrgyz parliament and unlike members of parliament in other Central Asian states, members of Kyrgyzstan's new Legislative Assembly were to work full time and were to be prohibited from holding positions in the state administration. In theory at least, these deputies were insulated from executive cooption.

After the dissolution of the parliament, however, Akaev convened an October 1994 constitutional referendum to unilaterally reassign the number of seats in each house. The Legislative Assembly, according to the terms stipulated in the referendum, was to be reduced to thirty-five seats and the Assembly of People's Representatives was to be enlarged to seventy seats.[30] Ostensibly Akaev favored this redesign because it would "give regional leaders more representation in matters of most direct concern to them."[31] "Territorial interests," according to the Kyrgyz constitution, were the domain of the Assembly of People's Representatives.[32] Furthering the "interests of the entire population of the Kyrgyz Republic," in contrast, was the task assigned to the Legislative Assembly.[33] Beyond these constitutional mandates, what this division meant in practice was that deputies in the considerably larger Assembly of People's Representatives, unlike Legislative Assembly members of parliament, could simultaneously hold state appointments while serving in the national parliament. Akaev explained the logic behind these differing portfolios as follows:

> The Constitution of the Kyrgyz Republic prohibits deputies of the Zhogorku Kenesh from holding state or judicial appointments or conducting business ventures while serving in the legislature. In my opinion, this prohibition applies only to the professional [full-time, Legislative Assembly] deputies. . . . It is a different matter when we consider the other chamber, the Assembly of People's Representatives. Meeting only on a part time basis, it is clear that these deputies cannot give up their regular employment. As a matter of fact, these deputies likely will be elected because of their regular employment, the work they are doing at the local level.
>
> Thus, with regards to the Assembly of People's Representatives, only those holding national-level appointments, for example state ministers—for whom pursuing local interests may conflict with their obligation to the state—should be prevented from running for election.[34]

Akaev's rewriting of Kyrgyz electoral law thus did more than simply increase regional representation. Far more fateful to Kyrgyz politics, the enlarged Assembly of People's Representatives allowed Akaev to rebuild patronage networks within the Kyrgyz parliament. Although oppositionists did win seats to the much reduced Legislative Assembly in the February 1995 parliamentary elections, the majority of seats in the Assembly of People's Representatives—and thus in the parliament as a whole—were filled by candidates with close ties to the state administration. Indeed, reading the roster of the 1995 Assembly of People's Representatives is like reading a who's who in the Kyrgyz state bureaucracy.

Among those elected were Chingiz Aitmatov, Kyrgyz ambassador to Belgium and architect of Akaev's rise to power in 1990; Baktybek Abdrisiaev, the Akaev administration's director of international affairs; T. Akmatbaev, the deputy minister of industry and trade; G. Asanaliev, the undersecretary of state; Isa Omurkulov, the chief inspector of Kyrgyz transport inspections; Bekamat Osmonov, the deputy head of the Osh oblast state administration; Dastan Sarigulov, the president of the state-owned Kyrgyz-Gold; Malabek Toktobolotov, the deputy head of the Jalal Abad oblast department of finance; and, perhaps most ironic, Bakhtiiar Fatakhov, the chairman of the state department on antimonopoly politics.[35] In total, of the seventy deputies elected to the assembly more than two-thirds were in the direct employ of the state administration—an outcome clearly welcomed by the Akaev administration.[36] Almambet Maturbraimov, Kyrgyzstan's deputy prime minister, for example, declared: "The Assembly of People's Representatives is ready to work in unity with the president and the government."[37] Maturbraimov would know, for not only was he deputy prime minister, he was also a newly elected member of parliament and speaker of the Assembly of People's Representatives.[38]

Akaev's control over the legislature was, neither in 1995 nor later in his administration, absolute. His stacking the upper house with state appointees reduced but did not eliminate opposition in the parliament. Deputies in Kyrgyzstan's lower house in particular—for example, Azimbek Beknazarov and Ishenbai Kadyrbekov—continued to criticize executive rule.[39] Arguably, however, such criticism served a purpose. The European Bank for Reconstruction and Development concluded as recently as 2002 that "the Kyrgyz Republic has continued to make progress towards the implementation of the principles of multi-party democracy, pluralism and market economy."[40]

In reality, though, Kyrgyz members of parliament in the 1990s could do little more than protest—and even this legislative freedom became increasingly embattled as Akaev sought to deepen and further institutionalize his patronage networks in the second half of the decade. In 1996, for example, he proposed yet another constitutional referendum. Because Legislative Assembly members of parliament, he explained, "instead of fulfilling their duties—making laws—are more occupied by personal concerns like raising their salaries, finding nice apartments, getting government cars and outfitting their offices," the executive needed to be freed from such shirkers and instead be given a free hand in staffing critical government offices with minimal parliamentary oversight.[41] Passage of the 1996 referendum gave Akaev the right to appoint all state ministers, administrators, and—critical to the further consolidation of executive power—judges. Although parliamentary approval for these appointments would be required, it was only Akaev's pocket parliament, the Assembly of People's Representatives not the Legislative Assembly, that voted on these appointments.[42] Akaev promised that this new appointment procedure would guarantee that the constitution's "mechanism of checks and balances would become more reliable."[43] This new procedure ensured a pliant judiciary that Akaev could turn to again and again in an effort to silence the growing number of defectors from his regime in the early to mid-2000s.

Through a series of constitutional referenda Akaev was able to rebuild patronage networks and directly tie the Assembly of People's Representatives to the Kyrgyz executive. How do we know, though, that he in fact distributed foreign aid windfalls through these newly revitalized patronage networks? One clue lies in the reports of the donors themselves. In 1994 the World Bank extended to Kyrgyzstan sixty million dollars in "rehabilitation credit" (RC) and "privatization and enterprise sector adjustment credit" (PESAC) to "support a fledgling reform program" and to "improve the quality of privatization of small, medium, and large scale enterprises, and to support substantial trade and price liberalization measures to improve private sector development."[44] Initially the World Bank's International Development Association (IDA) rated its implementation of Kyrgyzstan's Rehabilitation Credit and the Privatization Enterprise Adjustment Credit as "highly satisfactory." Eight years later, however, the bank's Operations Evaluation Department (OED) downgraded these ratings to only "marginally satisfactory."[45]

The World Bank's watchdog agency explained: "OED rated the outcomes of both RC and PESAC as marginally satisfactory. RC's rating was lowered because its funds were used to finance inefficient SOEs (state owned enterprises) and the TA (technical assistance) component had little government management and was under-managed by IDA. The outcome of PESAC was considered only marginally satisfactory because the objective of attracting strategic investors was not realized, serious corporate governance issues were not addressed, negligible enterprise restructuring followed privatization, and many of the loss-making enterprises intended to be liquidated or restructured continue to drag on the economy."[46] In short, the money was distributed according to the logic of the Kyrgyz political market, not the economic free market. Key to the relative stability of Kyrgyz politics between 1994 and 2000, this money was not stolen directly by Akaev; rather, it was doled out to Akaev appointees and supporters within the Kyrgyz bureaucracy. These appointees did not use the bank aid for enterprise restructuring; they used the aid to rebuild and solidify networks of patronage politics. Although the Asian Development Bank correctly concluded that the Akaev administration "lacked a sense of ownership of recommendations and commitment to their implementation," Akaev's directors of the state-owned enterprises were more than happy to take ownership of World Bank aid.[47]

The $12.5 million decentralization project of the United Nations Development Program (UNDP) similarly illustrates this dynamic of executive-assisted capture of foreign aid.[48] The UN's decentralization program was designed to provide "support to local governance and grass-roots organizations."[49] Curiously, this program was administered by, of all institutions, the Kyrgyz presidential administration.[50] The UNDP appears somewhat confused on this score. The UN's residential coordinator in Kyrgyzstan noted in 1999 that "the executing agency of the Decentralization Program is an NGO (the Congress of Local Communities)."[51] The Kyrgyz liaison for the UN decentralization program, in contrast, explained that "the President's Administration is the executing agency of the political and administrative Local Governance Programme."[52] Perhaps some of the confusion may result from the fact that the Congress of Local Communities, although it calls itself an NGO, shares not only its offices but also its staff with the presidential administration.[53]

Donors need not be duped for foreign aid to still be an effective support for patronage politics. Consider, for example, a few of the programs included in USAID's $29 million assistance package to Kyrgyzstan in 1999. Of this amount, $2.5 million was targeted for "financial reform" and involved cooperative projects between USAID contractors and the Kyrgyz "Central Bank, the Ministry of Finance, the Bishkek Stock Exchange, and the National Securities Commission."[54] USAID allocated two million dollars in assistance to advance "more effective, responsible, and accountable local government" and worked directly with the "Office of Local Government in the Presidential Apparat, the Academy for Management, and the municipal association NGO, as well as the parliament and local (and national) level officials, both appointed and elected" to achieve this aim. USAID also allocated two million dollars in assistance to supporting "citizens' participation," a program whose "beneficiaries include activists of NGOs, personnel of independent television and radio stations, lawyers, judges, members of parliament, and the public at large." By far the largest allocation in the 1999 USAID budget for Kyrgyzstan was $12.5 million for "special initiatives" encompassing the strengthening of "primary health care service sites," "reproductive health services," and the "transfer of technology in both tertiary and primary care."[55]

Did these funds flow directly to the executive? No—and for Akaev the fact that this aid did not directly accrue to him was a political asset rather than a liability. As the perestroika legacy model illustrates, in political environments where elites are few and fragmented, as they are in Kyrgyzstan, executives must share a large proportion of all economic resources available to the state if they hope to remain in power. Paradoxically, the diffuse nature of economic and political reform aid—the fact that reform aid is distributed not directly to the president but to ministries, regional and local governments, members of parliament, even NGO activists—forces leaders like Akaev to pursue the very wealth redistribution policies that are most likely to sustain autocratic rule. In contrast, when economic resources can be directly captured, executives may be tempted to take a disproportionate size of the economic pie themselves and in the process engender elite defections that can ultimately bring down tenuous autocratic rule.

In short, what drove Akaev's brief period of autocratic calm and the power of his patronage from 1994 to 2000 was not his direct control of economic resources, but rather his ability to determine who would be in positions to receive these economic resources. Akaev was dependent on the international community to provide aid; the Kyrgyz executive was able in many cases, however, to determine who the ultimate recipients of this international aid would be. This Akaev did through two mechanisms: the power to appoint and remove political elites to national, regional, and local administration offices; and the power to initiate judicial proceedings against political elites who were unmoved by his power to appoint and dismiss.

Consider the cases of three prominent Kyrgyz political elites: Bakyt Beshimov, Felix Kulov, and Zamira Sydykova. From 1991 to 1998, Beshimov was the rector of Osh State University—a position awarded by Akaev by way of the Kyrgyz Ministry of Education. Akaev had Beshimov sacked in 1998 when, as the Kyrgyz Ministry of Education explained, it discovered the rector "lacked a doctor's degree."[56] The true reason why Beshimov was dismissed, though, was that he had publicly defected from the Akaev leadership and had begun to use Osh State University as a platform from which to mobilize support for his own political aspirations. Beshimov's gambit was not without risk. The rector's son, Erdin, was in Dearborn, Michigan, at the time on a U.S. Information Agency–funded high school exchange; as such, Beshimov's active defiance of the Akaev government threatened not just his own fortunes, but those of his family members as well.[57]

Beshimov's gamble ultimately yielded big dividends. Later in 1998 he won a by-election seat to the Kyrgyz parliament, and by August 1999 he was polling among the ten most popular politicians in Kyrgyzstan. He looked to be a shoo-in for reelection in the March 2000 parliamentary ballot and was rumored as a potential contender for the October 2000 presidential election.[58] In early February 2000, however, Beshimov suddenly gave up his political ambitions and accepted President Akaev's offer to be Kyrgyzstan's new ambassador in India. Of this sudden change of heart, Beshimov explained to the Kyrgyz press: "Mahatma Gandhi, along with Winston Churchill, is one of my greatest political role models."[59]

Not all Kyrgyz elites have proven so flexible in their political inspirations. Felix Kulov, for example, though he too had spent much of the 1990s within Akaev's administration, would not be swayed by veiled government threats when he defected from Akaev's ruling coalition in 1999. Like Beshimov, Kulov began indicating in 1999 that he planned to run in both the March 2000 parliamentary and October 2000 presidential elections. Kulov by 1999 was a well-known figure in Kyrgyz politics. He had served as Kyrgyzstan's vice president, as an oblast governor, as minister of national defense, and, beginning in 1998, as mayor of Bishkek. He was (and remains) a savvy politician. As such, upon defecting from Akaev's inner circle, Kulov immediately quit his position in the mayor's office rather than wait for the dismissal directive that would surely come from above. Kulov's vacating his executive-appointed mayorship was not enough to assuage Akaev's concerns. The Kyrgyz president directed his judiciary to begin investigations into Kulov's alleged abuse of power while serving as minister of defense. The Kyrgyz courts found Kulov guilty and in January 2001 sentenced the former Akaev protégé to seven years in jail.[60]

Zamira Sydykova, in contrast to Kulov and Beshimov, never held an appointed office under Akaev. Rather, as editor of Kyrgyzstan's *Res publica* newspaper, Sydykova was throughout the 1990s Akaev's most vocal critic. Importantly, neither Sydykova nor her paper was independent of Akaev's influence. Whenever the Kyrgyz executive perceived *Res publica* as being too strident in its criticisms, Sydykova was either jailed or fined for libel. Even though she was outside the presidential administration, her fortunes were very much tied to the whims of the presidential administration. Thus, when the International Women's Media Foundation and Times Warner awarded Sydykova twenty-four thousand dollars in 2000, Sydykova was forced to turn this money over to the government to settle a twenty-five-thousand-dollar libel lawsuit.[61] Reflecting on her paper's many libel suits and her own incarcerations, Sydykova rhetorically asked in an editorial what the future of *Res publica* would be. Her answer: The "newspaper's fate is up to the government. . . . It seems that only the [Kyrgyz] White House knows how much longer we shall last."[62]

Sydykova, Kulov, and Beshimov were all prominent political elites. As such, it is understandable why the executive acted quickly to limit the contagion effect their defections might have on Akaev's fragile ruling coalition. It was not only prominent elites, though, that the presidential administration closely monitored. Take the case of Tyup city administrator Zh. Sharapov, who in 1997 was dismissed on charges of embezzling sixty thousand dollars in wages he was supposed to distribute to local schoolteachers.[63] Commenting on the regional administrator's dismissal, Akaev's own press secretary warned: "I trust that Sharapov's example will serve as a lesson for other state administrators who are considering such malfeasance."[64]

In these examples the presidential administration took an active role in admonishing disloyal or potentially disloyal political elites. Equally representative of Akaev's ability to distribute wealth during this period of growing foreign aid are the less well reported yet nevertheless widely discussed cases of everyday rent-seeking opportunities that accrue to Akaev's appointees. There is the governor in Naryn who appropriated a shipment of insulin from a Western relief agency and then instructed his staff to sell the insulin to the region's diabetics.[65] There are the local "tax, custom, and code administrations who all take cuts from business profits" and pass a portion of these "revenues" up to their bosses.[66] And there are the judges at every level of the Kyrgyz court system who make a comfortable living by "handing down decisions—political decisions—that the central government wants."[67]

Akaev's strength throughout the second half of the 1990s lay not in his own direct access to economic wealth, but rather in his ability to determine who among Kyrgyzstan's narrow political elite could receive foreign economic aid and foreign grants. The ability to determine who received this aid, as the Sydykova case aptly illustrates, was not limited to state appointees. Through strategic use of the Kyrgyz courts, Akaev could limit who among Kyrgyzstan's NGO and media elite received foreign aid. Neither Akaev's ability to appoint and dismiss nor his ability to use the courts against elites who sought to undermine his ruling coalition disappeared after 2000. Nor did foreign aid to Kyrgyzstan suddenly vanish. Indeed, the threat to Akaev's patronage rule after 2000 came not from what he lacked, but rather from what he and his family gained: direct payments from the U.S. government for use of Kyrgyzstan's Manas airfield.

Akaev Debased, 2001–2005

In December 2002 Rina Prizhivoit, the editor of the Kyrgyz paper *Moya stolitsa*, informed the Moscow-based Center for Journalism in Extreme Situations that her paper was on the "verge of closing."[68] A Bishkek city court had ruled that *Moya stolitsa* had libeled the U.S.-registered company Merlisaid and directed Prizhivoit to pay fifty-two thousand dollars in compensation. Merlisaid, the paper reported, had failed to pay taxes on its primary business venture in Kyrgyzstan: supplying jet fuel for the U.S. air base at Manas.[69] The primary actor behind Merlisaid, Prizhivoit told the Center for Journalism in Extreme Situations, was Adil Toygonbaev, a Kazakh citizen as well as President Akaev's son-in-law.[70]

The United States began using the air base at Manas in December 2001 as a central launching point for its post-9/11 "War Against Terror" operations in Afghanistan. Prizhivoit broke the Toygonbaev and Akaev family story the following month. Akaev attempted to gag Prizhivoit; not only was Prizhivoit subjected to onerous libel cases, but also the January 14, 2002, print run of *Moya stolitsa* (the issue in which Toybonbaev was first linked to the Manas fuel contracts) was censored. Other publications quickly picked up the story. On January 23 the Russian paper *Vremia novostei* informed its readers about the "the latest scandal in Bishkek" and suggested that the censoring of *Moya stolitsa* in addition to Akaev's dismissal of the minister of interior affairs as well as the director of national security were all connected to the Akaev family's financial machinations surrounding the new U.S. air base at Manas.[71]

Five months later, in an interview with David Stern of the *Financial Times,* Akaev conceded for the first time that Toygonbaev was supplying fuel to the Americans at Manas and that because of this arrangement "his son-in-law was 'doing well.'"[72] Stern continued to press Akaev and asked if any other of the president's family members, and specifically Akaev's son Aidar, were benefitting from contracts with the U.S. base. Akaev replied that there was no "family involvement beyond that of his son-in-law."[73] I asked Stern in April 2010 why he had pressed Akaev on his son's possible involvement with Manas. Stern replied he had done so because "Aidar's involvement was being spoken of openly when I wrote my piece."[74]

If in 2002 Aidar's involvement was being spoken of openly, by the summer of 2003 the end game of Aidar's involvement in Manas was also being openly discussed. Akaev's strategy of rule, Kyrgyz colleagues repeatedly told me in June 2003, had morphed from foreign aid redistribution to outright embezzlement. Tolekan Ismailova, the director of the nongovernmental organization Citizens Against Corruption, described this new strategy: "If we are to analyze Askar Akaev's behavior, then we can say that he's not thinking about the future of the country. He's thinking about how he can safeguard and legalize everything he's stolen. He probably won't be successful. But he's trying to make sure that when he goes, this wealth, these funds, will remain with his family, his relatives—this for him is what's most important. This is the strategy he's now working on. And in this vein we can now see which politicians are playing along with him."[75]

Akaev's days were numbered. Akaev himself knew this. Ismailova knew it. And most important, the Kyrgyz political elite knew it. For half a decade the nature of economic resources available to Akaev forced him to do what was in his political best interest. The diffuse nature of bilateral and multilateral foreign aid compelled him to share wealth among Kyrgyzstan's fragmented political elite and in the process temporarily shore up his tenuous autocratic rule. The Manas air base changed this dynamic, however. Although political and economic reform aid continued to flow, this aid was overshadowed both in the popular imagination and ultimately by the immense amount of wealth that was directly accruing to the Akaev family through American fueling contracts. Members of Akaev's winning coalition, perceiving they were not receiving their fair cut of the Manas wealth, began defecting and agitating for Akaev's overthrow.

We now have a clearer understanding of just how much Akaev and his family were withholding from his winning coalition supporters. Following Akaev's overthrow in March 2005, the U.S. government shared with the new Bishkek leadership an FBI report detailing the extent to which Kyrgyzstan's former first family benefitted from the U.S. air base. The report revealed that three private Kyrgyz companies—Manas International Airport (MIA), Manas International Services (MIS), and Aalam Services—provided fuel as well as other contract services to the Americans at Manas. Aidar Akaev controlled Manas International Airport. Adil Toyganbaev controlled Manas International Services and Aalam Services. Two investigative journalists who had access to the FBI report (David Cloud with the *New York Times* and Aram Roston with *NBC News*) have estimated that MIS and Aalam, through their fuel subcontracts with the U.S. Department of Defense, netted the Akaev family on average revenues of forty million dollars a year between 2002 and 2005.[76] MIA, which Aidar Akaev controlled, collected an additional two million dollars a year in rent for the U.S. air base as well as seven thousand dollars every time a U.S. military plane took off from Manas—all payments that never passed through official Kyrgyz government accounts.[77]

Manas was not the only source of rents for the Akaev family. One month before Akaev's overthrow, Prizhivoit appealed to her readers to double-check her own list of Akaev properties and inform her if she had inadvertently left something out. Her list included:

> The Kant cement and slate plant, the Kadamjay mercury combine, the Kara-Balta sugar refinery, the joint-stock company Aeroport Manas, the joint-stock company KyrgyzAlko, a network of filling stations ShNOS, OsOO MIS (fuel and lubricants for the Manas airport and the Ganci air base), Aalam Servis in the Bishkek free economic zone, the television channel KOORT, the newspaper *Vecherniy Bishkek,* the Ayrek advertising agency, the radio station Love Radio, the Kyrgyz-Info information agency, the Norus downhill ski base. . . .

EnergoBank, the NK Alyans network of filling stations, the BITEL and Fonex cellular networks, the Ysyk-Kol Avrora sanatorium, territory in the sanatorium Kyrgyzskoye vzmorye, the Gulkair pensionat, the Silk Way trading house, the Irish Pub restaurant, the First disco club, STARS restaurant, the Narodnyy supermarket network, the Bishkek Hotel, the Kumtor gold mining joint venture, the Internet Service Provider ElKat, the television channels Piramida and NBT, a beauty salon, the Tokmok Interglass glass plant, the Mercedes-Barat station, the Jalal-Abad cotton plant, and financial control of joint-stock companies Server-Elektro, OshElektro, Elektricheskiye stantsii, Kyrgyzgaz, Kyrgyzneftegaz, and Kyrgyz Telekom. . . . If the readers have corrections or additions to this impressive list—I welcome them![78]

In a February 2005 speech at the Carnegie Center in Moscow, Akaev's onetime foreign minister turned oppositionist Roza Otunbaeva was hitting a similar note, informing her Russian colleagues that "on our (party) website you can find an impressive list of businesses owned by the presidential family . . . family oligarchs and corruption make economic development impossible."[79]

Otunbaeva titled her Moscow speech "Will There Be a Tulip Revolution in Kyrgyzstan?" Akaev's erstwhile foreign minister might more appropriately have titled her talk "How We Will Run the Tulip Revolution in Kyrgyzstan." What Otunbaeva laid out in Moscow was, to a T, the strategy of disaffected elites as outlined in the perestroika legacy model. First, she noted the Kyrgyz political elites' disaffection with the executive's embezzling rather than sharing economic resources. Second, Otunbaeva identified the handful of key actors—all former members of Akaev's winning coalition—who would be spearheading the anti-Akaev movement: "We have five major party blocs. . . . I lead one of them, Ata Zhurt, or Homeland. . . . Another bloc, Kyrgyzstan's Popular Movement, is led by Kurmanbek Bakiyev, the country's former prime minister. The next bloc is the People's Congress of Kyrgyzstan. It includes the Ar-Namys party led by Felix Kulov. The next bloc is led by the former Foreign Minister Murat Imanaliyev. The name of the bloc is the New Course or Jany Bagyt. Finally, I would like to mention the movement the Civil Union for Fair Elections formed by the former Secretary of the Security Council Misir Ashirkulov, who stepped down from the post in April."[80]

Third, Otunbaeva explained that these key figures were now united in an effort to unseat Akaev: "The five of us have united and on December 29 last year we signed a memorandum of cooperation. The memorandum called for joint actions, moves, assistance, and joint activities in nominating and promoting candidates from our blocs, exchanges of information, regular meetings of the leaders of the blocs so they would be able to learn faster and promote opposition purposes. We have started working in this mode."[81] Lastly Otunbaeva hinted at the end game, at the fact that Akaev would not be unseated through the ballot box, but rather through street protests: "We arranged pickets, rallies, brought around 700 people to the President's office. In Ukraine they said: 'Kuchma get.' We say: 'Akayev ket.' 'Ket' is a Turkic word . . . it means 'go.' We stayed there near the President's office and shouted: 'Akayev ket, Tanayev [the Prime Minister] ket.' Rallies are actually the only instrument we, the opposition, have."[82]

What Otunbaeva described in February was precisely how the so-called Tulip Revolution unfolded in March. When perceived vote irregularities sparked demonstrations in Kyrgyzstan's provincial capitals following the first round of parliamentary elections in late February, Otunbaeva and her colleagues rushed to the regions and transformed local-level protests into a national anti-Akaev uprising.[83] On March 22 Otunbaeva informed the Russian press: "Today we are controlling six of the Osh region's seven districts, five of the Jalal Abad region's eight districts, one of the Naryn region's five districts, and three of the Talas region's four districts . . . we are close to controlling half of the republic."[84] Bakiev added that same day: "If the authorities don't change their position, I don't rule out that the events may take a radical turn."[85] Two days later, events did take a more radical turn. Demonstrators from the regions joined protesters in Bishkek in a march on Akaev's poorly guarded White House. By the end of the day the Kyrgyz and international press were snapping photos of young Kyrgyz men lounging in the now former President Akaev's seventh-floor office, an office that would be held for the next five years by Kurmanbek Bakiev.

The Second Presidency

One of the first actions the new provisional government took was to investigate the Manas fuel contracts. Daniyar Usenov, the vice premier of the interim government, declared reports that Akaev, now in Moscow, "had nothing apart from a flat and an old car" were ludicrous.[86] Usenov, one of Kyrgyzstan's most prominent bankers, asserted that he personally knew that Akaev's "son and son-in-law had a fairly prosperous business in Kyrgyzstan." Usenov went on to explain how Akaev's son and son-in-law profited from their Manas fuel contracts: "Jet fuel net cost amounts to $250 (per ton). These companies filled aircraft for $500 per ton. It will not do."[87] Instead, Usenov proposed an "open tender to change the situation." Similarly, Kyrgyzstan's new director of National Security, Miroslav Niyazov, noted that Bishkek and Washington had a deal "to find out about all the sales, all the affairs of Aalam Services and Manas. . . . There is a basis to believe there were serious embezzlements and harmful misdeeds."[88] In Washington, Kyrgyzstan's new ambassador, Zamira Sydykova, continued to press the Manas issue, pointing out in an interview with the *New York Times* that the U.S. Department of Defense "was paying inflated fuel prices to companies stolen by the family of the former president."[89]

Ultimately the U.S. government did assist the new Kyrgyz government. In September 2005 the FBI shared a report with Kyrgyz prosecutors detailing how Akaev and his sons engaged "a myriad of suspicious U.S. shell companies" to conceal their control over the air base fueling subcontracts and how the Akaev family had laundered profits from these subcontracts through Citibank and Dutch ABN Amro.[90] Bakiev—by this time no longer Kyrgyzstan's interim leader but now the newly elected president—used the FBI report not for its intended purpose (to prevent graft and money laundering within the new Kyrgyz government), but rather as a blueprint for how he and his family might use the American air base for personal enrichment. The Kyrgyz president's turn from democratic revolutionary to personal enrichment—and the consternation this caused within Kyrgyzstan's narrow political elite—was immediately apparent.

The same month the FBI delivered its report to Kyrgyz prosecutors, Kyrgyzstan's chief prosecutor, Azimbek Beknazarov was dismissed. The same day he was dismissed, Beknazarov held a press briefing to make clear what he perceived as the central reason why he was sacked: "The Kyrgyz prosecutor's office agencies have opened a number of criminal cases on corruption charges. We have not found support in this work. Moreover, there has been constant invisible pressure both from former and current high-ranking officials. . . . Instead of assistance in the investigation and the return of misappropriated money into state coffers, we have encountered strong resistance against our legitimate actions. The Prosecutor General's Office will never return to its previous practices and become a 'White House' appendage, a 'one family' prosecutor's office, or a 'pocket' prosecutor's office."[91]

Beknazarov's intimation that Bakiev was seeking to recreate Akaev's "pocket-prosecutor's office" proved well founded. In November 2005, for example, the director of the Kyrgyz-British joint venture Oxus-Talas Gold received a letter from the Kyrgyz executive noting that based on the findings of Kyrgyz lawyers, the "government has decided to refuse to restore the Oxus-Talas Gold's license to develop the Dzheruy gold mine."[92] Despite ongoing litigation and attempts at negotiation from the British diplomatic corps, including a letter from the British prime minister Tony Blair noting that the Bakiev regime's decision to revoke the Oxus license could lead to "a real danger of damage to Kyrgyzstan's reputation in the international financial market," the Bakiev administration nevertheless transferred mining rights to the Austrian-registered Global Gold. This company, reportedly owned by Russian and Kyrgyz actors close to the Bakiev administration, "had previously been unknown in the mining sectors," noted the mining publication Mineweb.[93]

The Oxus case is unusual in that given the involvement of foreign actors and the expectations these actors have regarding property rights and rule of law, the machinations of the Bakiev regime have been widely documented in the local and international press. The case is also notable because it demonstrated to potential foreign investors the unanticipated costs—including potential physical harm—one risks when attempting to defend property rights in Kyrgyzstan. In July 2006, Oxus's representative in Bishkek, Sean Daley, was ambushed and shot outside his home in central Bishkek. Daley survived. Other prominent businessmen—people typically portrayed by the Bakiev regime as mafia leaders—have not. For example, in September 2005 prominent businessman, member of parliament, and oppositionist Bayaman Erkinbaev was shot outside his Bishkek apartment and died later from his wounds. Testhtemir Aytbaev, Bakiev's then director of the National Security Services (NSS), told a parliamentary commission that Erkinbaev was murdered by drug traffickers who, according to the findings of an NSS investigation, were angered that Erkinbaev had failed to deliver a promised twenty kilograms of heroin.[24] Omitted from Aytbaev's accounting was the fact that Erkinbaev's considerable assets, including his ownership of the lucrative Kara Suu bazaar, would be soon "nationalized" by the Bakiev executive.

Oxus Gold and the Kara Suu bazaar were not the only assets Bakiev sought to appropriate in the months immediately after his July 2005 presidential election. Other prominent properties Bakiev secured in the fall of 2005 and winter of 2006 include Bitel telecommunications, the Kyrgyz Champagne and Distillery Plant, the Pinara luxury hotel, the Kant Cement Factory, the Jalal Abad Cotton Factory, and the Pyramid TV station.[95] What was particularly striking about these appropriations is how brazen they were. As Omurbek Abdrahmanov, the president of Kyrgyzstan's Union of Entrepreneurs, described in a May 25, 2006, interview with Radio Free Europe / Radio Liberty: "After the revolution, we talked about the properties of the ex-president and his entourage a lot. . . . But none of them were returned to the state or [formally] identified as Akaev's. Members of the new government and their entourage slowly took over property. That has caused disappointment. People even came up with a new slogan: 'Stop the Maksimization of Kyrgyzstan!'"[96] Maxim Bakiev is President Bakiev's son and was the principle person behind many of the Bakiev family appropriations. Oxus-Talas Gold, Kant Cement, the Jalal Abad Cotton—these were all certainly substantial business interests, particularly given the broader backdrop of Kyrgyzstan's small economy. The real plum of the economy remained the Americans at Manas. Once settled in as Kyrgyzstan's elected president, Bakiev, with the help Maxim, pursued the air base fuel contracts with the same zeal as had Akaev, his son Aidar, and his son-in-law, Adil Toygonbaev.

The Bakievs' machinations to gain control of the fuel contracts were readily discerned in both Bishkek and Washington. In December 2005, Bakiev publicly rebuked Ambassador Sydykova for discussing with the *New York Times* past malfeasance in the Manas contracts and suggesting reforms designed to prevent such malfeasance in the future.[97] Sydykova's indiscretion, Bakiev claimed, was that her comments were "made without the approval of the Kyrgyz Foreign Ministry."[98] An alternative interpretation for Bakiev's reprimanding of Sydykova was that the ambassador bluntly detailed the profits that could accrue to the Kyrgyz executive if the fuel contracts were not made transparent. More specifically, Sydykova shared with the *New York Times* information—details on how the Akaev family pocketed at least eighty million dollars by selling fuel to the Americans at Manas at artificially high prices—that Bakiev himself was now doing his best to keep hidden.[99] Around the same time Bakiev rebuked Sydykova, the Kyrgyz president also dismissed the services of an "independent corporate investigations company" that the interim Kyrgyz government had hired to explore the Akaev-era Manas contracts.[100] According to the investigator—an employee of "a major Washington-based law firm"—who personally met with Bakiev, the Kyrgyz president's response to the report was: "Thank you very much for your job. Your services are no longer needed."[101]

Even before Bakiev rebuked Sydykova and dismissed the Washington-based corporate investigations company, the U.S. Department of Defense had a good sense of where Kyrgyzstan's new president was headed. A May 19, 2005, Department of Defense Intelligence Information Report (IIR) noted that the Bakiev regime was attempting to gain control over all Kyrgyz aviation fuel and petroleum industries and supply.[102] Internal Department of Defense documents similarly detailed how in the weeks immediately after Akaev's March 2005 fall from power, fuel transport companies linked to the Bakiev family quickly replaced those once controlled by the Akaev family.[103] U.S. intelligence confirms what the Washington-based corporate investigator suspected: "They changed the names of the companies but the scheme remained the same."[104]

More specifically, the Department of Defense's Defense Energy Support Center continued to award fuel supply contracts to Red Star and Mina Corporation, and these two Department of Defense contractors in turn continued to subcontract to Kyrgyz fuel transport companies controlled by the Kyrgyz president's son.

Only, instead of Aidar Akaev running the Manas contracts, it was now Maksim Bakiev. The pivot that facilitated this relatively smooth transition of fuel subcontract from the Akaev to Bakiev family is Charles Squires, a retired U.S. Army lieutenant colonel and former U.S. Defense attaché to Bishkek. Kyrgyz prosecutors estimate that between March 2005 and April 2010, Squires's Red Star and Mina Corporation delivered 1.8 million tons of fuel to Manas.[105] Squires sourced this fuel through several companies, all of them thought to have been controlled by Maksim.[106] This fuel monopoly, Kyrgyzstan's interim leadership concluded in May 2010, netted Maksim Bakiev eight million dollars a month.[107]

Although we have a good sense of the Bakiev family's rent-seeking behavior, what is most important to the patronage legacy model is not ex post facto knowledge, but rather elite knowledge of this graft concurrent with the president's tenure in power. After all, it is this knowledge of inequitable resource distribution that drives elites to overthrow the executive in the first place. Did the Kyrgyz elite have any idea what they had received in return for their overthrow of Akaev in March 2005? Edil Baisalov, at the time the leader of Kyrgyzstan's largest NGO and one of the country's leading reform activists, was one among many who were optimistic that politics were changing for the better in his country. One year after Akaev's overthrow I visited Baisalov in his NGO offices in Bishkek. His optimism by that time had all but vanished. In April 2006 an unidentified assailant's violent blow had sent Baisalov to the hospital. Before our meeting, another Kyrgyz activist, summarizing the country's changed political mood, darkly joked that it was time for Baisalov to swap his orange T-shirt for an orange helmet.

During our interview I learned Baisalov was leaving his position as director of the Coalition of NGOs. The coalition had received approximately $800,000 in grants from the U.S. National Democratic Institute (NDI). For $133,000 a year Baisalov had maintained offices with full-time staff in nine different Kyrgyz cities, trained election monitors, and monitored Kyrgyzstan's local and national elections. NDI was terminating funding to the coalition, though, because Baisalov had become "too political."[108] Baisalov understood NDI's decision. At the same time, he explained, he had to become more political, he had to continue organizing new protests against the Bakiev government, because Bakiev, in a year and a half in power, had proven to be even more corrupt than Akaev.[109]

Melis Eshimkanov, a member of Parliament and deputy chairman of Kyrgyzstan's Social Democratic Party, echoed Baisalov's assessment. Before March 2005, Eshimkanov explained, he and his colleagues had fought Alga Kyrgyzstan, the Forward Kyrgyzstan party that had supported Askar Akaev. The fruits of this opposition, Eshimkanov mused, proved to be a new movement, Alga Bakiev

(Forward Bakiev Family).[110] Eshimkanov's colleague in parliament, Kubatbek Bai-bolov, agreed. He admonished those like Baisalov who had once been optimistic that March 2005 would lead to substantive reform: "The so-called Tulip Revolution did not let the democratic genie out of the bottle; rather, it unleashed a devil intent on eating everything up."[111] Roza Otunbaeva, though less colorful in her language, noted that since consolidating power in the July 2005 presidential election, Bakiev had directed all his attention to "personally privatizing all of Akaev's former assets."[112] Otunbaeva predicted that Bakiev's attempt to replicate Akaev's stealing of state assets would fail in the long run, that "after fifteen years of Akaev, the Kyrgyz people will not allow Bakiev to pursue similar power and property grabs."[113]

Not only did the Kyrgyz political elite know early in Bakiev's tenure that the new Kyrgyz president was stealing the most lucrative assets of the Kyrgyz state, this political elite was also actively rallying street protests in an effort to remove Bakiev from power. By November 2006, Bakiev's former key supporters—Otun-baeva (who had briefly served as Bakiev's foreign minister), Almazbek Atambaev (who had served as Bakiev's minister of industry and tourism), Baisalov, Eshim-kulov, and Baibalov—were leading twenty-thousand-people-strong street protests in Bishkek's Ala-Too central square. Baisalov explained the reason for the protest: "The nation feels it was cheated, and can no longer believe the authorities' hollow words."[114] Eshimkulov added: "There will be no more of negotiation process . . . the president actually went back on his word."[115] Otunbaeva justified the protests: "Yesterday's state officials who persecuted the opposition are sitting today near Bakiev, yesterday's thieves have remained in power. Bakiev took Akaev's chair, and he likes it very much! We made a big mistake a year ago. Bakiev appoints only his relatives to regional government posts. We call on the president to resign. Bakiev, leave! You did not carry out your promises!"[116]

Political protest, though not always on the scale of the November 2006 demonstrations, would present a steady challenge to Bakiev's rule for the next five years. At times Bakiev was able to mix economic incentives and coercion to mitigate these threats. For example, he enticed Eshimkanov back into the executive administration by first appointing him as director of the Kyrgyz National Broadcasting Corporation in October 2007 and then in November 2009 as chairman of the advisory board to the Kyrgyz Republic Development Fund (Maksim Bakiev, until his father's ouster in April 2010, was the director of the fund).[117] Bakiev, like Akaev, used the judiciary in an attempt to derail antigovernment mobilization. Thus the general prosecutor began proceedings against Baisalov for "causing large material damage to the state" and for "preventing the Kyrgyz Central Election Commission operating."[118] In what ultimately proved a trial run for the April 2010 protests that would overthrow Bakiev, the president's former supporters—Omur-bek Tekebayev, Bakyt Beshimov, and Roza Otunbayeva—were arrested in the Kyrgyz city of Talas in January 2009 for holding an "unsanctioned rally."[119]

In addition to using the courts to constrain his erstwhile supporters, Bakiev also used the judiciary in an attempt to deter the media's reporting on antigov-ernment mobilization. For example, Bakiev's Bishkek city prosecutor, Uchkum Kerimov, ominously warned journalists not to print "slanderous" articles about the president.[120] In April 2007 the Paris-based Reporters Sans Frontiers (RSF) published a "Letter to Kyrgyz Authorities" protesting violent attacks against two independent TV journalists, Talantbek Sopuev and Daniyar Isanov.[121] Although RSF did not directly implicate the Bakiev administration in these attacks, the ad-ministration's own director of the Presidential Human Rights Commission, Tur-sunbek Akun, acknowledged in an April 2007 interview with the Institute for War and Peace Reporting that "there have been cases of assaults on journalists by state officials and criminal elements, and I condemn them categorically. . . . This treat-ment of media employees undermines the [reputation of] the authorities in the international community."[122]

Bakiev's attempts at intimidation, in contrast to his Uzbek counterparts' heavy-handed repression, rarely were effective. Bishkek's political elite continued to protest and the media continued to cover these protests. Moreover, outside of Bishkek, Bakiev's authority was equally challenged. Travelling in the regions in May and June 2007, for example, I heard from merchants in Cholpon Ata who had refused the presidential administration's attempts to exert control over their city's bazaar.[123] In Ak Terek, a village on the southern side of lake Issyk Kol, Is-lamist activists told me how they began organizing for the provision of public works—for example, canal construction and the cooperative farming of apricot grooves—when it became increasingly clear that Bakiev's local appointees were incompetent.[124]

In Osh, in southern Kyrgyzstan, I discussed with Sadykzhan Kamalov—Kyr-gyzstan's former mufti—how religious communities were working together to provide social services and grow local business.[125] Back in Bishkek I met with Ab-dulla Usupov, an ethnic Uzbek mercenary whom Bakiev had tasked with monitor-ing Kamalov and other Osh-based ethnic Uzbeks who had exhibited "extremist" and "separatist" tendencies.[126] Several months earlier, Osh's governor, Zhantoro Satybaldiev, had similarly noted Kamalov's influence and his administration's comparatively limited legitimacy in the south.[127] Revealingly, our December 19, 2006, conversation was interrupted several times by protestors in the square ad-jacent to the governor's administrative headquarters. Satybaldiev assured me that such disturbances were "normal for Osh . . . we still have a Soviet style administration that is incapable of meeting post Soviet challenges." Later that same day Satybaldiev would be quoted in the press; Bakiev's prime minister had suddenly resigned, and Satybaldiev took this opportunity to urge his boss to create a government capable of ensuring "that waves of excited protest don't once again carry the Bishkek government away."[128]

Waves of excited protest would once again carry the Bishkek government away. In March 31, 2010, Rosa Otunbaeva, Almazbek Atambaev, Temir Sariev, and Isa Omurkulov convened a press conference in Bishkek and warned Bakiev that not only was the "opposition" united, but that the Kyrgyz political elite was once again ready to mobilize street protests to effect political change: "If the authorities do not meet the requirements of the people, people have the right under the Constitution to take power into their own hands."[129] Atambaev described the nature and strategy of this new opposition: "We are just performers, the people will decide themselves."[130]Atambaev's candid statement summarizes well the reality of Kyrgyz politics. He had served as Bakiev's prime minister from March to November 2007. Otunbaeva was Bakiev's foreign minister during the rule of Kyrgyzstan's 2005 interim government. Omurkulov's connection to Bakiev reached back to 2001 when Bakiev, then President Akaev's prime minister, appointed Omurkulov to serve as director of Kyrgyz National Railways. Of the four "opposition" politicians at the March press conference, only Sariev, who made his initial fortune as director of Kyrgyzstan's commodity exchange, could claim an independent "opposition" stance of any significant duration. With the exception of Sariev, the oppositionists now urging the Kyrgyz people to "take power into their own hands" all at one time had held ministerial-level positions in either the Akaev or Bakiev regimes or, in the case of Otunbaeva, in both governments.

I do not purport to have an explanation for why the Bakiev regime fell in April 2010 and not earlier—for example, during the large November 2006 protests. Otunbaeva and her colleagues, there is no doubt, did well to portray the president as nasty and brutish during the lead-up to the April 7 protests that ultimately brought Bakiev's rule to an end. The Kyrgyz government, for its part, presented the antigovernment movement ample material for portraying Bakiev as nasty and brutish. The prime minister, Daniyar Usenov, labeled the antigovernment elites as "bandits . . . criminals who have committed particularly grave crimes against the state," after the first day of protests in Talas, a regional city 190 kilometers southwest of Bishkek, and promised to bring these criminals to justice.[131] That same evening Usenov delivered on his promise and arrested several antigovernment leaders, including Ata-Meken vice chair Bolot Sherniyazov, who directed the Talas protests, as well as Ata-Meken chair Omurbek Tekebaev and Isa Omurkulov. Inexplicably, the Bakiev government quickly released these leaders, allowing them to rejoin the countrywide protests they had earlier planned for April 7.

Even if everyday Kyrgyz citizens were not enthralled with these antigovernment elites, they had ample reason to turn out for the protest day Otunbaeva and her colleagues urged for April 7. Many Kyrgyz were frustrated by recent utilities rate hikes. Earlier in March five thousand residents of Naryn, a tenth of the city's population, had already taken to the streets to protest electricity rate hikes.[132] Others were angered by recent revelations in the Italian and Kyrgyz press that the Bakiev government's financial consultant for the country's Development Fund, Yevgeniy Gurevich, "turned out to be the accountant for the Italian mafia."[133] Still others were frustrated by Bakiev's recent public dismissal of democracy as being "last century" and the president's assertion that what Kyrgyzstan most needed, more than "elections and human rights," was a "consultative democracy" based on the "deep roots in the traditions of our people."[134]

With no shortage of reasons to protest, the crowds gathered in Bishkek on April 7, 2010, as they had on November 7, 2006. This time, though, with the mounting frustration of three additional years of what many perceived to be Bakiev's corrupt rule, demonstrators did not retreat when riot police fired tear gas and snipers on the roof of the Kyrgyz White House fired live ammunition. Instead, the demonstrators broke through the White House gates and then, as some tended to the wounded and dead while others turned from demonstrating to looting, stepped aside to let the "opposition"—Bakiev's former supporters— form a new interim government.[135]

The Third Presidency

Although the perestroika legacy model cannot explain the exact timing of the April 2010 uprising that drove Bakiev from power, nor for that matter the earlier March 2005 protests that ousted Akaev and won Bakiev the Kyrgyz presidency in the first place, the model does offer considerable insight into why Kyrgyz politics is and likely will remain chaotic. The perestroika legacy left Kyrgyzstan with a narrow and fragmented political elite. This narrow and divided elite pose challenges to stable executive rule in Kyrgyzstan that do not exist in Uzbekistan and Kazakhstan. Kyrgyz political elites, believing their chances are good not only to successfully overthrow the president but to find themselves back in positions of power under a new government, are considerably more likely to defect from the executive's ruling coalition whenever they perceive the president to be appropriating a disproportionate share of state resources. As chapters 4 and 5 demonstrate in contrast, Uzbek and Kazakh political elites, because they know they can be readily replaced by any number of people within Karimov's and Nazarbaev's large presidential parties, are more likely to tolerate executive appropriations of state funds. As such, they are considerably less likely to defect from these presidents' ruling coalitions.

Paradoxically, the diffuse nature of political and economic reform aid to Kyrgyzstan during much of the 1990s worked to limit the executive's ability to appropriate state resources. As a result, this helped sustain Akaev's autocratic rule. Conversely, the emergence of readily exploitable rents with the arrival of American forces and lucrative fuel contracts after 9/11 freed the Kyrgyz executive from having to share the wealth. These lucrative fuel contracts by no means freed the Kyrgyz executive from the need to maintain the loyalty of elites within his ruling coalition. Ironically, Akaev's and then Bakiev's economic windfalls became their political downfalls. Disgruntled elites, knowing they could defect from the Kyrgyz executive and be rewarded for this defection in subsequent governments, did defect and indeed defected repeatedly. Kyrgyz political elites who were once members of Akaev's ruling coalition defected and became members of Bakiev's ruling coalition. They then defected again and became leading members in Kyrgyzstan's new interim government.

Will Kyrgyz politics become any less chaotic under post-Bakiev governments? The evidence thus far suggests that despite democratic reform efforts by leaders like the well-intentioned Roza Otunbaeva, elite fragmentation is difficult to overcome let alone manage. This reality became painfully apparent in June 2010 when, partially as a result of President Otunbaeva's effort to accelerate political liberalization, Kyrgyzstan's southern cities of Bazar Korgan, Jalal Abad, and Osh were engulfed in ethnic conflicts between Kyrgyz and Uzbeks that resulted in almost four hundred deaths. The inadvertently negative effect of Otunbaeva's reform efforts admittedly is only one contributing cause to the deadly violence in Kyrgyzstan's south. The many allegations of ethnically charged street beatings and rapes that surfaced in the atmosphere of political instability immediately following the April putsch likely also contributed to the wider-scale violence between Kyrgyz and Uzbeks in June 2010. That said, Kyrgyzstan has endured similar periods of political instability, most recently after the overthrow of Akaev in 2005. As such, the question arises: Why did ethnic violence accompany political instability after the 2010 putsch while ethnic relations remained peaceful after the 2005 anti-Akaev putsch? Although much remains unknown about the precise sparks that ignited the 2010 violence, three critical changes differentiate the immediate post-putsch 2010 setting environment from the post-putsch March 2005 political environment:

1. Variations in regional networks through which the interim leader can mobilize-support and instill a modicum of order.

2. Variations in how the interim leader negotiated with the holdover parliament from the previous regime.

3. Citizen perceptions of agency and more specifically of the perceived ability to change local and national politics through extra constitutional and violent means.

Analysis of these fundamental changes in the Kyrgyz polity between March 2005 and April–June 2010 suggests a causality that not only provides a more accurate explanation of the June 2010 violence, but also offers concrete prescriptions for how similar violence might be avoided in the future.

Regional Networks

The repertoire of identities available to elites for mobilizing support is vast. Which identity elites and more broadly society perceive as salient is largely the product of political context. Thus, although the Kyrgyz-Uzbek ethnic identity cleavage is enduring, the activation of this identity depends on changing incentive structures. Neither ethnic Uzbeks nor ethnic Kyrgyz perceived ethnicity as an identity cleavage worth pressing in the spring of 2005. Though clear in retrospect, this absence of ethnic conflict in 2005 could readily have been anticipated in the days immediately after the March 2005 ousting of President Akaev. Akaev's replacement, Kurmanbek Bakiev, is from Jalal Abad and draws support from southern regional and familial networks. Southern Uzbek activists understand the scope and capacity of these networks and recognized that spring 2005 was not the time to press ethnic identity claims.

Where local cleavages did produce conflict after Bakiev's assumption of power was in the north, an area where Bakiev's regional and familial networks were weak. In May 2005 supporters of the opposing politicians Ravshan Dzheen-bekov and Dzhusup Imanaliev clashed in Talas. In October of that year alleged Issyk Kol mob boss Ryspek Akmatbaev mounted a show of force outside the Kyrgyz parliament in which he and his supporters demanded the resignation of Prime Minister Felix Kulov. And in May 2006 Akmatabaev was gunned down as he was leaving a mosque in Bishkek. While political elites and mob bosses fought in the north, Kyrgyzstan's south remained quiet. Roza Otunbaeva, in contrast to Bakiev, does not enjoy strong support in Kyrgyzstan's south. Although she was born in Osh, Otunbaeva has lived most of her life outside of the south and has spent half of the post-Soviet period abroad in ambassadorial positions. Adding to Otunbaeva's weakness is her lame-duck status; her decision not to contest the October 2011 presidential elections undercuts her authority and her ability to cut deals with elites who could potentially exert power in the south.

This new environment of political uncertainty alters the perceptions of Uzbek political entrepreneurs and those with reason to fear these entrepreneurs. Thus Kadyrjan Batyrov, a prominent ethnic Uzbek leader in the south, created his own de facto police force in Jalal Abad as a counterweight to regional security services that had remained loyal to Bakiev. It is unclear whether the interim government directly requested Batyrov's help or if Batyrov acted independently. What is clear is that the interim government's failure to secure the south through the co-optation of alternative regional and familial networks gave political entrepreneurs like Batyrov an increasing voice. It also gave pro-Bakiev forces in Jalal Abad an opportunity to recast Batyrov's rise as a threat, not just to holdovers from the old regime but to all ethnic Kyrgyz.

The Parliament Problem

This analysis raises the critical counterfactual: Could the interim government have secured its southern flank by co-opting alternative regional networks, such as Osh-based regional and familial networks? Stated differently: To what extent are the June 2010 clashes the result of political instability that invariably accompanies sudden political transitions or the result of a failure of elite leadership within the interim government?

Otunbaeva made a grave error upon assuming office. She disbanded the national parliament rather than reaching out to the regional elites, particularly the southern regional elites within the legislature. This was a mistake that Bakiev, importantly, avoided. Although it was a wave of popular outrage against Akaev's rigging of the February–March 2005 parliamentary elections that brought Bakiev to power, Bakiev was quick to cut deals with rather than ostracize members of what initially was a pro-Akaev parliament. In contrast, the interim government's April 7, 2010, decree dissolving the Zhogorku Kenesh alienated critical southern elites who, had they maintained their member of parliament mandates, could have helped Otunbaeva and her colleagues solidify control in critical southern cities like Osh and Uzgen.

The interim government further bungled its ability to cultivate southern support when in early May security service personnel detained the newly elected speaker of the now unrecognized parliament, Iskhak Masaliev. Masaliev, a stalwart of Osh city and national politics and a southern elite adept at building alliances with diverse groups despite Kyrgyzstan's fragmented politics, issued a statement following his release stressing that the parliament "does not recognize the interim government's decree on its dissolution . . . [and] it will unlikely recognize the interim government given the ongoing situation in the republic."[136] In issuing its April 7 decree, the interim government needlessly undercut its own authority in three critical areas. First, the decree created a renegade parliament that publicly challenged the interim government's legitimacy. Second, the decree burned what were working institutional bridges to regional elites capable of helping the central government project authority in regions where central authority would be (and now in fact is) otherwise weak. Third, the decree removed a critical pressure valve in Kyrgyz politics through which members of parliament could voice the concerns of their regional and familial constituencies. In social scientist Albert Hirschman's classic formulation of state-society relations, Otunbaeva and her colleagues utterly failed the first round of the "exit, voice, and loyalty" game.[137] Rather than securing the preferred outcome of loyalty or the second best outcome of voice, the interim government's dissolution of parliament encouraged potential allies to exit.

The Power of the Street Mob

Achieving sudden political change through street protest was in 2005 not a strategy but rather a shock. Mass demonstrations have been commonplace in Kyrgyzstan since 1991, yet none of these previous demonstrations have led to substantive change. In March 2005, however, protestors stepped from central squares up to the curtain shielding the president and were surprised to discover that the slightest of touches exposed the fragility of the executive. The events of April 2010 provided a considerably more decisive lesson. Whereas it took weeks for protestors in the regions to descend upon Bishkek in March 2005, it took fewer than two days for the angry crowds that first formed in Talas in April 2010 to breach the gates of the presidential White House. The March 2005 events are no longer just a one-off; rather, April 2010 was proof positive that street violence and the storming of government buildings are effective means for compelling change at the regional and national level. Kyrgyzstan, once thought to be home to Central Asia's most vibrant civil society, is now hostage to stick- and steel rod-wielding flash mobs.

At the time of this writing, the events of June 2010 remain understudied. That said, these events suggest that explaining Kyrgyzstan's comparative instability relative to Uzbekistan and Kazakhstan is insufficient; scholars must explore pronounced within-case variations in Kyrgyzstan. Just as variations in the nature of economic resources shaped variations in the duration of President Akaev's and President Bakiev's tenures in power, so too have changed state-society relations and diverging executive strategies generated differing kinds of chaos under Bakiev and Otunbaeva. This variation, the relative peace of spring 2005 and the deadly riots of spring 2010, can be attributed to three critical differences in post-coup Kyrgyz politics.

First, Otunbaeva in 2010, unlike Bakiev in 2005, enjoyed neither regional nor familiar networks necessary for projecting power in Kyrgyzstan's restive southern cities. Second, Otunbaeva immediately disbanded the Kyrgyz parliament and thereby destroyed the one institution through which the interim government could have rallied powerful southern elites to the interim government's side. Lastly, the efficacy of mob politics in 2010, in contrast to the halting nature of street protests in 2005, was not questioned. Just as the protestors in Talas and Bishkek in April 2010 anticipated that through coordinated action they could undermine Bakiev's rule, so too did opposing societal groupings in Osh and Jalal Abad anticipate that through street violence they could further the interests of their own ethnic group. The paradox that Kyrgyzstan's new leaders now confront is that this learned behavior that brought them to power is the same behavior that produced the deadly June riots in Jalal Abad, Osh, and Uzgen. Whereas the power of the mob was a novelty in March 2005, it is now the norm in Kyrgyzstan. Convincing a population, particularly a youth population whose only sense of political efficacy is mob mobilization, to unlearn and disavow street violence will prove an enduring challenge.

4 Uzbek Violence

UZBEKISTAN AT FIRST glance appears politically stable. In contrast to the elite turmoil in Kyrgyzstan, Uzbek elites thus far have proven remarkably deferential to President Islam Karimov. When one investigates deeper, though, potential weaknesses in the Karimov state begin to emerge. I focus on two of these weaknesses: the increasingly tense relation between state and Islam in Uzbekistan and the looming challenge of Karimov's aging Soviet-era political elite. At the local level, in cities and villages, Islamic civil society has already demonstrated an ability to mobilize populations to meet the many needs the central Uzbek state does not. This Islam-centered mobilization, though not oppositionist in nature, nevertheless exists largely outside the control of the central government. As such, it poses a threat to Uzbek autocratic rule. Uzbekistan's aging political elite is also a challenge to Karimov's continued hold on power. The united Soviet political elite Karimov inherited is an ever shrinking portion of the Uzbek population, and it remains unclear if the Uzbek president will be able to find ready recruits among younger generations who have been less acculturated into Soviet-style patronage politics.

Since the early 1990s, however, Karimov has effectively limited direct challenges to his authority. The Uzbek political opposition enjoys no representation in the Uzbek parliament and with few exceptions has been driven out of the country or into Uzbek jails. Karimov himself has maintained his hold of the presidency through a mixture of carefully choreographed elections and referenda. He used a December 1991 ballot to change his formal title from Uzbek first secretary to

Uzbek president. He convened a referendum in February 1995 to extend his first term in office to 2000 rather than stand for election in 1996, as stipulated in the constitution. Karimov's concern was not that he would not be reelected—he was with 90 percent of the vote—but rather constitutionally imposed term limits that potentially could force him from power after his second term in office. Karimov subsequently added more time to his presidential clock through a January 2002 referendum that, like the February 1995 ballot, added more years to the constitutionally stipulated five-year term. Predictably, in 2007, when Karimov had exhausted the extra two years in power he had won through the 2002 referendum, he dispensed with the constitution and ran for office again. As in 2000, Karimov won with 90 percent of the total vote. As far as any discontent or dissent from within Uzbekistan's political elite in response to his machinations, there was not a peep. Just the opposite in fact. Karimov's "challenger" in the January 2000 ballot, Abdulhasiz Dzhalov, informed the press after casting his own ballot: "I voted for stability, peace, our nation's independence, for the development of Uzbekistan. . . . I voted for Karimov."[1]

Such orchestrated stability is what our understanding of the perestroika legacy model would lead us to expect. Karimov, thanks to Gorbachev's intervention to restore political order after Uzbekistan's 1989 ethnic riots, entered into the post-Soviet period with a large proexecutive political elite. This large executive-oriented elite has enabled Karimov to maintain a loyal winning coalition while expanding the Uzbek state's repressive capacity and his family's own wealth. Gulnara Karimova, when not in Madrid serving as her father's ambassador to Spain, applies her considerable wealth to bring international stars to Tashkent.[2] For example, in return for one million dollars, the singer Sting accepted Karimova's invitation to perform at Tashkent's opera hall in October 2009 and to accompany the president's "tiara-wearing" daughter to a fashion show.[3] The entertainer Julio Iglesias was Karimova's escort to the fashion show the previous year, and at the opera the two performed a duet version of "Besame Mucho."[4] Karimova funded these indulgences—and her father abided them—through her control of Zeromax.[5] According to Zeromax's now defunct Web site, the company invested in "oil and gas, agriculture, textiles, construction, mining and logistics," and its operating revenues for 2008 were three billion dollars. How much of these revenues directly accrued to Karimova is unclear. In May 2010 the Uzbek government shuttered Zeromax and assumed direct control over what had been the company's most lucrative asset, Uzbekistan's natural gas exports. Although Karimova may no longer have direct control of what was once Zeromax's vast riches, we do know the Uzbek first daughter has fared financially well. Karimova owns a $16.3 million property in Geneva.[6] And the magazine *Bilan*, in its 2009 annual review of "The

300 Most Wealthy Swiss," estimates Karimova's Swiss accounts hold between $540 million and $630 million; the magazine also notes that Karimova disputes this estimate.[7]

As in Kyrgyzstan, the Uzbek executive uses his children to amass and manage wealth. Where Uzbekistan differs from Kyrgyzstan, however, is that thus far the Karimov family has managed to enrich itself while maintaining control of the presidency. This, as the patronage legacy model suggests, is what we would expect given Karimov's ability to draw from a large pool of bureaucrats when filling key government positions. Because of this large pool of elites—the renamed but largely unchanged Communist Party from the perestroika period—Karimov need not worry about elite disloyalty. In the rare cases elites prove problematic, the Uzbek president can eliminate them, confident that a replacement bureaucrat can be readily found. In the even rarer cases political oppositionists attempt to contest Karimov's hold on power, these oppositionists are quickly repressed. Erk and Birlik, two opposition parties that formed during the late perestroika period, were effectively driven underground and their leaders driven out of the country in the early 1990s. Sanjar Umarov, the leader of Uzbekistan's third short-lived opposition movement, was sentenced to eleven years in prison in March 2006 on money-laundering charges. Umarov's imprisonment effectively put an end to his Sunshine Coalition's eleven-month attempt at contesting Karimov's autocratic rule.[8]

Not all has been quiet in Uzbekistan, however. Karimov's focus on personal enrichment and his inattention to public welfare has encouraged Uzbeks, much like their Kyrgyz counterparts, to turn to local charities (particularly local Muslim charities) to fulfill everyday needs not met by the Tashkent government. In contrast to their Kyrgyz counterparts, Uzbeks incur a considerable degree of risk in working with Muslim charities. The Karimov government perceives these charities, especially the business and clerical elites who organize them, to be a threat to government rule. Although Tashkent has repeatedly sought to bring Islamic civil society under the control of state institutions, many of Uzbekistan's Muslim organizations operate independently of the central state. In several cases they have even co-opted Tashkent's appointees at the local level. Two events—the city of Namangan's de facto secession from Uzbekistan from November 1991 through March 1992 and the Andijan uprising in May 2005—provide the most prominent examples of Islamic civil society and how the Karimov government perceives this as a threat to continued autocratic rule.

Although Karimov has proven adept at controlling would-be political oppositionists, he continues to struggle in his effort to control Uzbekistan's independent Muslim leaders. Karimov represses these leaders as he does the political opposition but, because Muslim elites neither see themselves nor portray their activities as in opposition to Tashkent, it is considerably more difficult for the Uzbek executive to identify who among these Muslim elites might ultimately prove to be a threat. Often, it is only after the mobilization potential of these leaders is already apparent, as it was with the Namangan protests or the Andijan demonstrations, that the Uzbek executive initiates wide-scale repression. That said, a tense relationship between state and Islam pervades everyday Uzbek life. This chapter illustrates the nature of this tense relationship and explores how religious clergy, the backbone of Uzbek Islamic civil society, are frequently the targets of preemptive repression—that is, the Uzbek state's attempt to limit and dampen the clergy's popular appeal.

I also explore what this charged state and Islamic civil society relationship means for the future of Uzbek politics. I focus precisely on Uzbekistan's future— the country's youth—and how the Karimov government, through the state-run youth group Kamalot, is attempting to ensure that young Uzbeks who turn to Islam do not turn against Uzbek authoritarianism. This youth, problematically for Karimov, has fewer and ever more distant connections to the united political elite the Uzbek president inherited in 1991. It is questionable whether Karimov will be able to count on the same loyalty from this new generation that he has enjoyed with the Soviet-era holdovers who continue to fill positions of power in the Uzbek bureaucracy.

Islamic Civil Society as Perceived Threat to Autocratic Continuity

Most studies of Islam in Uzbekistan have emphasized militancy and radicalism. To some degree, this focus on radical Islam is understandable. Militant Islamists have repeatedly sought to destabilize the Uzbek government. Paradoxically, though, militant Islamists are considerably less threatening to Karimov than is Uzbekistan's significantly more widespread and less political Islamic civil society. Militant Islam is fleeting; Uzbekistan's Islamic civil society is growing and provides a constant challenge to Karimov's autocracy and legitimacy. Islam presents a challenge on two levels. First, Islam's ethics and the sense of community that these shared ethics generate stand in stark contrast to the corrupt and often repressive Uzbek state. Second, this sense of community, this shared Islamic capital, generates real economic wealth. This society-based wealth undermines the state's economic comparative advantage and threatens to attract regional and local bureaucrats out of Karimov's top-down patronage system and into alliances with local business and religious elites.

Karimov, recognizing these threats, has attempted to incorporate Islamic

elites into Uzbekistan's broader patronage politics system. Tashkent has maintained, with few changes, the Soviet practice of a state-controlled muftiate, a de
facto state-administered spiritual directorship. Through its post-Soviet muftiate
Tashkent has created a coterie of loyal Islamic leaders. Regional Islamic leaders—those who oversee the activity of Uzbekistan's many local or *mahalla*-level
imams—are watched particularly closely by, and are largely compliant with, the
government's Committee on Religious Affairs and the government-controlled
Muslim Spiritual Board.[9] The head imams of Quqon in the Fergana Valley and of
Qarshi near the Afghanistan border, for example, noted in interviews that given
what they saw as the Uzbek population's susceptibility to radical Islamic teaching,
the government needed to regulate religion. Qarshi's head imam concluded that
the government was correct to imprison one of the city's local Islamic leaders who
purportedly taught Wahhabi, or extremist, Islam.[10]

In addition to his continuation of the Soviet-era muftiate, Karimov has also
created new institutions in an effort to create what perhaps can best be described
as a novel secular Muslim elite. Most prominent among these institutions is the
Tashkent Islamic University (TIU). Founded by presidential decree in 1999, the
university differs from Uzbekistan's older—and considerably less well funded—
madrassas in that it emphasizes instruction in the sciences and the humanities as
much as it does religious studies.[11] The university's pedagogy differs from that of
the madrassas as well. Whereas madrassas instruct students in Islam the religion,
TIU's approach is almost devoid of religious belief; that is, students are taught the
history and philosophy of Islam rather than the inviolable truth of Islam.[12] Students convey this secular state-defined Islam to broader Uzbek society through
weekly television and radio programs. Tashkent Islamic does produce a handful
of imams, but the religious leaders TIU is most keen to graduate are secularized
agitprops who can instruct Uzbek society in a Karimov-friendly and state-centric
Islam. Accordingly, among the courses students pursue at TIU are marketing,
management, and the history of Islamist extremism.[13]

Not all Islamic leaders and community activists toe the government line,
however. Imams, although they may obey some governmental regulations—such
as submitting to yearly attestation exams and registering their mosques with the
Muslim Spiritual Board—will flout restrictions they perceive as unjust. Islamic
leaders in Tashkent, Quqon, and Qarshi, for example, confided that they regularly hold Quran discussions despite the fact that the 1998 Law on Freedom of
Conscience and Religious Organizations prohibits the "private teaching of religious principles."[14] Other leaders, such as a village imam near Quqon and a Sufi
imam in the Ferghana Valley, lead prayers despite having no authorization from

the Muslim Spiritual Board.[15] And Islamic activists—community organizers and business elites—operate outside of and thus do not perceive an immediate need to be accountable to the Uzbek government's Islamic oversight institutions.

This independence, though beneficial to Uzbek society, has also elicited devastating central government repression. In at least two cases (in Namangan and in Andijan), Uzbek government troops have forcibly repressed Islamic activists and their community supporters. Far more typical of this repression—and far less reported in the Western press—is the everyday repression of Islamic leaders and community activists. This repression is illustrated with the changing fortunes of three Muslim activists: Uzbekistan's former mufti, Muhammad Sodik Muhammad Yusuf; Qarshi imam Rustam Klichev; and Klichev's advocate, an unnamed Quqon imam. Their changing fortunes as well as the uprisings in Namangan and Andijan illustrate that the Karimov government perceives Islamic civil society as a threat to patronage rule and is willing to use extraordinary force in repressing it.

Namangan and Security

The 1991–92 events in the Fergana Valley city of Namangan, depending on the sources one reads and the eyewitnesses and participants with whom one speaks, was either Uzbekistan's first post-Soviet manifestation of radical Islam or the first example of the Karimov government repressing grassroots Islamic civil society. The historian Ahmed Rashid has described the events as being led by "young militants . . . who had no respect for official Islam, no patience with tradition, and no fear of the political regime."[16] The scholar Adeeb Khalid has portrayed the events as protests led by "various informal groups, many of them religious," and with demands ranging from converting Communist Party headquarters into an Islamic center to the "legalization of Islamic parties and the establishment of an Islamic state."[17] Uzbekistan's mufti at the time, Muhammad Sodik Muhammad Yusuf, has attributed the protests to mass frustration and, more specifically, to the regional administration's not fulfilling its promise to turn the Communist Party headquarters over to the Mother and Child Health Protection Center, as the administration had originally said it would, but rather to the newly formed People's Democratic Party of Uzbekistan—which in reality was the old Communist Party with a new name.[18]

Militant or not, what we can say for certain is that many residents in Namangan were fed up with the disorder and lack of security that pervaded their daily lives. In December 1990 a brawl between drunken ethnic Russian soldiers and Namangan youths who were enraged by these soldiers' alleged inappropriate conduct toward several young women left eight people dead.[19] In response to what many perceived to be the Uzbek Interior Ministry's mishandling of the riot, Namangan residents formed "law-and-order squads" to patrol the streets and "maintain order."[20] Two of the central leaders of these law-and-order squads were Tohir Yoldosh and Juma Namangani (Juma Khojiyev), activists with the locally prominent Adolat (Justice) Islamic party.

It was not only drunken Russian soldiers that Yoldosh, Namangani, and other Namangan residents resented; many were infuriated that President Karimov's adviser, Shahabuddin Ziyamov, was meddling in their local mosques.[21] Yoldosh and Namangani seized on this anger and organized a series of rallies throughout the fall of 1991. They demanded that Ziyamov be removed from power and that local Namangan government be brought into conformity with Muslim norms. The rallies—at times more than twenty thousand strong—unnerved Karimov and won Yoldosh and Namangani a face-to-face meeting with the Uzbek president in November.[22] Karimov, in an attempt to placate the Adolat activists, agreed to turn the Communist Party building into a new Islamic study center. Karimov's November 1991 bargain was strategic and short-lived, however. Four months later, in March 1992, the Uzbek president ordered the Islamic center closed and its property unceremoniously dumped into the street.[23] The closure of the Islamic center was the least of Adolat's worries. March 1992 marked the beginning of what has since proved to be the wide-scale repression of Islamic religious and community activists.

After the closing of the Islamic center, Yoldosh and Namangani fled to Tajikistan to avoid what the *Nezavisimaya gazeta* termed at the time "an open attack on Muslim self-government movement in Fergana valley."[24] Yoldosh and Namangani would return to Uzbekistan later in the 1990s and the nature of their return—as the leaders of the Islamic Movement of Uzbekistan (IMU)—goes a long way toward explaining why analysts like Rashid have interpreted the 1991 Namangan events as Uzbekistan's first case of militant Islam. Although there is no justification for the terrorist attacks Yoldosh and Namangani's followers are believed to have orchestrated, it is worth exploring why militant groups like the IMU emerged and have found some resonance with members of Uzbek society. These acts include the deadly bombings of government buildings in Tashkent in February 1999, deadly border clashes with Uzbek and Kyrgyz soldiers in the summers of 1999 and 2000, and more bombings in Tashkent in the summer of 2004. Here Clifford Bond, the acting principal deputy of the Office of the Special Adviser to the Secretary of State, provides valuable insight. Asked during a House International Relations Committee hearing on June 6, 2001, to explain the rise of the IMU, Bond observed:

The IMU, which is a foreign terrorist organization, designated a foreign terrorist organization by the United States, grows out of repression in the Ferghana valley that occurred early in the 1990s. Most of its leaders are there.

I guess my response to you is that we do not see Islamic fundamentalism right now as a threat to the states of Central Asia, but that the policies that are being pursued by the governments now are driving the young, particularly because there is a lack of economic opportunity, into the arms of extremists. And that's a message which we have to make and continue to make with the leadership in Central Asia.[25]

The U.S. Department of State's *Report on International Religious Freedom for 1999*—the first in what has become a series of State Department annual reports on religious freedom—provides specific detail on the nature and extent of the Uzbek government's state-led repression before the February 1999 IMU Tashkent bombings. All across Uzbekistan, the report documents, Muslim leaders had vanished. Among the disappeared, the 1999 report lists: Aboullah Utaev, leader of the Islamic Renaissance Party—disappeared 1992; Imam Abduvali Kori Mirzaev, leader of Andijan's Central Mosque—disappeared 1995; Nematjon Parpiev, assistant to Imam Mirzaev—disappeared 1997; and Imam Abidkhon Nazarov, leader of Tashkent's Tokhtaboi Mosque—disappeared 1998.[26] What this report does not capture is the everyday pressure Uzbekistan's other Islamic activists and leaders faced and continue to face. Many of these activists, such as Muhammad Sodik Muhammad Yusuf, Rustam Klichev, and the Quqon imam, do not turn to militant Islam. That some, like Yoldosh and Namangani, do turn to militant Islam can in part be explained by the logic ambassador Bond offers. What is critically important is that we do not mistake, as Rashid does, Islam-inspired civic activists with Muslim militancy simply because mixed in with these activists are militants or people who may ultimately become militants. This is the logic President Karimov would have us follow in interpreting the May 2005 events in Andijan—a logic that most independent observers have rejected.

Andijan and Economic Welfare

The human tragedy of the Andijan protests was devastating at the time and continues to grow. The Karimov government acknowledges that 187 people died. Half of these fatalities, the government concluded, were Islamist "terrorists." Thirty more fatalities came from the ranks of soldiers and policemen who battled the purported terrorists. Fewer than a third of the Andijan fatalities, Tashkent concluded, were Andijan residents, presumably in the wrong place at the wrong time. Indeed, if we are to believe Karimov's narrative of the events, Andijan was almost a ghost town on May 13, 2005: "In Andijan fundamentalist extremist groups tried to carry out their plan . . . they hoped to achieve in Uzbekistan what the crowds had done in Kyrgyzstan, where the local and central governments proved to be weak. The fundamentalists attempted to use their poisoned rhetoric to rally youth into capturing Andijan's administrative buildings and, in this manner, create a so-called 'Islamic caliphate.' The fundamentalists hoped that the local population would support them. But no one came out to the square, no one supported them."[27]

Tashkent refused international offers for an independent fact-finding mission that could have corroborated Karimov's account. Were it true, one would think such fact-finding missions would have been in the Uzbek president's interest. Nongovernmental organizations that did have access to Fergana (such as the International Crisis Group) were quick to dispute Karimov's fatality estimates and instead concluded that "as many as 750" died when government forces fired on demonstrators gathered in Andijan's central square.[28] Although I have data neither to confirm nor disprove the International Crisis Group's estimates, my own field research in Andijan and with refugees from the Andijan events suggests an unfolding of events that differs markedly from President Karimov's portrayal. I visited Andijan twice in 2004—once in August and once again in November. At the time Andijan did not strike me as all that different from other Uzbek cities where I was conducting field research.

As in Qarshi and Quqon, in Andijan there were several dozen women and a handful of men picketing the local prosecutor's office in protest of the detention of husbands, fathers, and sons who, these protestors told me, had been jailed on false charges of Islamist extremism. Many of the detained in Andijan were associates of imprisoned local businessmen—twenty-three prominent Muslim businessmen who had pooled economic resources and who (through their bakeries and construction, clothing and furniture companies) employed a considerable portion of the city's population. Unlike their counterparts in Quqon and Qarshi, however, the Andijan protestors decided, after repeated government delays in the trials of the Muslim businessmen, to take justice into their own hands and free the businessmen through an armed jailbreak. As had happened in Namangan in 1990, when enraged youths dispensed street justice to the drunken Russian soldiers, in Andijan in 2005 the dispensation of street justice brought supportive crowds into the city square. This time, however, Karimov, did not negotiate. Rather, he ordered a "special service" (*spets sluzba*) contingent from within his

Ministry of Internal Affairs to disperse the crowds with bullets and armored personnel carriers.[29]

This repression did not stop in May 2005. The 2009 U.S. Department of State's human rights report on Uzbekistan notes "a credible report cited the deaths in custody" of one of the Andijan Muslim businessmen and two of the Andijan protestors.[30] Alisher Saipov, the journalist whose unsolved murder I discussed in this book's introduction, observed in June 2007 that his reporting on Andijan and his work with Andijan refugees in Osh had resulted in his being constantly tailed by Uzbek security agents.[31] Alisher's father, Avas Saipov, has repeatedly testified that immediately before his son's murder "two representatives of the Uzbek security forces came to our house with a civil servant well known in the town of Osh accompanying them. . . . They talked to my son and threatened him."[32] These same agents maintained close watch of the Andijan refugees who visited Saipov's newspaper offices for advice and support. To deter these refugees from making secretive trips back to Andijan to see their families, Uzbek police would regularly "check our wives for any signs of intercourse."[33]

Three Islamic Activists and State Coercion

Despite this considerable evidence of government-ordered repression before, during, and after the May 2005 protests, some scholars have continued to argue that Karimov's response to Andijan was simply that of a government responding to a militant Islamist threat. Just as Ahmed Rashid had characterized the Namangan events of 1991 and early 1992 as the work of Islamist militants, the Central Asia scholar Shirin Akiner has characterized Andijan as "a carefully prepared attack . . . not a demonstration mounted by peaceful civilians."[34] That Akiner's assessment and mine vary may be the result of the differing conditions in which we conducted our respective field research. My interviews in Andijan and with Andijan refugees in Osh were conducted independent of Uzbek government appointees. Akiner, in contrast, notes of her May 25, 2005, fact-finding trip to Andijan: "At the border of Namangan province we were met by the deputy governor (*hokim*) of the Andijan province. He had been informed of my visit and he told me that he had been asked to help me see and do whatever I wished. He remained with us for the rest of the day."[35] Akiner candidly acknowledges how the presence of government officials can change the narratives interviewees provide. Of her meeting with a prisoner in Andijan, she notes: "This account could have been fabricated for my benefit, particularly as it was recounted in front of the prison governor [administrator of the prison]."[36]

Akiner's and Rashid's research, their findings of Islamist mobilization in contrast to what I describe here as Islamic civil society, might give us more pause if
it were not for the fact that Namangan and Andijan are but two cases of what in
reality is a pattern of Uzbek government-coordinated repression of Islamic civil
society. Below I provide brief sketches of three Uzbek Islamic activists and their
struggles with the Karimov state. One of these activists, former mufti Muhammad Sodik Muhammad Yusuf, is well known both in Uzbekistan and abroad. The
other two activists, imam Rustam Klichev and an imam in Quqon (whose name
has been withheld by mutual agreement), are less well known. What all three men
share is a common history of being coerced by the Uzbek state. All three enjoyed
significant support in their respective communities, and ultimately this support—
a popular legitimacy that accrued from local activism rather than a state-gifted
position—proved too threatening for the Karimov government to silently abide.

I identified these three Islamic activists with the help of focus group participants in August and November 2004. I held these focus groups in the Fergana Valley cities of Andijan, Namangan, and Quqon, as well as in Tashkent (the
country capital) and the southern city of Qarshi. Though not a random sample of
the Uzbek population, the focus groups did nevertheless capture a cross-section
of Uzbekistan's "active" Muslim population—those Uzbeks who are interested
in topics relating to Islam but not necessarily those who are themselves devout
Muslims. My central goal was to discover what Uzbeks perceive as the qualities
of a respected Islamic community leader. To contextualize this question within
perceptions of Islam more broadly, I asked for respondents' attitudes toward such
topics as sharia law, politics and Islam, women and Islam, education, and religion.
Perceptions of what makes for a respected Islamic leader varied little according
to the answers given to these supplemental questions. Among all but one focus
group, independence from the Uzbek state and knowledge of the Quran were
what was most valued in an imam. The Uzbeks with whom I spoke preferred that
their religious leaders not engage in politics, be it the politics of the state or of the
opposition.

Human rights activists helped in arranging focus groups in Andijan, Namangan, and Qarshi. In addition to two local human rights defenders, the Namangan group also included three members of the city's "unofficial clergy"—Islamic
scholars and imams who study and teach independently without the accreditation
of Uzbekistan's muftiate. The Namangan respondents were the most anti-Kari-
mov of all the Uzbeks with whom I spoke. All members had grievances against
the government. One respondent, for example, stated that he had been falsely
charged with drug possession, a charge he attributes to the local authorities' dis-
pleasure with his religious and community activism. Another respondent claimed

that he had lost his job as a truck driver for a state-owned company because he refused to shave his beard. A third expressed frustration at the refusal of his local mahalla to subsidize the funeral of a young acquaintance who had died in police custody after being charged with Islamic extremism. The Namangan group was uniform in asserting that imams must be independent if they are to be respected at the local level. The group underscored, however, that finding such independent imams was difficult; the Karimov leadership, they explained, had systematically replaced older clergy with new younger imams. These interviewees emphasized that the younger imams, though less knowledgeable, are considerably easier for the Uzbek government to control.

The Andijan respondents were the most diverse of the five focus groups. One member of the nine-person group, a Hizb ut-Tahrir activist in his mid-twenties, quickly became frustrated with the others and left a mere fifteen minutes into the discussion (I met individually with him the following day). In addition to the Hizb ut-Tahrir activist, respondents included a human rights activist, a school-teacher who had studied Islam for several years in the Middle East, two journalists, and two Islamic teachers from neighboring villages. Similar to the Namangan group, the Andijan cohort lamented the lack of "authoritative" Islamic leaders. Several in the group distinguished between official and unofficial leaders, emphasizing that the unofficial clergy and *aksakals* (elders) are both knowledgeable and free from government control. Others, most notably the Hizb ut-Tahrir member, disagreed. He asserted that the aksakals were ignorant and that many among the unofficial clergy were in reality controlled by government imams.

The most candid and in many respects the most helpful respondents were those in Quqon and Qarshi. I met with the eight-member Quqon group during *gap*, the weekly Saturday-evening talk session during which classmates from the same cohort gather to share news and advice. Several members of these talk sessions recalled police visits to their homes and intimidation as early as in the 1990s and more recently, after the March 2004 bombings in Tashkent. They attributed this intimidation to their association with Muhammed Rajab, Quqon's charismatic and independent head imam whom the government jailed in 1994. Despite their shared hardships, however, the Quqon focus group was considerably more sanguine than their Namangan and Andijan counterparts about the potential for knowledgeable, independent Islamic leaders and the positive role such leaders could have in their local community. This optimism was in large part due to their assertion that despite Rajab's imprisonment, other independent imams in and around Quqon continue to preach and that these local mosques help provide a sense of community free—at least for now—from the unwelcome reach of the central state.[37]

The Qarshi group, which consisted of eight women, was less optimistic. They invited me to meet with them to discuss the recent imprisonment of their local imam, Rustam Klichev, along with the imprisonment of many of their husbands. Understandably, in contrast to the Quqon group, the Qarshi women questioned the future of independent Islam in Uzbekistan. The fifth focus group consisted of five students enrolled at Tashkent Islamic University (TIU). Unlike respondents in other focus groups, the Tashkent students were reticent to discuss state relations with Islam, despite the focus group interviews being conducted not at the university but in a student apartment. Although all five students attended TIU, only one sought to become an imam (and even this student declined to discuss the Karimov regime's policy toward religion). After his friends had left the apartment, the future imam asked me about my work in Qarshi. He was from that city and was visibly distressed when I mentioned the Klichev case. He and Klichev, he explained, were acquaintances; there was nothing in Klichev's behavior, the student recalled, that suggested the young imam had sympathized with extremist groups such as Hizb ut-Tahrir.

I was unable to interview the jailed Qarshi imam, but in addition to speaking with focus group participants in Qarshi, I was also able to speak with Klichev's mother. I did meet with the other two imams. These meetings and interviews confirmed that Uzbekistan's imams and their followers face considerable pressure, but they also revealed the limits of Tashkent's influence. Although in command of political elites, the Karimov government is markedly less influential when it comes to Uzbekistan's Islamic elite. Religious leaders face different incentive structures than do their political counterparts, and it is these incentive structures—as much society driven as they are state manipulated—that ensure the continued future of independent Islam in Uzbekistan.

Muhammad Sodik Muhammad Yusuf

Studies of Islamic elites often emphasize the role that the political opposition plays in the construction of popular religious leadership.[38] Of the three imams examined here, only one, Muhammad Sodik Muhammad Yusuf, can be associated with the Uzbek opposition (and even in Sodik's case, this association is largely involuntary). Rather, focus groups suggest that for the most part Uzbeks prefer their Islamic leaders to be independent of all politics and to be beholden neither to the government nor to the opposition. Focus group respondents preferred that religious leaders refrain from all politics and instead devote their attention to religion and religious instruction. To some extent, these misgivings toward political imams stem from Uzbek society's dissatisfaction with the changing roles that Uzbekistan's most prominent Islamic leader, Muhammad Sodik, has played in national politics. In the years immediately following the Soviet collapse, Sodik was championed by his supporters as an alternative to President Karimov's authoritarian rule. By 2000, however, to the dismay of much of Uzbekistan's Muslim population, Sodik could be heard on television and the radio supporting Islam Karimov's presidential election bid. Despite his continued support for the president, Sodik nevertheless remains Uzbekistan's most prominent Islamic figure. Indeed, when I asked focus groups to identify national-level Islamic leaders whom they respected, his was the only name that emerged with any frequency.[39] Sodik, though seen as partially co-opted by the Karimov regime, nevertheless remains popular and in several important respects independent.

Following the Soviet collapse, Sodik's avoidance of the Islamist opposition and his current support for Karimov is likely as much a strategy for survival as it is the product of political ambition. As Uzbekistan's most prominent and popular Islamic leader at the time of the Soviet collapse, Sodik was seen as a natural leader by Islamists. He had served as Central Asia's mufti and director of the Central Asian Muslim Spiritual Board from 1989 to 1991. During this tenure, he had won widespread praise for his efforts to bridge the differences between Central Asia's Islamic elites.[40] Even after the Soviet collapse in 1991, Sodik continued to press for unity among the region's religious leaders.[41] While Sodik pressed for regional cooperation, many of those with whom he was negotiating were, however, pressing their own agendas—agendas that often challenged the continued rule of Soviet-era political elites.

In 1992 Tajikistan's mufti, Qazi Akbar Turajonzoda, broke with the Dushanbe government and sided with the paramilitary Islamic Rebirth Party in Tajikistan's increasingly bloody civil war. Turajonzoda's decision, though not supported by Sodik, nevertheless demonstrated to Central Asia's rulers, and in particular to President Karimov, the real challenges that an Islam-centered opposition could pose to continued secular autocratic rule. Sodik, for his part, attempted to distance himself from Turajonzoda, stating that he had repeatedly warned the Tajik mufti not to take sides in the civil war.[42] Moreover, Sodik added that he, unlike his Tajik counterpart, had no political ambitions and shared "nothing in common with the Islamic Rebirth Party."[43] Despite the mufti's public disavowals, or perhaps seeing in these statements a strategy for the mufti to avoid government suspicion, many Muslims in Uzbekistan continued to champion Sodik as an attractive alternative to Karimov's continued patronage-based authoritarianism.

In September 1991, for example, angry demonstrators in Quqon hoisted signs calling for the resignation of Islam Karimov and for Sodik to become president.[44] Three months later, in nearby Namangan, protestors demanded that Islam

Karimov evict the successor to the Communist Party—the People's Democratic Party of Uzbekistan—from its offices to make room for an Islamic community center. In both Ququn and Namangan, Karimov saw firsthand that his administrative authority was waning because of growing Islamic-centered and society-based mobilization. In Namangan, Yoldosh and Namangani's Adolat movement had wrestled security powers from the local police. Through Adolat's neighborhood watch patrols the group had begun to assert society-based policing in the city. For these Adolat activists Muhammad Sodik—whether he intended this or not—was a powerful symbol: he was a local figure with a nationwide reputation and a potential ally in their fight against continued nomenklatura rule. To the Uzbek president, Sodik was a threat, a rival with proven charismatic legitimacy.

Although Sodik may have sympathized with the discontent of the protestors in Ququn and Namangan, it is unclear if he himself desired political power. He had built his career in the religious hierarchy, rising to the chairmanship of the Muslim Spiritual Board by maintaining good relations with Uzbekistan's secular elite. At least in public statements following the Soviet collapse, Sodik expressed a desire to maintain this status quo. In a 1992 interview, for example, he told reporters that it was the Turkish—and not a theocratic—model that should guide Uzbekistan's post-Soviet political transition: "The Turkish path of development with secular power, economic reforms, Muslim religion and, certainly, the existence of any other confessions is close to us. The republican government shares our view."[45]

Sodik's press releases, however, did not allay the president's concerns. Like all Central Asian rulers, Karimov has a record of identifying threats—in particular, Islamist threats—where in all likelihood none exists. In August 1997, for instance, Karimov recalled two thousand Uzbek students from Turkey on the grounds that they had been exposed to radical Islamist groups while attending the university.[46] Any associations, voluntary or involuntary, in what the Uzbek executive perceived to be Islamist groups were suspect. In 1993, Sodik left Uzbekistan for Libya, ostensibly to pursue research and writing but also to escape growing pressure from the government.[47] The Karimov regime had accused Sodik of being an Islamic extremist, and he was suspected of harboring radical leanings that stemmed from a relationship with Akbar Turajonzoda, the former Tajik mufti and a subsequent supporter of the militant Islamic Renaissance Party.[48] Eight years later the Karimov government oddly reversed its position and called Sodik home, this time to fight extremism. Sodik returned to Uzbekistan briefly in 2000 and then permanently in 2001. Sodik explained he returned because Uzbekistan's Muslims wanted him home.[49]

Although there indeed was continuing widespread popular support for the former mufti, it was not only Uzbek society that wished to see Muhammad Sodik back in Tashkent. The Uzbek government also saw benefits in having the popular former mufti home. Karimov's relation to Islam and Uzbekistan's Islamic community was, to say the least, strained. Sodik could help the president reform his image among practicing Muslims, an ever growing portion of the Uzbek population. This the former mufti did. For example, speaking to television reporters during a trip to his hometown Andijan just before the January 2000 presidential elections, Sodik instructed his Fergana Valley compatriots: "The candidates are known. . . . The people's trusted son who has done so much for our people and cares for them, namely Islam Karimov, is one of the candidates. . . . God willing, a majority of people, all, will vote for him. . . . I pray to God that our people stay well on election day and that they will reelect the man they love to the post of head of state."[50]

Following the elections, Sodik appeared on television in February alongside the president and pledged that he was "determined to work with Karimov."[51] Sodik has remained true to this pledge. He regularly uses his weekly radio broadcasts to denounce the "radical and violent ideas" of Hizb ut-Tahrir and the Islamic Movement of Uzbekistan, thereby advancing the Karimov government's attempts at self-legitimation by portraying itself as a bulwark against militant extremism. Sodik has also championed what he stresses are the moderate values of Uzbekistan's Hanafi school of Islam—a school that, as the former mufti's recent behavior illustrates, encourages deference to autocratic rule.[52]

To dismiss Sodik as a puppet of the Karimov regime would, however, be a mistake. As he did before his departure in 1993, Sodik continues to fault the government for placing onerous restrictions upon Islamic education. In Uzbekistan the opportunity to study Islam with learned scholars is rare; clergy are cowed by threats of imprisonment should they conduct classes without "permission from a corresponding central administration body."[53] Sodik thus believes it is only natural that some Uzbeks might turn to extremist groups willing to operate outside the law: "People who want to learn Islam have no possibility to do that in an easy, correct and free way. That's why Hizb ut-Tahrir and other radical groups have had a chance to spread their radical and violent ideas by illegal and secretive ways and to introduce their ideas to ordinary people as true Islam. To stop this process, Islamic education should be put on the right track."[54] Sodik holds few delusions that the government will lift restrictions and allow Uzbekistan's imams to expand Islamic instruction. The Karimov government, he notes, has promised to "fight ideas with ideas."[55] By maintaining controls over the moderate Islamic leadership, the government has instead allowed radical ideas to go unchecked. Had the

Uzbek government "really done what it said it would," Sodik reasoned in a 2002 interview, "we would not have the Hizb ut-Tahrir."[56] He believes that "to be an imam in Uzbekistan today is to be dependent on and controlled by the government."[57]

Although Uzbeks in my focus groups disagreed with this statement, maintaining instead that there were indeed independent imams, Sodik's observation may be correct as a self-assessment. The former mufti, once an attractive alternative to Karimov, is now perceived as having been partially co-opted by the presidential political machine. As one member of the Andijan focus group observed, Sodik is now a "servant of the government." A respondent in Qarshi expressed similar sentiments, labeling Sodik as "Karimov's man." An Andijan schoolteacher added in frustration that "there are more religious prisoners in jail now than there are criminals, yet Sodik does nothing about this, he doesn't protest against the government." Other respondents were forgiving and pragmatic. They regretted the mufti's close ties with Karimov but acknowledged that Sodik had little alternative but to compromise with the president. A respondent in Namangan asked rhetorically: "What, in reality, can Muhammad Sodik Muhammad Yusuf possibly do?" One member of the Andijan focus group said that "Muhammad Sodik is a bird locked in a cage; it is to be expected that, perched next to the president in Tashkent, Sodik will repeat those phrases that are constantly shouted at him."

Sodik's cage is as much his prominence as it is his location. Authoritarian rulers do not welcome competition; as Sodik's case demonstrates, they repress, exile, or co-opt those they perceive to be a challenge.[58] In 1993 the Uzbek government chose coercion, using charges of Islamist extremism to chase Sodik out of the country. In more recent years Karimov has pursued a strategy of co-optation. Sodik, in return for being allowed to return to Tashkent, lent his name to Karimov's reelection campaign as well as to the president's crusade against Hizb ut-Tahrir and the Islamic Movement of Uzbekistan. This exchange, at least in the eyes of some Uzbeks, has not been in Sodik's favor. The mufti, once the icon of the Islamist opposition, is now seen as a partial client of the Karimov state.

Rustam Klichev, Former Head Imam

Muhammad Sodik's national prominence has been both an impediment and an asset. His popularity led the Karimov regime to perceive him as a threat. This same popularity likely protected Sodik from more severe forms of repression. Not all Islamic leaders, as Qarshi imam Rustam Klichev's case clearly demonstrates, have enjoyed such protection. Klichev is popular today for many of the same reasons that Muhammad Sodik was popular in the early 1990s. Imam Klichev, his supporters emphasize, is intelligent and devoted to teaching Islam. Much like Sodik, he is not political. Unlike other local imams he does not sing the praises of the Karimov government during Friday prayer.

Klichev was arrested in April 2004. Six months later he was sentenced to fourteen years in prison. He was found guilty of attempting to undermine the constitutional order, establishing a militant Islamist organization, and plotting to bomb the Khanabad air base, a U.S. installation adjacent to Qarshi and home to a thousand U.S. military personnel before closing in November 2005.[59] I spoke with Klichev's supporters both before and after the imam's October 20 sentencing. His backers insisted that the government's charges were fabricated. Klichev was not an extremist and had neither the skill nor the desire to bomb the air base.[60] Klichev is an admired imam and community leader. The twenty-nine-year-old imam, despite his youth, is the leading local authority on Islam. He won a regional Quran knowledge competition in 2002.[61] He is fluent in Arabic. In contrast to Qarshi's head imam, Klichev wrote his own sermons rather than adapting the notes that the Muslim Spiritual Board in Tashkent sends all imams for Friday prayers.[62] Klichev insisted on independence, his followers maintain, not because he opposed the government but rather because he wanted Islam to speak to the local challenges—unemployment, poverty, illness—that people in Qarshi faced. Klichev, by all accounts, found a wide audience. Three thousand people regularly attended his Friday sermons. His followers—from Qarshi and beyond—were both more numerous and considerably younger than those of other imams in the region. It was this growing cohort of devoted young believers, local human rights defenders told me, that alarmed the regional and central government authorities.

Other aspects of Klichev's practices and training likely troubled the government as well. Klichev, though far from being a radical, was not the pliable imam that the Uzbek government prefers to install in its mosques. At first glance his Islamic education appears unremarkable. Like most young Uzbeks who seek to become an imam, Klichev enrolled in a state-run madrassa.[63] After graduating from the madrassa, Klichev considered attending Tashkent Islamic University (TIU), the state's flagship institution for preparing religious elites and, oddly enough, computer programmers and business managers.[64] Klichev, unimpressed with the combination of religious and secular education at TIU, decided instead to intern as a deputy imam in Qarshi. In 2000, after a one-year apprenticeship, Klichev was appointed head imam of Qarshi's new Navo Mosque, a mahalla mosque designed to serve residents of Qarshi's sixth microregion. Word of Klichev's knowledge and sermons spread quickly and by 2002 the young imam's neighborhood mosque had become the regional center of the Islamic community, drawing worshippers from as far away as Samarqand and Bukhara.

Just as Klichev's growing number of supporters would later draw unwanted government attention, so too would his contacts abroad eventually raise government suspicion. Klichev made the hajj (pilgrimage to Mecca) in 2002. During his travels, Klichev's supporters explained, the young imam was befriended by several Saudis. In addition to supplying Klichev with Islamic texts, these Saudis helped him financially. Although Saudi support of Uzbek mosques and imams had been commonplace during the years immediately following the Soviet collapse, most Uzbek imams stopped accepting private Saudi money in the late 1990s. Rakhmatulla qori Obidov, for example, one of Tashkent's most prominent imams, acknowledged that in the early 1990s Saudi donors had given one million dollars to support the construction of his Kokcha mosque. Obidov emphasized that today, however, the mosque operates only with the funds of its congregation.[65] Obidov's desire to distance himself from Saudi money is understandable. Wealthy members of Saudi Arabia's Wahhabi sect (which adheres to a strict fundamentalist version of Islam) have actively funded the Islamic Movement of Uzbekistan and Hizb ut-Tahrir, the two groups that are most vehemently contesting Karimov's rule.[66] Klichev, in contrast to Sodik, maintained his Saudi contacts despite these associations. Qarshi human rights activists claim that the government exploited these Saudi ties in its prosecution of Klichev. Indeed, few were surprised when police declared that they found a Wahhabi leaflet while searching the imam's house.[67]

Klichev's popularity, despite these charges of extremism, remains high in Qarshi. Outside of southern Uzbekistan, however, few know of Klichev and his recent imprisonment. In August 2004, Muhammad Sodik told me that he had not heard of Klichev. Indeed, it is likely that this lack of a national profile was what made Klichev, like other independent local imams, expendable in the eyes of the Tashkent government. In the eyes of his supporters, Klichev has not bargained with the government and thus remains uncompromised. In addition to Klichev, there are other imams at the local level who likewise believe Uzbekistan's mosques should not be instruments of government propaganda. Klichev's case raises important questions: Why do these local imams persist in maintaining their independence? Why not follow Sodik's strategy of compromise and avoid government persecution? As I learned in my discussions with an independent imam in Ququn who fortunately has not been repressed by the government, many imams choose a strategy of compromise. For others like himself, the imam suggested, submitting to government threats would be worse than going to prison.

An Independent Quqon Imam

I attended one of the imam's Friday prayers in late November 2004. Despite poor weather, hundreds had come to hear the sermon. The central prayer hall where I sat was filled to capacity; outside the mosque hundreds more endured the rain and cold to hear the imam speak. In many respects his sermon was unremarkable. There was no expression of distaste for the current regime, no call to resist Karimov's authoritarian rule. Rather, similar to imams' sermons I had heard in American mosques, the Qoqon imam counseled the congregants as to how they might apply the principles of the Quran to challenges encountered in everyday life. I spoke with this imam following his sermon and asked for his thoughts as to why some imams prove more popular than others. In many ways his answer paralleled those I had received in focus groups throughout the Fergana Valley, Tashkent, and Qarshi. His answer suggested what was so different about his seemingly normal sermon. He concluded that "some imams are too radical, whereas others are clearly government imams . . . in fact, some imams do no not speak of anything other than the government."

He underscored the fact that although few Uzbeks want their religious leaders to be government figureheads, neither do they want their Islamic leaders to be extremists or oppositionists. Abstaining from politics, however, does not in and of itself make for influential leadership. Not all Uzbek imams, he lamented, have sufficient knowledge and charisma to deter their followers from the attractions of fundamentalism. This imam is well aware of the risks that popular and independent Islamic leaders face in Uzbekistan. Several respondents in my Quqon focus group likened him to Muhammed Rajab, the city's charismatic head imam whom the government jailed on charges of extremism in 1994. This flattering and troubling comparison has not been lost on him. The imam knows his position is tenuous; understandably he concluded our discussion by requesting that he not be identified by name in any publications.

Uzbek religious elites, in contrast to political elites, must be responsive to their constituencies. Whereas the average Uzbek has little recourse if he dislikes his local government administrators, he is free to choose his religious leaders. Should he dislike one imam, he can travel to the next district or the next city to seek spiritual guidance from another imam. In contrast to Uzbekistan's political elite who respond almost exclusively to government incentives, Uzbekistan's religious leaders must balance government directives from above with society's demands from below. In Uzbekistan there is a market for independent Islamic leaders but no such demand for independent political leaders.

Although it may not be possible to assess how many independent Islamic leaders there are in Uzbekistan, such leaders clearly exist and are increasingly central to local communities across the country. In contrast to their political counterparts, these religious leaders cannot readily be controlled by patronage politics and coercion. Imams' freedom from the state provides pockets of space where ordinary citizens can gather and, building on the trust engendered by shared religious norms, coordinate community activities. This last point is deserving of particular emphasis. Likely a large reason why we see events like Namangan and Andijan—that is, Islam-centered mobilization—is because Islamic elites provide one of the few safe havens in everyday Uzbek life where society enjoys some protection from the authoritarian state. If this indeed is the case, then the "Islam" component of mobilization events like Namangan and Andijan to a large degree may be epiphenomenal. Were other societal actors—academics or nongovernmental activists, for example—able to provide the same protection that independent imams do, then we might equally see university or NGO-based mobilization. Neither academics nor NGO activists face the same demands that imams face from their local communities, however. As such, it may well continue to be only Uzbekistan's religious leaders who feel compelled to risk snubbing the state in favor of Uzbek society.

Looking to Uzbekistan's Future

Focusing solely on Uzbekistan's political elite would leave one with the sense that Karimov's autocratic rule is secure. Analysis of state-Islam relations suggests the opposite, however. Although Uzbekistan's political elite may be deferential to President Karimov, Uzbek society broadly is increasingly turning away from the central state and toward their local communities—local communities patterned by networks of Muslim faith and charity. Which of these two opposing trends currently defines the Uzbek polity? These two trends are actually interconnected. When seen as such, it becomes increasingly apparent that the Karimov government is not as strong as it outwardly appears to be. Signs that the regime might collapse would not be readily apparent if one's analytical framework derived solely from the political science transitions literature. Although political scientists are preoccupied with change, our leading theories emphasize continuity. We stress path dependency, institutional stickiness, and enduring ethnic, national, and indeed civilizational identities. When change does arrive, we attribute it to sudden disruptions, "exogenous shocks," "punctuated equilibriums," mobilization "cascades," and the contingencies of "elite miscalculation."[68] So much for predictive social science theory.

What if, however, we jettisoned the ex post causal parsimony of transitology and instead rolled up our analytical sleeves and actually mucked around in the messiness of day-to-day autocratic politics? What indicators, short of the familiar stability-collapse dichotomy, might we use to assess the pulse of authoritarianism? Might these indicators actually help us, ex ante, predict political change? I believe that we can evaluate the health and furthermore the likely longevity of autocracy. By taking seriously that which political scientists often do not—symbols, spectacle, and discourse—we can identify the stress points where authoritarian governments—specifically the Karimov government—are most likely to crack. The spectacles discussed below involve the Karimov government's efforts to mobilize the soon-to-be majority of the Uzbek population through the youth group Kamalot. To a certain degree, this discussion parallels the familiar social science model of inquiry; Kamalot became suddenly prominent in the early 2000s. My analysis of this past variation is decidedly forward looking. By understanding the causal factors behind changes in symbolic politics, we can understand the processes and the likelihood of Uzbek regime change. That is, the same factor that is driving symbolic politics in the Kamalot case—the spreading failure of patronage-based politics in the regions—will lead to Uzbek regime change in the near future.

That this is a case study need not lessen the implication of the analysis's broader methodological findings. Political change and revolutions are seldom "now out of never."[69] Rather, political change is almost always foreshadowed by identifiable changes in discourse, symbols, and spectacles. Lamentably, political analysts rarely acknowledge these changes in symbolic politics until it is too late, until well after dramatic institutional changes come to pass. Sovietologists, for example, not only failed to acknowledge the potential importance of the changed discourse embodied in the 1975 Helsinki Final Act, they smugly derided the human rights language of this diplomatic effort.[70] Thus the journalist Anthony Lewis wrote of the Final Act in August 1976: "Only a fatuous optimist would have expected its [the Soviet government's] attitudes to be transformed by the Helsinki Declaration."[71]

Fast forward twenty-five years and the political scientist Daniels Thomas has offered a differing assessment: "That the unraveling of the Communist party-state enabled by Gorbachev's reforms proceeded in a democratic and largely peaceful direction across Eastern Europe is explained by the continued salience of those activists and independent organizations who had made 'Helsinki' a watchword for human rights nearly a decade earlier."[72] Thomas's book *The Helsinki Effect* is a superb study. Of Sovietology and transitology more broadly, though, one cannot help but conclude that although our punch lines are good, our delivery is frequently too late. Political scientists justify our discipline's collective tardiness by appealing to the need for methodological rigor. The social scientist John Hall in his essay "Ideas and the Social Sciences," for example, has written: "Given the sloppiness to which facile idealist analysis is prone, this sort of explanation should, in my opinion, be entertained only after more structural accounts have been exhausted."[73]

Thus we are instructed that ideas—the shorthand political scientists use for symbols, discourse, norms, for causal variables that neither rational choice nor institutionalist explanations adequately address—should be treated as the residual, something to be analyzed only as a last resort when all other explanations fail. Coauthors Judith Goldstein and Robert Keohane's book *Ideas and Foreign Policy*, mandatory reading in almost every American political science graduate program, instructs aspiring PhDs that for their "null hypothesis" they should assume political outcomes as the result of actors following "egoistic interests in the context of power realities." Only when this "null hypothesis is carefully addressed and comparative evidence brought forth," Goldstein and Keohane instruct, will we be in a position to evaluate the role ideas play in political change.[74]

There are dissenters, of course. "Symbolic change," the anthropologist David Kertzer has written, produces "important political and material consequences."[75] And political actors recognize this, even if political scientists often do not. Thus the political scientist Alison Brysk has stated that actors, even those who pursue egoistic interests, seek "to achieve social change through symbolic collective action."[76] This is what President Islam Karimov is attempting through Kamalot. No longer able to count on patronage politics to ensure monopoly power, he is seeking to rally youth to his side through symbolic collective action. His efforts may not (and likely will not) prove successful. That Karimov is engaging youth politics in symbolic collective action, though, is a ready indicator of the political change that is likely to come.

In my analysis of Kamalot, I discuss the emergence of this state-led Uzbek youth group and the extraordinary spectacles it conducts. I explore what Kamalot's spectacles potentially tell us about the health of the Karimov regime and the potential for change in Uzbek politics. The image I present, that of an aging and ailing autocratic leader attempting to enlist youth support, is notably at odds with the portrayal of liberalizing youth politics in other post-Soviet contexts—for example, in Georgia, Serbia, and Ukraine. Critically, though, just as reformists see youth as vigorous and symbolically potent allies in the fight against moribund autocracy, so too do autocrats see youth as a way to revitalize stalled authoritarianism. I conclude by exploring the implications of youth mobilization for the future of Uzbek governance, showing that Karimov's attempts at youth mobilization are an indicator of failing patronage politics. If the septuagenarian president's gambit at winning youthful affection fails, if Kamalot is but a one-sided romance, then Karimov's political star will quickly fade.

Kamalot

For any student of Soviet politics, Uzbekistan's Kamalot youth organization is immediately familiar. Modeled after the Soviet Komsomol, Kamalot is designed to capture the hearts and minds of Uzbekistan's burgeoning youth population. It may be trite to conclude a country's youth is its future. Nowhere in Central Asia, though, is this more the case than in Uzbekistan. In 2015, 47 percent of Uzbekistan's population will have been born after the Soviet collapse. This fourteen-million-strong youth cohort (twenty-four and under) will be larger than the total 2015 country populations of Kyrgyzstan, Tajikistan, and Turkmenistan and just two million shy of the total population in Kazakhstan.[77] Numeric strength need not equal political power. The Karimov government is intent on enlisting the support of younger generations through Kamalot's carefully crafted programs and events.

My description of Kamalot's activities is derived largely from secondary sources, primarily from Uzbek media accounts of the youth organization. This reliance on secondary sources is the result of political necessity rather than any lack of desire to research the organization firsthand. A few months after I returned from my last research trip to Uzbekistan in June 2005, a Human Rights Watch representative informed me that several Uzbek colleagues—all human rights activists—were either under threat of state repression, actively being repressed, or in exile and seeking refugee status. The Human Rights Watch representative further added that one of my Uzbek colleagues noted in his United Nations High Commissioner for Refugees (UNHCR) asylum application that his collaborative research with me was what had elicited Uzbek government threats of repression. I have neither directly collaborated with Uzbekistan-based colleagues nor returned to conduct field research in Uzbekistan since June 2005.

Despite or perhaps because of these challenges, my interest in the Uzbek polity has grown. In light of my colleagues' trials and given what I had witnessed of youth and state interactions during my own field research, I have become increasingly puzzled about why Uzbek youth broadly did not appear to share the dismal view of the Karimov government that my Uzbek friends and I did. Upon reflection, I realized my research interests brought me into contact with youth who, understandably given the often fraught relations between the state and consumer goods traders and the state and Islam, likely harbored more animosity toward the Karimov government than did the average Uzbek teen or twenty-something.[78]

What if I could return now to study Kamalot? Would the Uzbek youths I encountered be any different from the frustrated traders and young religious scholars I had encountered during previous visits? If the following media-derived accounts are even partially true, the answer is almost certainly yes, that far from fearing the Karimov regime, many youths value the state-run Kamalot for the entertainment and education opportunities the organization provides. That this appreciation might translate into mobilized political support for the Karimov government, though, is uncertain.

Not all my waking hours in Uzbekistan were spent in markets, mosques, or madrassas. By June 2005 I had attended enough weddings, dance clubs, and football matches and frequented enough Internet cafes to know that Uzbek youth share the same aspirations and gravitate to the same forms of entertainment that youth the world over do. It is here, in the arena of entertainment, that Kamalot particularly excels. In January 2006, for example, Kamalot and the government's Forum on Culture and Art televised the Kelazhak Ovozi (Voices of the Future) ceremony, a government-sponsored celebration in which medals are awarded to promising young leaders in the arts, businesses, and sciences.[79] Headlining the event were the singers Tohir Sodiqov and Gulnora Karimova. Sodiqov, immensely popular in Uzbekistan, provided a fitting start to this now equally popular annual celebration of youth achievement. Kelazhak Ovozi has grown from three thousand competitors in 2005 to more than fifty-four thousand in 2008. To reach the broadest possible audience, Kelazhak Ovozi rotates the categories of competition every year—the fields in 2009, for example, included "architecture and design, information communication technology, traditional arts and crafts, and poetry and prose" as well as a competition for "the best collection of materials covering Kelazhak Ovozi contest."[80] Participants compete at the local level before advancing to the final national-level selection. Those who win, in addition to being honored on national television by household names like Sodiqov and Karimova, receive stipends to further their education.[81]

For the more athletically inclined, Kamalot sponsors a range of sporting institutions and events. The youth group runs summer camps for disadvantaged children. The goal of these camps "is to bring children up in the spirit of love and loyalty towards their motherland, to prepare them for service in the Uzbek armed forces, to strengthen their health, to temper them physically and spiritually."[82] Kamalot regularly sponsors sports festivals. In September 2003 it organized an "extreme sports" festival in Tashkent, where skaters competed while organizers worked the crowds to raise awareness about the dangers of drug abuse.[83] In December 2005, Kamalot coordinated a "mass marathon" from Termez to Tashkent to commemorate the thirteen-year anniversary of the Uzbek constitution.[84] In Andijan in July 2006, Kamalot held an "international youth martial arts tournament under the slogan: 'we are against terrorism and drugs.'"[85] Together with the Presidential Fund for the Development of Children's Sports, Kamalot sponsors the annual "student games" in which twenty-four hundred of the best athletes from secondary schools and universities converge in Tashkent to compete in basketball, tennis, Ping-Pong, football, track and field, swimming, chess, and wrestling.[86]

For Uzbek youths more interested in virtual games, Kamalot has opened computer cafes and free Internet access points throughout the country.[87] Should cerebral rather than virtual or athletic competitions be more attractive, Kamalot hosts "values, customs, traditions, and youth" contests in which university students are quizzed on the "uniqueness of national customs, traditions and values of various regions, peoples and nationalities."[88] For future lawyers and judges, Kamalot offers "do you know the law?" contests for high school students.[89] There are job fairs and seed capital to start small businesses for the entrepreneurially inclined.[90] For the more spiritually oriented, Kamalot's Andijan branch has established a resource center "to prevent the spread of drug addiction and religious extremist ideas among minors."[91] For history buffs Kamalot organizes tours of Tashkent's national monuments. The goal of these excursions, tour director Khilola Makhmudova explains, is "to shape in forthcoming generation the sense of love to Homeland, respect to its invaluable culture and history, which serves an important factor in upbringing the youth."[92] Should diplomacy capture an Uzbek teen's imagination, Kamalot organizes biannual cross-cultural exchanges with youth groups in neighboring countries. Occasionally, these exchanges result in diplomatic pronouncements. A 2005 visit to Azerbaijan thus concluded with Kamalot's vice president Shohret Gasimov's pronouncement on the Nargono-Karabakh conflict: "We also understand the problems of the Azerbaijani youth and we believe that the territorial integrity of Azerbaijan should be restored."[93]

Religious resource centers, Internet cafes, sports tournaments, academic competitions, small business loans, cultural exchanges, arts, and entertainment—these all sound like wonderful programs, but how broad is Kamalot's actual reach? Kamalot's target age group is fifteen to thirty.[94] In 2005 there were approximately eight million Uzbeks between these ages.[95] According to Kamalot's leader, Botir Ubaydullayev, the organization had 4.5 million members in February 2006.[96] This is an impressive figure and, if true, it begs the question why—why this concerted effort upon the part of the Karimov regime to reach out to Uzbekistan's younger generation? No other post-Soviet state can claim half the fifteen- to thirty-year-old population as active members of a state-sponsored youth association. Indeed, one must look back to the Soviet period, to the Komsomol, to find a state-led effort to engage younger generations on such a massive scale.

The answer to the questions surrounding Kamalot, about these carefully designed sporting events, concerts, and nationalism and state-oriented competitions, lies in the growing crisis of Uzbek governance. The spectacle of youth politics is an indicator that President Karimov's traditional source of power, the patronage politics that had throughout much of the 1990s secured the deference of regional elites, is failing. Youth politics is Karimov's attempt to "rebuild," to replace failing patronage networks among older Soviet-era elites with a new younger polity that coheres not only as a result of state largesse, but also as a result of individuals' perceptions of a postcolonial Uzbek-nationalist identity. Thus Kamalot's festivals, the organization's executive secretary Said-Abdulaziz Yusupov unabashedly notes, are designed to promote youth "loyalty to the mother land."[97] Through symbolism and spectacle, through "patriots' festivals," marathons celebrating the Uzbek constitution, and post-Andijan music concerts held under such slogans as "protect your motherland as you would a loved one," President Karimov is reaching out to a younger generation to replace an ossified political elite while redefining that which constitutes political legitimacy.[98]

State Patronage and Uzbek Society's Alternative Sources of Wealth

Problematically for the Karimov regime, resources for maintaining patronage politics are increasingly being overshadowed by the resources business elites—often Muslim business elites—hold at the local level. In contrast to the oil-rich Nazarbaev regime in Kazakhstan, Karimov has struggled to replace Moscow's Soviet-era largesse with easily exploitable industries or easily exploitable international supporters. To some extent, monopoly control over natural gas exports and the domestic purchase and international resale of Uzbekistan's large cotton crop has yielded rents Karimov can redistribute to the political elite.[99] The World Bank estimates that 25 percent of Uzbekistan's foreign reserves come from the international resale of cotton.[100] Declining cotton yields and the Karimov government's attempt in recent years to offset this decline through some liberalization of the industry have eroded cotton's ability to deliver patronage funds. Net tax transfers from cotton production have declined from 10 to 3 percent of Uzbek gross domestic product between 2000 and 2004.[101]

Some, most notably Craig Murray, the former British ambassador to Uzbekistan, would argue that beginning in late 2001, the Karimov government found in the United States a ready substitute for declining cotton revenues. In October

2001, U.S. troops began landing at Karshi-Khanabad, an Uzbek air base ninety miles north of the Afghan border. A marked buildup in U.S. troops at the base and a similarly marked increase in U.S. assistance to Uzbekistan quickly followed. In 2002 the United States extended $160 million in assistance to Uzbekistan, a figure equal to 77 percent of combined U.S. assistance to Uzbekistan from 1993 to 2001.[102] Murray would later conclude of this buildup, and of U.S. and U.K. military and intelligence cooperation with Uzbekistan more broadly, "we are selling our souls for dross."[103]

The U.S. military presence, and with it flush U.S. assistance budgets, ended in November 2005, following five months of strained relations in the wake of the Karimov regime's violent repression of the Andijan protestors. Although Uzbek experts like Murray may be correct to question the morality of Washington and London's partnering with autocratic regimes, human rights have only worsened with the decrease in U.S. assistance. The U.S. government devoted more than half of its 2002 U.S. assistance to Uzbekistan to democracy, community development, and humanitarian programs.[104] These programs proved critical in supporting, among others, Uzbekistan's human rights and democracy activists. In short, although U.S. assistance from 2002 to 2005 may have to a degree offset declining cotton revenues, thereby temporarily shoring up Karimov's weakening patronage system, U.S. assistance equally aided Uzbekistan's democracy and human rights activists.

Although it is difficult to assess the net effect U.S. assistance between 2002 and 2005 had on Uzbek politics, what is clear is that revenues from international aid and from the cotton industry are now in decline. While Uzbek regional elites continue to seek their ever shrinking cut from the state's economic pie, the long-run sustainability of Karimov's patronage politics is ever less certain. Patronage politics demand that the state maintains a near monopoly on economic wealth.[105] As soon as alternative sources of wealth emerge, the effectiveness of centrally defined patronage networks weakens.

Andijan, a Window into Weakening Patronage Politics

The May 2005 Andijan uprising illustrates this dynamic. The uprising also shows the potentially destabilizing demonstration effects mass mobilization generally and youth mobilization in particular may have on Karimov's weakening autocratic rule. Andijan, perhaps more clearly than any other event since the Soviet collapse, provides a window into why the Karimov government has initiated a new strategy of youth politics to preempt its declining power in the regions while persuading younger generations of the ills of color revolutions.

The Andijan protests, contrary to the Karimov leadership's claims of religious extremism, were a product of the leadership's failed attempts to reassert control over regional appointees and a regional population that had become more responsive to local rather than national-level sources of wealth. In May 2004, Karimov dismissed Qobijon Obidov, Andijan's governor, citing the negative effects of regionally based "personal connections."[106] Karimov's charge of corruption was an oblique reference to the growing influence a local cohort of wealthy Muslim businessmen—a group the Uzbek regime had labeled Akramiya—held both over Obidov's administration and among Andijan society more broadly. Karimov, however, was not content with simply sacking Obidov. Concerned that an administrative reshuffle alone was insufficient, Karimov proceeded to jail the Muslim businessmen on charges of religious extremism—an action that precipitated the May 2005 uprising.[107]

Andijan is the most prominent but by no means the only case of failed patronage. Given the state's control over the Uzbek press, it is often difficult to uncover the full extent of patronage breakdown. That said, Karimov's own pronouncements suggest central authority breakdown at the local level is a common and geographically widespread phenomenon. In 2000, Karimov sacked Jora Noraliyev, the governor of Surkhandarya, citing that the governor had cultivated an environment of "nepotism, cronyism and bribery."[108] In October 2004 the Uzbek president removed Alisher Otaboyev, the governor of Fergana, noting that his regional representative's "instructions and orders are beginning to lose, or possibly have already lost, their power in the localities."[109] In December 2008, Karimov dismissed three district hakims as well as the governor of the Tashkent region, Ziyovuddin Niyozov, for embezzling state land and selling housing plots to political supporters.[110]

Perhaps the most astonishing state acknowledgment of declining (and in this case altogether absent) control over its regional appointees is the case of regional hakim Isoqov. Isoqov, Uzbek Prosecutor-General Rashid Qodirov explains, "wanted to get rich and paid no attention to solving social, economic, cultural and everyday problems. Feeling himself to be invulnerable and all-powerful, he stopped taking into consideration people's views and did not pay heed to their problems and needs. This former official gathered around him people loyal to him. He created an atmosphere of unlimited autocracy in the locality by exerting duress on his subordinates . . . the arrogant governor was given a long prison term."[111]

Complementing these challenges at the elite level have been further mass mobilization challenges at the local level. The Andijan protests, for example, were preceded by a string of "market uprisings" in September 2004 in Andijan, Fer-

gana, Qarshi, and Quqon in which retailers marched on and in several cases occupied local administration buildings in protest of new central government laws
regulating local commerce. These protests ended when regional administrators
quietly ceased implementing Tashkent's directive.[112] Uzbeks throughout the country as well as regional leaders learned from these demonstrations that protest
was possible, that Karimov's control was not absolute. Uzbeks learned from their
own success in these protests as well as from the March 2005 Tulip Revolution
in neighboring Kyrgyzstan and from the earlier Rose and Orange revolutions in
Georgia and Ukraine that uprisings could be successful, that citizens could constrain and in some cases turn out their autocratic rulers. Giving voice to this new
optimism, Mukhammed Salikh, the leader of the Erk opposition party, declared
in the days following the Karimov government's violent repression of the May 13,
2005, Andijan protests: "We can transform this movement into a velvet revolution, just as in Georgia, Ukraine and Kyrgyzstan, without arms and bloodshed."[113]

Given Uzbeks' growing inclination to protest and Tashkent's increasingly
failed rule at the local level, it is understandable that the Uzbek president might
pursue new strategies of control. Karimov's old regional elite no longer are responsive and reliable. In some cases, as in the September 2004 market protests,
this elite simply lacks the power to be responsive. In other settings, though—for
example, in the case of regional hakims Obidov, Isoqov, Noraliyev, and Niyozov—
these elites chose not to be responsive. In all cases Tashkent's authority is in retreat. It is in this environment of central government retreat that the Karimov
government initiated its new strategy of youth politics in an effort to restore executive rule in the regions.

The Spectacle of Youth Politics

Youth movements are portrayed both in the popular media and in the social
science literature as drivers of liberal political reform. Empirically and, no less
important, symbolically, youth mobilization causalities enjoy considerable support. Any reflection on the recent prodemocracy revolutions in Georgia, Serbia,
and Ukraine immediately evokes images of young protestors challenging—and
winning over—equally young and armed government soldiers. Substantive explanations do exist for why younger generations appear so willing to challenge the
authoritarian leanings of their elders. Closer analysis suggests that the causality
scholars attribute to youth protest may be mistaken. That is, although choreographed youth mobilization is an indicator of impending political change, youth
mobilization need not be an indicator that liberalizing political change is near.

This observation is soberingly at odds with the "end of history" optimism

that characterizes much of the study of youth in post-Soviet transition. The political scientists Valerie Bunce and Sharon Wolchik, for example, have told us that
there are compelling reasons to believe younger generations are more inclined to
liberal change than their elders. Writing of the Georgian, Serbian, and Slovakian
revolutions, Bunce and Wolchik find that youth, in addition to bringing "fresh
approaches [and] new techniques," are also "untainted by the compromises many
members of the opposition had made [with the old regime]."[114] Although Bunce
and Wolchik's argument helps explain the demographics of revolutionary mo-
ments and the enduring youthful face of postrevolutionary successor regimes, we
should not be deluded that this younger demographic is any more committed to
reform than their elders. The thirty- and forty-somethings of the United National
Movement who dominate post-Shevardnadze Georgian politics, we now know,
are no more democratic than the pre-2003 Georgian political elite. President
Mikheil Saakashvili's cohort may be less tainted by associations with the Soviet
state. But these young Western-educated leaders—champions of NATO, the European Union, and a Euro-Atlantic future—are now compromised in the eyes of
Georgian voters by other associations: associations with ballot rigging, corruption, and Dr. Dot.[115]

Even if one accepts the hypothesis that younger generations are more open
to change, there is little evidence that youth are any more inclined toward *liberal* rather than *illiberal* change. Perhaps because analyses of post-Soviet politics
have centered on liberal or partial reform rather than authoritarian retrenchment,
the question of illiberal youth politics has received comparatively little attention.
New research, most prominently the political scientist Lucan Way's analysis of
Ukraine's Orange Revolution, suggests that youth mobilization may be an indicator of autocratic weakness rather than a causal force behind liberal reform. Way
questions Orange Revolution interpretations that attribute the winter 2004–5 de-
feat of the Kuchma-Yanukovych alliance to mass youth protest. He instead argues
that it was internal discord within the Kuchma regime in the fall of 2004, not "the
idealistic youth who braved Kyiv's ice-cold streets," that precipitated the Orange
Revolution.[116] This does not mean youth politics is inconsequential. Just the opposite, if as the political scientist Joel Migdal has suggested, we can assess a government's strength by the degree to which it ensures "compliance, participation,
and legitimation," then sudden shifts in the nature of compliance, participation,
and legitimation may well indicate eroding, or a government's perception of eroding, state capacity.[117]

The events in Andijan suggest that the nature of compliance, participation,
and legitimation is shifting in Uzbekistan. Given Tashkent's fading economic
clout relative to the growing resources of local Muslim business elites, Soviet-style

patronage politics no longer guarantees President Karimov the loyalty of regional appointees. Rather, the Uzbek president must cultivate new sources of legitimacy and, having lost the economic game, Karimov is turning to nationalism in an effort to cultivate a new less mercenary following among Uzbekistan's younger generations. Will Karimov, Central Asia's oldest remaining Soviet-era autocrat, be able to reinvent himself and find legitimacy anew as the nationalist leader of a country where the majority of people were born after the Soviet collapse? Given the forced nature of Kamalot's many productions, it is tempting to conclude that Karimov has not a hope at rallying Uzbekistan's youth. His efforts to cultivate nationalist mobilization are awkward and contrived: a countrywide celebration of Uzbek culture that culminates with the televised performance of the president's aspiring pop star daughter; "do you know the law" contests for a country that has no rule of law; sporting events that honor the Uzbek constitution, this despite Karimov's running roughshod over his country's founding document.

Yet it is the very inanity of these spectacles that may hold the key to their potential success. Here political scientist Lisa Weedan's analysis of the Syrian president Hafez al-Assad's similar use of spectacle is instructive: "The images of citizens delivering panegyrics to Assad's rule, collectively holding aloft placards forming his face, signing oaths in blood, or simply displaying pictures of him in their shop windows communicated to Syrians throughout the country the impression of Assad's power independent of his readiness to use it. And the greater the absurdity of the required performance, the more clearly it demonstrated that the regime could make most people obey most of the time."[118] Ultimately Karimov's political future rests not in Kamalot's ability to stage slick nationalist productions, but rather in the organization's ability to seemingly effortlessly rally youth en masse despite the artificiality of these clearly choreographed events. To achieve this appearance, Karimov must recognize that the power of spectacle exists only so far as his government is perceived as not expending considerable effort in the staging of Kamalot's rallies. Assad's absurdity is compelling because the Syrian president appears aloof from spontaneous displays of public fealty. Indeed, in addition to learning from Assad, Karimov would do well to study the same youth he is attempting to mobilize; the perfected detachment of adolescent youth is exactly the image the Uzbek autocrat needs to convey to his target audience.

In Karshi, a city in southern Uzbekistan not far from the Afghan border, there is—or at least there was during my last visit in November 2004—a large billboard of President Karimov holding a young soldier aloft in a powerful bear hug. My colleague, Tulkin Karaev, and I would regularly joke about the obvious symbolism and the equally obvious insecurity this billboard conveyed. Karaev, the father of two adolescent boys, was acutely aware of the billboard's true meaning. The Uzbek leader's embrace of youth politics was too tight. Karimov was suffocating the very population he hoped would breathe new life into his fading presidency. If Kamalot's recent activities are accurate indication, it is clear that neither Karimov's embrace nor his insecurity has lessened in the intervening years. What is less clear is if Uzbek analysts broadly and political scientists in particular will take Kamalot and the spectacle of youth politics seriously.

As I have argued, taking Kamalot seriously need not mean we ascribe symbolism and spectacle some invariably determinative causality. Karimov's effort to mobilize youth may (indeed, most likely) fail. What taking Kamalot seriously does mean, though, is that we recognize Karimov's clumsy attempt at youth mobilization as a sign of growing autocratic strain and, as such, a portent of change to come. Political scientists and Uzbekistan's international partners have thus far all proven slow to recognize and interpret such signs of existing regime weakness. From a discipline-specific point of view, this reticence to recognize and interpret symbols and spectacle is unfortunate in that it impedes a central goal of social science—the development of predictive causal theories. From a policy-specific point of view, this reticence is equally unfortunate in that it leads to ephemeral alliances with embattled autocrats. Such alliances, as the United States has discovered in Central Asia and South Asia, may yield fleeting gains, but these gains come, more often than not, at the expense of long-run strategic and no less important humanitarian interests.

5 Kazakh Dynasty

THE KAZAKH CASE, similar to the Uzbek and Kyrgyz cases, closely conforms to what the perestroika legacy model predicts. Kazakh president Nursultan Nazarbaev, thanks to Gorbachev's restoration of political order after the Almaty riots in December 1986, began the post-Soviet period with a united and executive-oriented political elite. The incentive structures characteristic of this inheritance, in contrast to the incentive structures that define Kyrgyzstan's narrow and fragmented elite inheritance, heighten ruling coalition members' loyalty to Nazarbaev. At the same time, they also reduce the payoffs Nazarbaev must extend to secure elite loyalty. The outcome of post-Soviet Kazakh politics is what we would expect, given an understanding of the perestroika legacy model: Kazakh politics remains stable and the Kazakh executive has become phenomenally wealthy.

The Kazakh case, like the Uzbek and Kyrgyz cases, also presents challenges that the perestroika legacy model alone cannot fully answer. In the Kyrgyz example, although we indeed have seen the chaos the legacy model predicts, we nevertheless were confronted with the question of why President Askar Akaev was able to maintain power for fifteen years while President Kurmanbek Bakiev was ousted after only five. In Uzbekistan, although the elite stability the perestroika legacy model predicts has emerged, we are confronted with the vexing issue of bloody state-society relations. The challenges in Kazakhstan are twofold. The first relates to international relations—more specifically, to the question of why Kazakhstan's partners (in particular, Kazakhstan's Western partners) believe that by engaging and rewarding Nazarbaev, they might compel the executive leader to abandon dynastic politics in favor of political reform. The answer, I suggest, rests in Western governments' misinterpretation of Nazarbaev's partial political reform, in their mistaking managed and often orchestrated conflict for real political contestation. The second dilemma is Kazakhstan's future political stability.

This future stability will depend on two dynamics, both of which Nazarbaev cannot control. First, Nazarbaev's government, like all governments that depend on windfall revenues from natural resource extraction, remains vulnerable to fluctuations in commodity prices. An oil shock like the one that debilitated Soviet patronage politics in the 1980s could similarly undermine the stability of Nazarbaev's autocratic rule. Second, Nazarbaev is now in his seventies and, despite two decades of enjoying a united political elite, the president's advancing age adds a new twist to how his supporters calculate returns to continued loyalty or future defection. Unless Nazarbaev establishes clear and effective rules of dynastic succession, two decades of political stability could quickly turn into a cascade of elite defection.

Misreading the Politics of Partial Reform

In January 2010 the Kazakh secretary of state, Kanat Saudabaev, was inaugurated as the chairperson-in-office of the Organization for Security and Cooperation in Europe (OSCE). In addition to working to enhance security, the OSCE is tasked with monitoring and evaluating the elections of its fifty-six member states. The OSCE's election-monitoring arm, the Office for Democratic Institutions and Human Rights, has yet to certify any Kazakh election as being in compliance with "OSCE commitments and other international standards." Oddly, despite Kazakhstan's consistent failure to meet its elections commitments, the Nazarbaev government nevertheless was accorded the honor of leading the OSCE. When presented with this troubling divergence between Kazakhstan's unmet OSCE commitments and Kazakhstan's chairmanship of the OSCE at a May 2009 congressional hearing, Ambassador George Krol, the deputy assistant secretary of state, explained why the U.S. government supported Nazarbaev's bid to lead this international organization: "Our broader vision is for a strong, independent and democratic Kazakhstan that is a leader and anchor of stability in the region. We believe Kazakhstan's service as chairman in office for the OSCE will help serve that broader vision."[1]

In fairness to Krol, the U.S. acquiescence to Kazakhstan's becoming OSCE chair happened before his appointment as deputy assistant secretary. That said, one nevertheless wonders why the United States, along with fifty-four other OSCE members, agreed to putting Kazakhstan in charge of an organization that has as one of its central tasks promoting "the principles of democracy by building, strengthening and protecting democratic institutions."[2] One answer to this question might be that member states simply do not see the OSCE as meaningful. If one rejects this cynical explanation though, one has to worry that U.S. policy makers and their international counterparts have fundamentally misinterpreted the politics of Kazakh partial reform.

To the outside observer, Kazakh politics appears considerably more tumultuous than Uzbek politics. Whereas in Uzbekistan there is no open political opposition, in Kazakhstan a vocal opposition does exist. This opposition contests and occasionally wins seats in the national parliament and regularly criticizes Nazarbaev in the domestic and foreign press. This comparative openness relative to Uzbekistan has won the Kazakh government qualified praise. Though still "not free" according to Freedom House's annual assessments of "freedom in the world," Kazakhstan has escaped Uzbekistan's dubious distinction of being among the world's worst autocracies. Furthermore, whereas 98 percent of all countries score better than Uzbekistan does on the World Bank's "voice and accountability" governance indicator, a somewhat less astounding 84 percent of countries score better than Kazakhstan.[3] Is it possible, though, that Freedom House and World Bank's World Governance Indicators have misread what it takes as political contestation in Kazakhstan? A brief review of this contestation answers this question.

In October 1992 Nazarbaev stated in a national address: "The executive must be extremely tough now so that people can feel the strength of the state."[4] Yet, at the same time that Nazarbaev was expressing executive resolve, the Kazakh parliament—the inherited Supreme Soviet—was working with the Zheltoksan nationalist movement to undermine the president's proposal to accord Russian the status of an official state language. The Supreme Soviet members of parliament argued that Kazakhstan was now "a unitary state and only the language of the indigenous population can be its official language."[5] Similarly indicative of contested executive-legislative relations was the January 1993 dispute between the Supreme Soviet's chairman, Serikbolsyn Abdildin, and the president. Abdildin insisted that the parliament should have greater oversight over the design of the Kazakh national budget, whereas Nazarbaev argued the parliament's role should be limited to merely approving the budget. The deadlock between the chairman and the president was so severe, the government newspaper *Kazakhstanskaia pravda* wrote that Kazakhstan's future peace and stability was in question: "From the outside Kazakhstan would seem not to be subject to the cataclysmic struggle for power into which Russia is now plunged. But our republic's internal political processes only appear to be calm and measured. In actuality, the skirmish between the legislative and the executive branches is just as acute."[6]

These skirmishes continued to characterize executive-legislative relations even after the Supreme Soviet disbanded and a new parliament was elected. In 1994, for example, in response to severe economic downturn, Kazakh members of parliament once again demanded greater oversight over the national budget and national economic policy. Leading the parliamentary charge was Olzhas Suleimenov—at the time Kazakhstan's second most prominent statesman and internationally acclaimed for his role in organizing the Soviet-era Nevada-Semipalatinsk antinuclear movement. Someone needed to stand up to Nazarbaev, Suleimenov urged, otherwise the parliament would be "turned into a subsidiary of the executive. . . . They draft all the laws and we are just expected to pass them."[7]

Three years later the Kazakh parliament was still attracting oppositionist ire. On November 30, 1997, former member of parliament Petr Svoik, tired of his failed efforts working with the Nazarbaev government as a "soft oppositionist" in the hopes of encouraging political reform, led his new "hard oppositionist" Azamat party in a six-hundred-person-strong march on the parliament in protest of what he described as Nazarbaev's increasingly "arbitrary rule."[8] Svoik's new "hard oppositionist" stance appears to have inspired others—even some elites within the president's ruling coalition. Akezhan Kazhegeldin, for example, shortly after he stepped down as Kazakh prime minister in October 1997, declared his intentions to challenge Nazarbaev in the January 1999 presidential elections. Similarly, Mukhtar Ablyazov, who served as director of the state-owned power company KEGOC as well as Nazarbaev's minister of energy, broke ranks with Nazarbaev in November 2001 and formed the opposition party Democratic Choice of Kazakhstan. Even Nazarbaev's own son-in-law, Rakhat Aliev, broke ranks with the president in May 2007 and joined the Kazakh opposition.

All these prominent cases of political contestation—with the exception of the Aliev defection—proved either to be minor affairs or events directly orchestrated by Nazarbaev himself. The 1992 language law dispute between the parliament and the president in actuality provided political cover for Nazarbaev as he rapidly indigenized Kazakh government posts. In 1985 half of all regional and central state administration posts in Kazakhstan were held by nonethnic Kazakhs.[9] By 1992 this number had dropped to 41.5 percent, and by 1994 only a quarter of all administrative posts were held by non-Kazakhs.[10] Abdildin's 1993 dispute with Nazarbaev was prompted by Abdildin's proposed "law on the control chamber"— legislation that would have given future parliaments increased oversight over the Kazakh national budget.[11] The *Kazakhstanskaia pravda* article and Nazarbaev's own January 1993 reprimand of the parliament for its "crafty interpretations" were, as the *Izvestiia* correspondent in Kazakhstan would call it, "veiled rebukes to the Supreme Soviet."[12] All of these rebukes the outgoing Supreme Soviet would ultimately heed. On December 9, only days before the Supreme Soviet was scheduled to disband, Kazakhstan's members of parliament granted Nazarbaev the authority to appoint 42 of the future parliament's 177 members, thus ensuring that the next parliament would be as accommodating as the first.[13]

Suleimenov, in the intervening years since his 1994 public criticism of Nazarbaev for Kazakhstan's poor economic performance, has not made a peep. In 1995 Nazarbaev appointed Suleimenov ambassador to Italy. Suleimenov continues to serve abroad, only now he is serving in Paris as Kazakhstan's permanent representative to UNESCO. As for other members of parliament who joined Suleimenov in his 1994 critique of Nazarbaev's mishandling of the economy, they all lost their jobs. In March 1995 an Almaty resident, Tatyana Kviatkovskaia, petitioned the Kazakh Constitutional Court and claimed the March 1994 parliamentary elections were unconstitutional.[14] Kvyatkovskaya argued that her right to equal representation had been violated because her Almaty electoral district contained considerably more voters than did districts elsewhere in the country.[15] The court ultimately agreed with Kviatkovskaia and ruled the 1994 ballot invalid. The court held firm to its ruling even when Nazarbaev formally protested the decision. As a result of the court's steadfastness, Nazarbaev was forced to dissolve the parliament. "What could I do?" Nazarbaev asked in an interview with the Russian daily *Izvestia*, "disobey the court?"[16] Clearly not, Nazarbaev answered his own question. "If a president is true to democratic principles, if he intends to be the guarantor of the constitution, then he has no choice . . . he must abide the rule of law."[17]

The oppositionists Svoik and Ablyazov were dealt with in a less roundabout way. The week after leading his six-hundred-person-strong march on parliament in November 1997, Svoik, along with his wife, democracy activist Natalya Chumokova, were beaten by "four masked assailants" while the two were on a working visit to neighboring Kyrgyzstan.[18] Former energy minister Ablyazov, not long after he established his oppositionist Democratic Choice of Kazakhstan in November 2001, was sentenced to six years in jail for abuse of power and corruption.[19] Akezhan Kazhegeldin, the former prime minister turned 1999 presidential contender, would also be found guilty of corruption. Kazhegeldin left Kazakhstan in 1998 and was not present for his 2001 court trial. After being disqualified on an "administrative offense" from contesting the January 1999 presidential ballot, the ex–prime minister understood he was no longer welcome in Kazakhstan.[20]

In short, in all of these cases of seeming contestation, political oppositionists were either co-opted or coerced before they could mount any real challenge to

Nazarbaev. This well-established pattern of permissiveness and subsequent co-optation and coercion suggests that perhaps OSCE member states were too quick to accept the Kazakh foreign minister Marat Tazhin's 2007 pledge in Madrid that "in the context of future Chairmanship," Kazakhstan would: "develop media self-regulation mechanisms . . . and liberalize the registration procedures for media outlets," "implement ODIHR [Office for Democratic Institutions and Human Rights] recommendations in the area of elections and legislation concerning po-litical parties in Kazakhstan," and "further liberalization and greater openness and transparency of political-governmental processes."[21] Might not Tazhin have been making this pledge for instrumental reasons, for securing Nazarbaev the prestige of the OSCE chairmanship while all the while knowing that Nazarbaev would not follow through on this promise to reform? Indeed, in accepting Tazhin's pledge, the OSCE failed to recognize in Nazarbaev a trait that characterizes many auto-cratic leaders who "want power but also want to be admired and adored."[22] Po-litical scientist Adam Przeworski and his colleagues have noted of such leaders: "Ideally, they would hold office as a result of elections. Yet the hunger for power overwhelms other motivations: They prefer to remain in office by force rather than lose power. Incumbents have some notion of how likely it is they will win the next election. If they think they will win, they hold elections. If they think they will lose, they do not. If these assumptions are correct, then the observed sample of regimes that hold regular elections is biased in favor of 'democracies,' that is, regimes that look like democracies in the sense that they permit contestation and fill offices by elections, yet are not democracies in the sense that the opposition has a chance to assume office as a result of elections."[23]

Przeworski's claim that such leaders want to be "admired and adored" might seem fanciful but, as the details of a September 6, 2005, state dinner with former U.S. president Bill Clinton illustrate, this claim is spot on in the Kazakh case. For most of the guests attending the dinner in Kazakhstan's capital Astana, the goal of the evening was economic gain. Nazarbaev, in contrast to his guests, was the only one at the table not seeking money. Rather, what he wanted was prestige and respect—more specifically, Clinton's support for Kazakhstan's bid to chair the OSCE. The state-run newspaper *Kazakhstanskaia pravda* captured this aspect of the dinner well:

> Bill Clinton summarized the commonly-held position of the American politi-cal elite, "I am strongly impressed by the pace of Kazakhstan's economic growth. We can all see the fruits of your economic reforms. I think your country is ready for this [OSCE] mission.

Addressing Nursultan Nazarbaev and, at the same time, making his views clear to the international community, Clinton concluded: "Kazakhstan's time has come."[24]

What the *Kazakhstanskaia pravda* article did not mention, though, was that accompanying Clinton to the dinner was the Canadian businessman Frank Giustra. Less than a week after the dinner Giustra signed an agreement with the state-run company Kazatomprom. The deal granted Giustra control over several lucrative uranium-mining ventures. As for Clinton, a few months after the Kazakh dinner, his charitable foundation received a $31.3 million donation from Giustra.[25]

Clinton, along with the broader international community, has misread Nazarbaev. Kazakhstan now chairs the OSCE, but the time for Kazakh democracy has not come. Kazakhstan's citizens are no closer to Krol's vision of a "strong, independent and democratic Kazakhstan that is a leader and anchor of stability in the region" than they were before the question of the OSCE chairmanship first emerged. In one key respect—societal activism—Kazakh citizens may be further away from this vision of a democratic Kazakhstan than they were at the time of the Soviet collapse. For this they have Nazarbaev's effective continuation of the Soviet socialist contract to thank. Nazarbaev is now wealthy beyond measure, and because of his immense personal wealth, he feels free to use state resources to achieve goals beyond personal enrichment. He has created a sovereign wealth fund to spur employment and economic growth, and he has invested considerable government resources into improving Kazakhstan's health, education, and social welfare infrastructures. Lastly, as Nazarbaev's bid to chair the OSCE illustrates, he has also invested state resources to burnish his own as well as the Kazakh national image.

In addition to Kazakhstan's growing stature abroad, Nazarbaev's investments have created among Kazakhs a real sense that their standard of living is considerably better than that of other Central Asians. As figure 5.1 illustrates, Kazakh gross domestic product (GDP) per capita has expanded since the early 1990s to the point where it is now more than four times greater than GDP per capita in Uzbekistan and Kyrgyzstan. This economic growth is not disproportionately concentrated at upper income levels. Gini coefficients for Kazakhstan, Kyrgyzstan, and Uzbekistan are nearly identical (the Kazakh and Uzbek Gini coefficients in 2002 were thirty-five, while the Kyrgyz coefficient was thirty-two).[26]

Moreover, as figure 5.2 illustrates, not only do average Kazakh income levels compare favorably to Kyrgyz and Uzbek income levels, Kazakh GDP per

Figure 5.1. GDP per Capita (Purchasing Power Parity) in Kazakhstan, Uzbekistan, and Kyrgyzstan

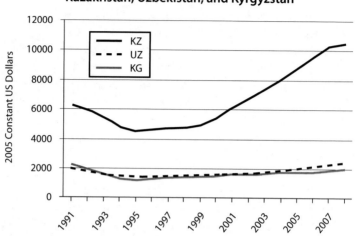

Source: World Bank World Development Indicators, available at http://data.worldbank.org/ data-catalog/world-development-indicators.

capita also compares favorably to mean income levels in the broader post-Soviet context.

Where Kazakhs at the individual level do exhibit lower scores than their Uzbek and Kyrgyz counterparts, curiously, is in areas of community association-alism (figure 5.3). Thus, although Kazakhs' economic means may be four times greater than the wealth of their neighbors, my colleagues and I found in our 2008 surveys that Uzbeks and Kyrgyz citizens are twice as likely to donate money or time to voluntary and community-based organizations.

This finding parallels the research conducted on civic associationalism in other resource-rich states. As the political scientist Kiren Chaudhry has observed in the case of Middle Eastern states, executives with easy access to oil rents can "ameliorate political conflict by directly distributing resources through gifts, sub-sidies, loans, and state contracts," thereby mitigating the draw to independent community based activism while at the same time encouraging the rise of a new class of "bureaucratic and private elites with strong links to the state."[27] This dy-namic is readily acknowledged by Kazakh elites who are closely affiliated with the state as well as by the handful of community activists who have attempted to maintain independence from Nazarbaev's influence. For example, Roza Akyl-bekova, the director of the Information and Education Center at Evgeny Zhovtis's Kazakh International Bureau for Human Rights, has noted that most Kazakh NGOs are actually "progovernmental and depend on the state for funding . . .

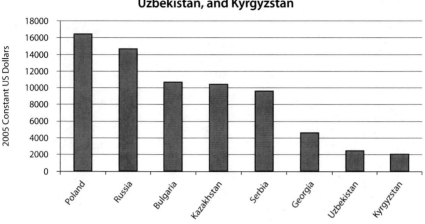

Figure 5.2. GDP per Capita (Purchasing Power Parity) in Poland, Russia, Bulgaria, Kazakhstan, Serbia, Georgia, Uzbekistan, and Kyrgyzstan

Source: World Bank World Development Indicators, available at http://data.worldbank.org/ data-catalog/world-development-indicators.

these NGOs do not even want to associate with us because they fear that if they do, the state will cut off their oxygen."[28] As for why Kazakh society tolerates this, an activist with the opposition party Democratic Choice of Kazakhstan has explained: "Nazarbaev rules like the Sultan of Brunei. He takes a portion of the profits from each barrel of oil and distributes it to the people of Kazakhstan. We're a country with a vast territory and with vast resources. Yet we have only fifteen million people—a whole country whose population is equal to that of Moscow. You do what Nazarbaev does and the people will carry you in their hands . . . you'll be in power for the rest of your life."[29]

Petr Svoik, the leader of the opposition Azamat party, has similarly noted that this immense oil wealth has enabled Nazarbaev to maintain in effect the Communist social contract in which people abide authoritarianism because authoritarian rulers continue to deliver economic welfare: "Although we now have a market economy and we are open to the world, in terms of ideology and how the government is run, we continue to think like we're still living in the USSR."[30] As Nazarbaev's own adviser, Ermukhamet Ertisbaev, has explained, Kazakhstan can be best understood as "an authoritarian democracy." In contrast to Karimov, Nazarbaev tolerates a degree of media freedom and opposition, yet "the head of the state has enormous authority compared to the parliament. . . . Nazarbaev is the supreme arbiter . . . he presides over the judicial, executive, and legislative branches . . . he embodies supreme power."[31]

Figure 5.3. Percentage of Respondents Who Donate Time or Money to Voluntary or Community Organization

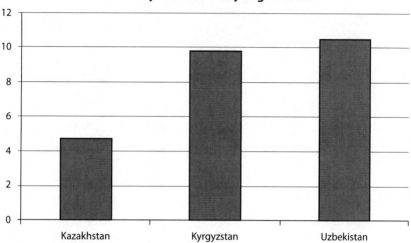

Source: Countrywide surveys of Kyrgyz, Kazakhs, and Uzbeks (1,000 respondents per survey), conducted in June 2008 by the Central Asian polling agency Brif as part of the author's National Science Foundation–funded project "The Effect of the Internet on Central Asian Society."

The Future of Kazakhstan's Authoritarian Democracy

Two decades of Nazarbaev's executive rule—rule that, in contrast to the Kyrgyz executive, has faced no significant elite-based challenges and that, in contrast to the Uzbek executive, has faced no society-based threat—provide strong empirical support for Ertisbaev's assessment. However, two future dynamics that are likely to occur threaten this comparative equanimity the Kazakh executive has thus far enjoyed. First, a collapse in oil prices and a subsequent erosion of the economy could encourage what has been a largely passive Kazakh population toward greater activism and potentially antistate protest. Second, as Nazarbaev ages and the question of presidential succession becomes more pressing, the uncertainty that accompanies presidential succession may encourage a cascade of elite defections from what has proven to be Nazarbaev's remarkably stable ruling coalition.

We have seen similar elite cascades in the past—for example, in the wake of the December 1986 protests in Almaty. Moscow intervened then to restore cohesion among the Kazakh political elite. Were such a cascade to occur in today's post-Soviet environment, the absence of an outside power to reimpose elite order means the nature of Kazakh politics, even if Nazarbaev's chosen successor were to gain control of the executive, would fundamentally change. The nature of this change is difficult to predict. Although the collapse of a united and executive-oriented political elite might encourage liberal reform, post-Soviet scholars' identification of enduring regional, clan, and ethnic identities serve as sobering warnings that the fragmentation of the Kazakh state elite could also lead to a fragmentation of Kazakh society.[32]

Declining Oil Prices

The World Bank describes Kazakhstan's economy as "highly resource dependent" and estimates that in 2008 "minerals, oil and gas, accounted for 73 percent of exports and 39 percent of GDP."[33] The Kazakh national budget is similarly highly resource dependent. How dependent the budget is on oil, however, is not clear; Kazakh budget legislation does not detail government revenues by sector.[34] We do get a rough sense, though, of oil's importance from the Kazakh finance minister Bolat Zhamishev's account for why in 2008 the government receipts were slightly lower than anticipated. Zhamishev explained in February 2009 that total receipts would have been 8 percent rather than only 0.4 percent below projected estimates if it were not for "the important role of the export oil duty in boosting last year's budget revenues."[35] In other words, the state underestimated by 7.6 percent of the total budget the amount of revenue that would accrue from oil export taxes. Actual oil receipts, one would anticipate, were considerably higher than this windfall equal to 7.6 percent (approximately two billion dollars) of the total Kazakh national budget.

What would have happened if the Kazakh government had not underestimated oil revenues in 2008, and state spending subsequently needed to be slashed 8 percent? Or, even more problematic, what would happen if the price of oil drops below the Brent crude mark of sixty-five dollars per barrel the Kazakh government assumed in constructing the 2010 budget?[36] Collapsing oil prices, as chapter 2 presented in the Soviet case and as the comparative politics literature demonstrates more broadly, can prove devastating for autocratic regimes. If, as Chaudhry has stated, oil rents serve to "ameliorate political conflict," then we would expect the sudden absence of these rents might spark dissent. Such dissent, granted, might not arrive immediately. In the case of the Venezuelan government, as Terry Karl has written, "social spending, subsidized by petrodollars, became the key mechanism for delivering jobs and services to the middle and lower classes (preempting more radical demands for redistribution)."[37] When the price of oil collapsed in the 1980s, the Venezuelan government substituted growing debt for oil to continue generous social spending for nearly a decade. Ultimately, though, this public spending only delayed (and made "more painful and disruptive") the protests that would debilitate Venezuelan politics in the early 1990s.[38]

Currently Nazarbaev is enjoying the polity-pacifying dividends of a strong economy. In our 2008 surveys, for example, 60 percent of Kazakh respondents reported satisfaction with the national government while, in economically struggling Kyrgyzstan, only 43 percent of respondents reported they were satisfied with the national government. That Kazakh citizens might more closely resemble their Kyrgyz and Venezuelan counterparts if Nazarbaev's petrodollars were to vanish suddenly is an outcome worth considering.

Dynasty and the Uncertainty Elite Succession Generates

As the Uzbek case illustrates, social mobilization does not invariably lead to elite instability. The challenges the 1980s oil collapse posed to the Gorbachev government suggest we should not dismiss the collateral political damage a sudden and protracted decline in oil prices could have on the Kazakh government. At the same time, though, there is a much more pressing challenge facing Nazarbaev—the question of leadership succession. In the early to mid-1990s this question of leadership succession did not appear so pressing. Nazarbaev was in his sixties, and it was clear to everyone that his son-in-law, Rakhat Aliev, was next in line to the presidency. Aliev, married to the president's eldest daughter, Dariga Nazarbaeva, held lofty posts in multiple executive branch agencies during his apprenticeship for Kazakhstan's top job: tax police (in the mid-1990s), Kazakh national security committee (from 1999 to 2001), presidential guard (from 2001 to 2002), ambassador to Austria (from 2002 to 2005), foreign ministry (from 2005 to 2007), and for a brief stint in 2007 once again ambassador to Austria. In 2007, though, Aliev suddenly fell from favor. On May 26 he was stripped of all government posts, and by the end of the month the Kazakh government had issued an Interpol request for Aliev's arrest. One month later, and against Aliev's wishes, he and Dariga Nazarbaeva were divorced.

There are several theories for Aliev's spectacular fall. Some attribute his disgrace to his mishandling of the *Borat* affair; serving as Kazakhstan's deputy foreign minister during the *Borat* film release in October 2006, Aliev quipped: "I'd like to invite Cohen [Sacha Baron Cohen, the British comedian who plays Borat] here. . . . He can discover a lot of things. Women drive cars, wine is made of grapes, and Jews are free to go to synagogues."[39] An explanation perhaps closer to the truth is the one Aliev himself gives: "The president ordered his secretary of state, Kanat Saudabaev, and the director of the presidential administration, Bulat

Utemuratov, to Vienna. They demanded I hand over, without compensation, all my media assets. They took my refusal back to Astana. . . . My media outlets are the most popular in Kazakhstan and, in the run up to the August parliamentary elections, Nazarbaev wants to ensure favorable press for his 'Nur Otan' party, he wants to prevent all criticism and any dissenting opinion."[40]

Most revealing of all, though, is the twenty-year jail sentence a Kazakh military court handed Aliev and fifteen others in March 2008. As Amangeldy Shabdarbaev, chairman of the Kazakh national security committee, explained of the sentence: "From interrogations of persons closest to R. Aliyev, it becomes clear that he and A. Musayev [former head of the presidential guard and the Kazakh national security committee] had long ago gotten the idea of acquiring supreme power, and in fact they had begun making preparations for the takeover of power already in 1998–1999, when R. Aliyev headed up the tax committee. And although the purpose of the crime group at the initial stage was the personal enrichment of its organizers, still, as they say, the appetite comes while eating."[41]

Although Aliev and Shabdarbaev may differ on the specifics of Aliev's fall from grace, both accounts nevertheless capture the fundamental dilemma the Kazakh president, or for that matter any aging autocrat, faces. To safeguard his legacy and his family's economic interests, Nazarbaev has groomed a sympathetic successor, yet as the potential successor becomes increasingly empowered, his incentives for turning against his mentor increase. Nazarbaev knows this dynamic well; this was the path he himself pursued in undermining his own mentor, the Kazakh first secretary Dinmukhamed Kunaev, in May 1986. Not only do the potential successor's incentives to defect increase, so too do other elites within the president's ruling coalition begin questioning the payoffs they might receive if they throw their support to someone like Aliev.

An elite's decision to support an insurgent is risky. For example, if a member of Nazarbaev's ruling coalition were to defect and support an insurgent and if this insurgent were to win, there is no guarantee that the insurgent-turned-president would actually reward those who defected from Nazarbaev. For much of Nazarbaev's rule, though, this question of defection likely did not even come up in most elites' minds. Rather, given Nazarbaev's comparative youth in the 1990s and the legacy of a large executive-oriented political elite, most clear-headed Kazakh elites understood that defection would lead to pain, not profit. Figure 5.4 summarizes this logic, the Kazakh defection game, when leadership succession is not an issue.

The insights of the perestroika legacy model have been borne out; ruling coalition elites constituting Nazarbaev's ruling coalition have not defected in mass numbers because before the mid-2000s, the question of executive turnover was

Figure 5.4. Central Asian Defection Game—Kazakh Case
(Assuming Elite Unity and Executive Stability)

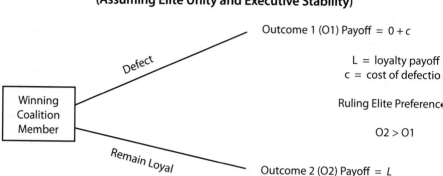

Outcome 1 (O1) Payoff $= 0 + c$

L = loyalty payoff
c = cost of defectio

Ruling Elite Preferenc

$O2 > O1$

Winning Coalition Member

Defect

Remain Loyal

Outcome 2 (O2) Payoff $= L$

Source: Author's rendering.

not an issue. Those elites who did defect were not able to rally others to their cause. Instead, in return for their defections, these elites lost their privileged positions in government and in a few cases were repressed. In short, Nazarbaev's ruling coalition members, when considering the choice of loyalty versus defection, have chosen the loyalty payoff (represented as L in the figures 5.4 and 5.5) rather than the defection payoff (represented as $0 + c$, the executive-imposed cost of defection).

Nazarbaev is now entering his seventies and, as reluctant as he may be to loosen his grip on the presidency, the question of who will be the next president is increasingly pressing. This eventuality of elite succession fundamentally changes elite calculations; Nazarbaev's ruling coalition members must now make decisions under conditions of imperfect information. Ruling elites must begin to evaluate how likely it is that the president will effect a successful transfer of power to a chosen successor or, alternatively, how likely someone like Aliev might prove successful in taking power from the president before the president is ready to cede authority. Is the probability of Nazarbaev effecting a successful transition, denoted as p in figure 5.5, considerably high, say 0.80 or 80 percent? Or is the probability of a successful transition low, say 0.40 or 40 percent, thereby making the likelihood of failure, denoted as $(1-p)$, 0.60 or 60 percent? This is the changing and uncertain reality in which Kazakh elites must now operate. As a review of the payoff structures of this new elite defection game illustrates, the potential implications this changing reality may have on the future of Kazakh politics are profound.

Looking only at the outcomes, an initial preference ordering can be readily discerned. Members of Nazarbaev's current winning coalition least prefer out-

Figure 5.5. Central Asian Defection Game—Kazakh Case
(Executive Succession Uncertainty)

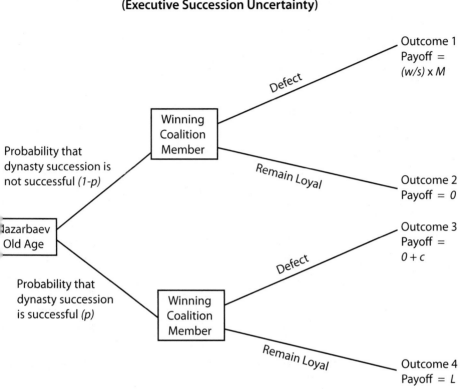

w = size of winning coalition (the Kazakh executive's ruling coalition)

s = size of "selectorate" (the total body of political elites from which the executive can constitute his ruling coalition)

w/s = probability that any given political elite will be a member of the executive's winning coalition

M = maximum payoff to members of the challenger's winning coalition

c = cost of defection when dynasty succession is successful

L = loyalty payoff when dynasty succession is successful

p = probability that dynasty succession is successful

$(1-p)$ = probability that dynasty succession is not successful

Source: Author's rendering. See chapter 1 for a discussion of w, s, w/s and the treatment of the selectorate model by Bruce Bueno de Mesquita, James D. Morrow, Randolph M. Siverson, and Alastair Smith, "Political Institutions, Policy Choice, and the Survival of Leaders," *British Journal of Political Science* 32, no. 4 (October 2002): 559–90.

Table 5.1. Central Asian Defection Outcomes and Associated Payoffs Given Executive Succession Uncertainty

Outcome	Description	Payoff
1	Dynasty not successful and defect from Nazarbaev	$(1-p) \times [(w/s) \times M]$
2	Dynasty not successful and remain loyal to Nazarbaev	$(1-p) \times 0$
3	Dynasty successful and defect from Nazarbaev	$p \times c$
4	Dynasty successful and remain loyal to Nazarbaev	$p \times L$

come three—that is, an outcome where they defect, wrongly anticipating dynastic succession will fail. Should elites defect in this case, not only will they lose the loyalty payoff that comes from supporting the Nazarbaev family, they also face potential costs for defecting—for example, retaliatory coercion from Nazarbaev's chosen successor. The second least preferred outcome is two—that is, wrongly anticipating dynastic succession when in fact dynastic succession fails. Here elites lose the reward they might have received had they shifted their support to the successful challenger. Elites in this case likely do not suffer coercion for failing to support the challenger. Lastly, although elite's ranking of outcome one relative to outcome four is not immediately apparent, it is clear that both of these outcomes—defection when dynastic rule fails and loyalty when dynastic rule is successful—are preferable to outcomes two and three.

Although the rank ordering of preferred outcomes is relatively straightforward, the process of elite strategic choice under conditions of incomplete information is considerably more complicated. A member of Nazarbaev's current ruling coalition thus must assess the likelihood of successful dynastic succession, p. He must determine the likelihood that he will be a member of a challenger's ruling coalition (w / s) should dynastic succession fail $(1-p)$. He then must explore what the maximum payoff (M) is for elites who have the good fortune of being in the challenger's winning coalition should Nazarbaev's attempt at dynastic rule fail. Lastly, this elite must determine what the actual cost of defection (c) might be in the event he defects, wrongly anticipating dynastic succession will fail. Table 5.1 summarizes these calculations.

Several insights can be drawn from these payoffs. First, if elites perceive dynastic succession as probable—that is, if p is close to 1.0 or 100 percent—the

Formula 5.1

Expected Payoff (Loyalty)	>	Expected Payoff (Defection)
$p \times L + (1-p) \times 0$	>	$p \times c + (1-p) \times [(w/s) \times M]$

actual payoffs (L) that Nazarbaev needs to extend to maintain the loyalty of his current ruling coalition are low. Nazarbaev merely needs to ensure that outcome four ($p \times L$) is greater than outcome one ($[1-p] \times [(w/s) \times M]$). This situation of assured dynastic succession in many respects resembles the status quo of Kazakh politics since the Soviet collapse. Should Kazakh elites begin to perceive managed succession as less probable (p), however, Nazarbaev can attempt to limit elite disloyalty through a combination of two methods. First, he can attempt to offset elite doubts—and thereby hope to encourage elite loyalty—by increasing payoffs (L) to current ruling coalition members. Second, Nazarbaev can increase the costs (c) of defection to encourage elite loyalty. Both strategies, taken together, help Nazarbaev in that they increase elites' expected payoffs for loyalty and decrease expected payoffs for defection with the ultimate goal of ensuring that the elites' expected loyalty payoff is greater than their expected defection payoff.

This theoretical analysis lays bare the increased likelihood of coercion under conditions of growing dynastic uncertainty. This is an eventuality to which, problematically, Kazakhstan's foreign partners have paid little attention. Instead, the international community has extended Nazarbaev the benefit of the doubt, not to mention the chairmanship of the OSCE, at exactly the time that monitoring organizations like the OSCE should be increasing pressure on the Kazakh executive to observe human rights, civil liberties, and free elections. Evgeny Zhovtis, who joined Ambassador Krol in the May 2009 congressional hearing on Kazakhstan's bid to chair the OSCE, explained why this need for additional international pressure was necessary. Within the Kazakh government, Zhovtis lamented, there exist no checks on executive authority: "The current parliament and the local representative power bodies consist almost by 100 percent of the representatives of only one party, Nur Otan, [whose] functioning methods and propaganda scope reminds one more and more of the Communist Party of the Soviet Union."[42]

Kazakh ambassador Erlan Idrissov, who sat next to Zhovtis during the May 2009 hearing, demurred and assured that the Kazakh government would deliver on Foreign Minister Marat Tazhin's 2007 pledge to reform and democratize the Kazakh political system and to respect media freedoms. The Kazakh government still has not delivered on these commitments, yet in an indicator of its growing willingness to coerce, the government has delivered Zhovtis, the Nazarbaev regime's most vocal and internationally prominent critic, to jail. In September 2009, four months after he informed congressmen at a U.S. Helsinki Commission hearing that Kazakhstan was unfit to hold the chairmanship of the OSCE, a Kazakh court sentenced Zhovtis to four years in prison for vehicular manslaughter.

Through a recent and decidedly undemocratic tactic, Nazarbaev might obviate the need for further imprisonments and coercion. Here his power-hungry and now estranged son-in-law, Rakhat Aliev, may have taught the Kazakh president a valuable lesson. Nazarbaev has two sons-in-law, a nephew, and a grandson who all can potentially fill the new role of heir-apparent. To ensure their aspirations and their elite-followings do not prematurely eclipse his own authority, Nazarbaev has begun laying the groundwork for his own continued influence once he formally relinquishes the presidency. In May 2010 the Kazakh parliament approved a law that would grant Nazarbaev a new status: "leader of the nation." This law proposes that future presidents be required to "secure the agreement of the first president when developing new initiatives that shape Kazakh domestic and foreign policy."[43] Nazarbaev's political adviser, Ermukhamet Ertisbaev, acknowledged there was a chance that the parliamentary bill could be vetoed, although he assured that he would strongly advise Nazarbaev against such an action: "The president enjoys colossal authority among the Majlis [lower house] and Senate [upper house] deputies. If he vetoes this bill, he will set the entire parliament against him. They see Nazarbayev as the main guarantor of the country's stable and sustainable growth until at least 2020."[44]

Ertisbaev's comments may elicit a cynical chuckle; one cannot fault the presidential adviser, though, for not having a shrewd understanding of politics and of the destabilizing effects an unmanaged executive succession could have on the Kazakh polity. For a country with as many prominent identity-based divides as Kazakhstan has, it is remarkable that none of these divides has led to social conflict nor the blatant distribution of state resources in favor of one or another region, clan, or ethnicity. A central reason why such conflict and favoritism likely have not occurred is Nazarbaev's perestroika legacy, his inheritance of a united political elite, and the loyalty to the executive this institutional legacy engenders. To the degree that Nazarbaev, through clever legislative design, can reduce the uncertainty that otherwise would accompany the question of dynastic succession, the stability that Ertisbaev describes may well persist. If, however, Nazarbaev's legislative gambit fails and clear mechanisms for the transfer of executive power are not established, then the growing uncertainty of presidential succession may well lead to the fragmentation of Kazakhstan's political elite along regional, clan, and ethnic lines.[45]

Conclusion

We began with the following questions: Why do Central Asian states with similar pasts exhibit dissimilar post-Soviet outcomes? Why is Uzbek politics violent? Why is Kyrgyz politics chaotic? Why, in contrast, is the only real threat to enduring Kazakh stability the question of elite succession and the Nazarbaev dynasty? The answers to these questions lie as much in Moscow as they do in Astana, Bishkek, or Tashkent. In the second half of the 1980s Mikhail Gorbachev and the Central Communist Party leadership intervened in Kazakhstan and Uzbekistan to restore political order in the wake of violent mass protests. Gorbachev intervened in Kazakhstan to restore order after the December 1986 mass uprising against the appointment of an ethnic Russian to the republic's top administrative post. Moscow intervened again in June 1989, when ethnic riots in Uzbekistan's Fergana Valley undermined First Secretary Rafik Nishanov's authority. Gorbachev did not intervene in June 1990, however, when deadly ethnic riots on the Kyrgyz side of the Fergana Valley eroded First Secretary Absamat Masaliev's legitimacy and led to the fragmentation of the Kyrgyz political elite.

In February 1990, in an effort to sideline establishment elites opposing perestroika reforms, Gorbachev decreed an end to the Communist Party's monopoly hold on power. His goal was to revitalize the party and eliminate dead wood through political competition. In the Kyrgyz case competition eliminated Masaliev and with him the elite unity that once characterized the Kyrgyz polity. Whereas Islam Karimov and Nursultan Nazarbaev carried their united parties—

albeit under new names—into the post-Soviet period, the new and narrowly elected Kyrgyz executive, Askar Akaev, struggled to solidify authority while balancing the competing interests of Kyrgyzstan's now fragmented political elite. Through the use of formal modeling, I demonstrated how we could have anticipated even in 1991 that these diverging perestroika-era legacies of elite rule would lead to the chaos, violence, and dynasty we now see throughout Central Asia.

My airplane analogy serves as shorthand for this formal model. The Kyrgyz executive, flying a small Cessna, must remain attentive to the demands of the few influential elite riding in the passenger cabin. Should the Kyrgyz executive expropriate rather than share state wealth, this narrow elite can readily coordinate a mutiny. Coordinated collective action is a considerably more risky proposition in Uzbekistan and Kazakhstan. Those who are lucky enough to find themselves in Karimov's and Nazarbaev's ruling coalition are unlikely to revolt because these elites understand that the likelihood they will find themselves back in the inner circle of the next leader is low. A small number of Karimov's or Nazarbaev's ruling coalition members may occasionally defect. Given the hundreds of party members in both executives' 747 passenger cabins, however, the ability of elites to coordinate a cascade of defection is limited. Karimov and Nazarbaev in turn, because they know ruling-coalition elites are unlikely to defect, are considerably more free than their Kyrgyz counterpart to use state wealth as they desire—for personal enrichment, for building coercive capacity, for investing in public goods, or for bids to advance their international prestige.

Diverging perestroika legacies and formal modeling, although they help us understand why Kyrgyz politics is chaotic and Uzbek and Kazakh politics is stable, do not explain variation in the degrees of repression we see in Uzbekistan and Kazakhstan. Nor can diverging perestroika legacies and formal modeling alone tell us why Kyrgyzstan's first president, Askar Akaev, was able to hold power for fifteen years while his successor, Kurmanbek Bakiev, held power for only five years. The answer to the first question can be found in Uzbekistan's and Kazakhstan's differing economies and diverging abilities to provide public goods. Kazakhstan's oil wealth and the stunning amount of foreign direct investment this wealth attracts generates real economic growth, which allows Nazarbaev to maintain the social contract that long enabled his Soviet predecessors to secure autocratic rule with little risk of social dissent. Uzbekistan's wealth is considerably more constrained. Although Karimov has sufficient resources to fund effective institutions of repression and to support his daughter's increasingly lavish lifestyle, the Uzbek president has little left over to meet even the most basic social welfare needs of the population. Other institutions, most notably local Muslim charities and businesses, have stepped in to provide social services that the Uzbek state cannot deliver. As we have seen most prominently in the protests in Namangan and Andijan, the local legitimacy and authority the leaders of these charities and businesses command threatens the central Uzbek state. Karimov responds to this threat by repressing both Muslim elites and their supporters.

The answer to the second question, to Akaev's considerably longer tenure in office than Bakiev's, can be found in the shifting nature of economic resources available to the Kyrgyz executive. Before 2001 the lion's share of resources available to the Kyrgyz executive came from international economic and political reform aid. This aid is considerably more difficult for the Kyrgyz executive to expropriate than, for example, the oil rents Nazarbaev enjoys. The best Akaev could do was to appoint Kyrgyz elites as directors to the target organizations of this diffuse reform aid—to differing government ministries and to quasi nongovernmental organizations. In short, the nature of reform aid forced Akaev to share the wealth among Kyrgyzstan's narrow and fragmented political elite. Paradoxically, economic and political reform aid helped Akaev maintain authoritarian rule. The post-9/11 arrival of readily exploitable financial flows in the form of executive-controlled fuel contracts for the U.S. air base at Manas, in contrast, led to first Akaev's and later Bakiev's outright expropriation of state wealth. As we would expect from the perestroika legacy model, in both cases Kyrgyzstan's narrow political elite temporarily put aside their differences and overthrew presidents who were stealing rather than sharing state wealth.

How far might these findings on Kazakh dynasty, Kyrgyz chaos, and Uzbek violence travel beyond the Central Asian cases? The causal arguments offered here, though in large part inductively derived from comparative analysis of these three countries, can be readily explored and tested beyond the borders of Central Asia and the former Soviet Union. My analysis has both built on and challenged three fields within the comparative politics literature. First, and most directly, I have engaged the literature on postcolonial institutionalism and offered the following hypothesis:

Hypothesis 1: Newly independent states that inherit large executive-oriented political parties from colonial rule will exhibit greater executive stability than newly independent states that inherit a small and fractured political elite.

Second, I have engaged the rentier state literature and argued that the degree as well as the nature of economic resources available to an executive shapes the nature of autocratic rule. More specifically, building on insights from the Kyrgyz case, I offered my second hypothesis:

Hypothesis 2: The diffuse nature of foreign aid—that is, the inability of executives to assert monopoly control over foreign aid inflows—paradoxically forces what otherwise would be vulnerable autocrats to share state wealth with the broader political elite. This sharing of state wealth in turn increases the likelihood that postcolonial executives will maintain a durable winning coalition and, consequentially, their hold on power.

Building on the Uzbek and Kazakh comparison, I offered my third hypothesis:

Hypothesis 3: Even in cases where postcolonial presidents have inherited large executive-oriented political parties, the degree of available state wealth has pronounced effects on state-society relations. Governments with middling economic resources, such as Uzbekistan, will see their presence erode in the regions as locally based religious and community organizations step in to provide public goods that the economically strapped postcolonial state cannot. In resource-rich states, such as Kazakhstan, postcolonial central governments can continue providing public goods and, as a result, can avoid the dilemma of having to choose between de facto decentralization or violent repression of increasingly influential religious and community organizations in the regions.

Lastly, my work intersects with the comparative politics literature on Islam and state-society relations. Here I have suggested that movements that are frequently identified in the literature as "political Islam" are in fact little different from other locally based community self-help organizations except for the fact that Islamic charities are forcibly politicized by insecure autocrats. Not all autocrats, importantly though, perceive the need or have the wherewithal to politicize—and repress—Islamic charities. Rather, the Uzbek case suggests the following hypothesis:

Hypothesis 4: Islam-centered state-society conflicts are most likely to emerge in postcolonial environments where presidents inherit large executive-oriented political parties yet do not inherit economic resources sufficient to provide robust public goods and thereby preclude local communities' gravitation to Islamic charities.

In short, although my particular region of focus has been Central Asia, it is my hope that the questions I have addressed and the causal arguments I have offered throughout this book can inform the broader comparative political science literature on postcolonial autocracy as well as policies informed by this broader comparative politics literature.

I must confess I did not begin this book with the intent of providing policy advice. As the analysis suggests, however, policy assessments are unavoidable given that Central Asia's foreign partners have had a role in diverging Kazakh, Kyrgyz, and Uzbek political outcomes. Most prominently, the United States, however inadvertently, has had a hand in the uprisings that led to the collapse of two Kyrgyz governments. The United States air base and the lucrative fuel contracts that arrived with this base transformed the Kyrgyz executive from a distributor of diffuse foreign aid to an expropriator of concentrated economic rents. This transformation of executive-elite relations led, in short order, to the 2005 uprising that ousted Akaev and to the 2010 uprising that unseated Bakiev. Unmanaged political chaos does not advance Washington's goal of maintaining its important air base in Kyrgyzstan. More important, unmanaged political chaos is not in Kyrgyz citizens' interests. This latter fact alone is sufficient cause to prompt a rethinking of how the United States structures base and fuel payments; the coincidence of Washington's geopolitical interests and Kyrgyz citizens' interests only adds to the urgency for rethinking how the U.S. government compensates international partners for the provision of critically important services—particularly international partners with elite institutions as fragile as Kyrgyzstan's.

More broadly, though, these three Central Asian cases suggest we pause and reevaluate the interlinked academic and policy discussions on post-Soviet transitions. These discussions have as their starting point an assumption that political change is not only possible, but that such change is probable. What is particularly striking about the Central Asian cases, however, is that although Kazakhstan, Kyrgyzstan, and Uzbekistan as a group exhibit diverging post-Soviet outcomes, at the individual country level they are remarkably stable. Kyrgyz politics, though chaotic, has been consistently chaotic since 1990. Likewise, Uzbek politics has been consistently violent, and Kazakh politics consistently autocratic yet comparatively benign. These are not countries in transition, but rather polities in stasis. Despite this reality, much of the academic literature and most governance-related foreign aid programs targeting Central Asia has focused on pathways to change—more specifically, to democratic change. Normatively this is an admirable goal. Analytically and empirically, however, this goal is divorced from post-Soviet Central Asian reality.

Consider, for example, the efforts of U.S. Congress–funded National Democratic Institute (NDI) and the International Republican Institute (IRI). Much of the work of these party institutes has been devoted to assisting Central Asian elites craft political parties that have coherent platforms and wide membership bases. This strategy has met with little if any success. In Kazakhstan and Uzbekistan this lack of success is, in part, due to the Karimov and Nazarbaev governments' severe restrictions on party aid. As the Kyrgyz case suggests, however, this lack of success is also due to the party institutes' overlooking of the incentive structures that define post-Soviet Central Asian patronage. These incentive structures are not conducive to the formation of political parties with coherent platforms and wide membership bases. In the Kyrgyz case the depersonalization of political parties would force what is now a narrow group of individuals rotating in and out of power to share state wealth with a broader political constituency. As for the Uzbek and Kazakh cases, the collective action costs entailed in forming such broad and depersonalized parties far outweigh the benefits of cooperating with the Karimov and Nazarbaev regimes.

If not political party promotion, what other activities might groups like NDI and IRI or, for that matter, any international aid organization pursue? First, the preceding analysis suggests that academics, policy makers, and the directors of international organizations operating in Central Asia recognize and take seriously country-level variations in the nature of authoritarian rule. This is not an argument in favor of particularism and against theory-driven policy. Rather, one can begin with a broadly deductive theory about how elites in authoritarian environments make decisions and then, based on this deductive model, investigate how differing country-level institutional, economic, and cultural constraints further shape political behavior. This approach allows social scientists and policy makers to identify pressure points—areas where sudden changes in structural constraints might lead to changes in the broader polity. Not all pressure points, admittedly, can be anticipated. An event similar to the polity-changing effects Gorbachev's end of Communist Party monopoly rule had on Kyrgyz elite politics, for example, would be hard to predict.

Much easier for policy makers to anticipate, though, are the likely consequences of decisions their own governments might make. For example, policy makers could anticipate, ex ante, the destabilizing effects the sudden injection of rents from fuel contracts would have on Kyrgyz politics. Similarly, a sober review of the incentives that define Kazakh elite politics may well have dampened hopes that extending Nazarbaev's chairmanship of the Organization for Security and Cooperation in Europe (OSCE) might somehow lead to Kazakh political reform. Lastly, and perhaps most difficult to acknowledge, Western European and American policy makers might have anticipated how publicly identifying and actively engaging the Uzbek government as a partner in the fight against militant Islam might provide an air of legitimacy for President Karimov in his unwavering policy of repressing Islamic charities and business elites he perceives as threatening to his continued autocratic rule.

Equally important for policy makers, and even more important for Central Asians themselves, is to anticipate how high-probability future developments may fundamentally reshape authoritarian rule. In Kyrgyzstan the most immediate of these eventualities is the end to easily exploitable rents from the Manas air base. These rents might end sooner rather than later if the U.S. fuel payments are restructured in a way that precludes rents directly accruing to the Kyrgyz executive. These rents certainly will disappear once the U.S. government winds down operations in Afghanistan and vacates Manas. If other foreign governments do not replace the funds the U.S. government withdraws, the possibility for substantive and positive political change in Kyrgyzstan exists. Here the experience of the 1990s is instructive; foreign aid that cannot be readily captured by the executive, although it might not yield democratic reform, can limit the extent of Kyrgyzstan's political chaos.

Kazakhstan's two most likely pressure points are a sudden drop in the price of oil and the unavoidable question of leadership succession. A rapid drop in oil prices could void the social contract that Nazarbaev has effectively maintained since the Soviet collapse. Although the state's inability to deliver the degree of public goods and economic growth it has for the past two decades might not lead to instability among the Kazakh political elite, Nazarbaev's inability to maintain the social contract would encourage Kazakhs to mobilize to provide the public goods the central government suddenly could not. This mobilization, as we have seen in Uzbekistan, can lead to erosion of peaceful state-society relations. Far more certain than a possible collapse in oil prices is the unavoidable question of leadership succession. Growing uncertainty over who will replace Nazarbaev can alter how Kazakh elites calculate the costs and rewards of loyalty to and defection from Nazarbaev's ruling coalition. Absent the establishment of clear rules— and these need not be democratic rules—of leadership succession, Kazakh elites will be tempted to shift their loyalty to any number of potential aspirants to the Kazakh presidency. Nazarbaev appears to be increasingly aware of these changing cost calculations. The Kazakh parliament's May 2010 vote to grant Nazarbaev what in effect are veto powers for life if and when he steps down both dampens the incentives of potential successors to prematurely wrest power from Nazarbaev and reduces the likelihood that Kazakh elites will see it in their interest to defect from his ruling coalition.

Uzbek president Karimov faces the same challenge of leadership succession. Complicating matters, he must deal with the added challenge of de facto decentralization. The Uzbek government's inability to provide social welfare has given rise to a parallel system of elite authority in the regions. Although Karimov's appointees continue to occupy formal institutions of power, everyday Uzbeks more and more are looking to local economic elites—and often these are Muslim businessmen—to provide the collective goods the Karimov government cannot provide. Were Karimov content to cede legitimacy and authority to these local elites, he likely could maintain his hold on power, albeit an ever more circumscribed power. His unwavering determination to repress these Muslim elites, however, and the growing political uncertainty engendered by the pressing question of leadership succession, suggests that the stability that has characterized Uzbek politics since the early 1990s could rapidly evaporate.

Exploration of all these pressure points illustrates that further change is possible in Central Asia. None of these pressure points in and of themselves suggests that the direction of this change will be away from authoritarianism and toward democracy. This does not mean that Kazakh, Kyrgyz, and Uzbek reform activists and international partners should close shop and leave Central Asia to the whims of autocrats. It does mean, though, that activists and policy makers would do well to reassess what is possible given the incentive structures and institutional constraints that drive post-Soviet Central Asian patronage politics. One area where immediate action is possible is in crafting policies that raise the costs and thereby reduce the incentives executives have for using coercion. The 2010s is a good time for crafting such policies. Providing support to Kyrgyz NGOs, for example, that work to expose corruption and coercion of the Bakiev regime can encourage Kyrgyzstan's new leaders to consider how their own stint in power will be viewed following the next round of political upheaval.

As for Karimov and Nazarbaev, leaders who still have an opportunity to reshape their political legacies, Uzbek and Kazakh activists can redouble efforts to expose state repression and corruption. The international community, rather than rewarding Karimov and Nazarbaev with unmerited state visits and honorary posts to international organizations, can support the courageous efforts of Uzbek and Kazakh activists by punishing executive abuses of power with unwavering sanctions. The sooner the international community recognizes that promoting democracy while rewarding autocrats is a fantasy, the sooner we can begin providing real assistance to Central Asian activists who risk their lives in the hope of a better future.

Notes

Introduction

1. The online news source Fergana.news is at http://enews.fergananews.com/.

2. Karen L. Remmer, "Neopatrimonialism: The Politics of Military Rule in Chile, 1973–1987," *Comparative Politics* 21, no. 2 (January 1989): 149–70, 165.

3. Stephen Kotkin, "Trashcanistan: A Tour through the Wreckage of the Soviet Empire," *New Republic,* April 15, 2002, 26–38.

4. The term "color revolution," of course, is a misnomer. The only place where the Georgian, Kyrgyz, and Ukrainian color revolutions continue to exist are in the pages of Western political science journals. What Karimov most feared in May 2005 was not democratization, but rather that some other autocrat would replace him.

5. As quoted in Daniel Kimmage, "Uzbekistan: One Witness's Testimony Forces Courtroom Collision," *Radio Free Europe / Radio Liberty*, October 23, 2005.

6. Saipov informed me, during my June 2007 visit to Osh, that plainclothes agents were constantly following him. He was sober about the risks he was assuming but hopeful that his links with the West might provide some measure of protection.

7. "Kulibayev to Chair Boards of Directors in Three National Companies," *Kazakh Oil & Gas Weekly*, May 25, 2009.

8. Anna Mikhailova, Daniel Foggo, and Steven Swinford, "Prince Andrew, His £15m Home, and the Kazakhstan Connection," *Sunday Times*, July 27, 2008; and Geoffrey Levy and Richard Kay, "The Duke, the Dame, and the Dictator," *Daily Mail*, March 14, 2009.

9. Daniel Kaufmann, Aart Kraay, and Massimo Mastruzzi, "Governance Matters VII: Aggregate and Individual Governance Indicators, 1996–2007," *World Bank Policy Research Working Paper*, No. 4654 (June 2008).

10. WGI measures, which the World Bank has been aggregating since 1996, are standardized with a sample mean (WGI covered 212 countries in 2008) of 0 and a standard deviation of 1. Thus, for example, Uzbekistan, which scored −1.9 in 2008, is nearly 2 standard deviations below the average "voice and accountability" score of all countries surveyed in 2008. In other words, 98

percent of all other states surveyed in 2008 allowed more freedoms to their citizens than did the Uzbek government.

11. Kaufmann, Kraay, and Mastruzzi, "Governance Matters VII."

12. Andre Grabot, "3,500 Demonstrate against Kazakh President," Agence France Presse, December 8, 1996.

13. "Uzbekistan: Thousands Protest Trade Restrictions at Uzbek Market," Radio Free Europe / Radio Liberty, November 2, 2004.

14. Michael Bratton and Nicholas Van de Walle, "Neopatrimonial Regimes and Political Transitions in Africa," World Politics 46, no. 4 (July 1994): 453–89, 458.

15. William Reno, "Congo: From State Collapse to 'Absolutism,' to State Failure," Third World Quarterly 27, no. 1 (2006): 43–56, 51.

16. H. E. Chehabi and Juan José Linz, Sultanistic Regimes (Baltimore, Md.: Johns Hopkins University Press, 1998), 7.

17. Ibid., 46.

18. Bratton and Van de Walle, "Neopatrimonial Regimes and Political Transitions in Africa," 487.

19. Karimov was quick to differentiate himself from his predecessor by calling for a "resurrection of Uzbek traditions." D. Makarov, "Chem vyshe kreslo, tem dal'she ot liudei. Islam Karimov: 'Tverdyi' poriadok pri polnoi ekonomicheskoi svobode," Argumenty i fakty, April 11, 1991; accessed via Eastview Universal Database of Russian Language Newspapers.

20. The airplane metaphor first appeared in my April 2010 op-ed; see Eric McGlinchey, "Running in Circles in Kyrgyzstan," New York Times, April 10, 2010.

21. By "predatory states" I have in mind the historian Peter Evans's definition: those that "extract at the expense of society . . . [and] lack the ability to prevent individual incumbents from pursuing their own goals"; see Peter B. Evans, Embedded Autonomy (Princeton: Princeton University Press, 1995), 12.

22. "The Kazakh Government Is Lacking Funds to Raise Wages of Social Workers and State Officials on January 1," Kazakhstan General Newswire, October 19, 2009.

23. "Kyrgyz Teachers Sue Government over Debt for Long Service," Kyrgyz Channel 5 TV / BBC Monitoring, February 6, 2008.

24. The IFES 1996 Kyrgyz survey included 1,494 respondents. The IFES 1996 Kazakh survey included 1,500 respondents. The IFES 1996 Uzbek survey included 1,830 respondents. Our 2008 surveys included 1,000 respondents each for Kyrgyzstan, Kazakhstan, and Uzbekistan. IFES, "Public Opinion in Kyrgyzstan, 1996" (April 1997), available at http://www.ifes.org/Content/Publications/Survey/1997/Public-Opinion-in-Kyrgyzstan-1996.aspx; IFES, "Public Opinion in Kazakhstan, 1996" (April 1997), available at http://www.ifes.org/Content/Publications/Survey/1997/Public-Opinion-in-Kazakhstan-1996.aspx; and IFES, "Public Opinion in Uzbekistan, 1996" (January 1997), available at http://www.ifes.org/Content/Publications/Survey/1997/Public-Opinion-in-Uzbekistan-1996.aspx.

25. "Five-hour Power Outage a Day Planned in Kyrgyzstan from 1 October," AKIpress.com, September 29, 2009.

1. A Post-transitions Research Agenda for the Study of Authoritarianism

1. U.S. Senator Tom Coburn, "Coburn Amendment 2631—Prohibits the National Science Foundation from Wasting Federal Research Funding on Political Science Projects," 2009, available online at http://thomas.loc.gov/cgi-bin/bdquery/z?d111:SP2631.

2. National Science Foundation, "nsf.gov—SES—Funding—Political Science—US National Science Foundation (NSF)," available online at http://www.nsf.gov/funding/pgm_summ.jsp?pims_id=5418&org=SES.

3. Stephen Kotkin, "A World War among Professors," New York Times, September 7, 2002.

4. Ibid.

5. Barbara Geddes, "What Do We Know about Democratization after Twenty Years?" *Annual Review of Political Science* 2 (1999): 115–44, 121.

6. Frances Hagopian, "Review: After Regime Change: Authoritarian Legacies, Political Representation, and the Democratic Future of South America," *World Politics* 45, no. 3 (April 1993): 464–500, 464.

7. Thomas Carothers, "The End of the Transition Paradigm," *Journal of Democracy* 13, no. 1 (2002): 5–21, 6.

8. Hagopian, "After Regime Change," 499.

9. "Excerpts from Remarks by Gorbachev before Central Committee of Party," *New York Times,* February 6, 1990, A16.

10. Michael McFaul, "The Fourth Wave of Democracy and Dictatorship: Noncooperative Transitions in the Postcommunist World," *World Politics* 54 (2002): 212–44, 232.

11. Kathleen Collins, "The Logic of Clan Politics Evidence from the Central Asian Trajectories," *World Politics* 56, no. 2 (2004): 224–61, 247.

12. Eugene Huskey, "The Rise of Contested Politics in Central Asia: Elections in Kyrgyzstan, 1989–90," *Europe-Asia Studies* 47, no. 5 (July 1995): 813–33, 829.

13. Author interview with Bermet Akaeva, June 1, 2007, Bishkek, Kyrgyzstan.

14. Bruce Bueno de Mesquita, James D. Morrow, Randolph M. Siverson, and Alastair Smith, "Political Institutions, Policy Choice, and the Survival of Leaders," *British Journal of Political Science* 32, no. 4 (October 2002): 559–90.

15. Ibid., 561.

16. Again, contrast this to democracies where, as Mesquita and his colleagues (ibid.) have noted, "the selectorate is the electorate, and the winning coalition is determined by the specific electoral rules."

17. For the mathematics and proofs behind the example provided here, see ibid. as well as Bruce Bueno de Mesquita, Alastair Smith, Randolph M. Siverson, and James D. Morrow, *The Logic of Political Survival* (Cambridge: MIT Press, 2005).

18. Author interview with Tursunbek Akun, ombudsman for human rights, December 16, 2006, Bishkek, Kyrgyzstan.

19. Author interview with Marat Kaipov, the Kyrgyz minister of justice, December 22, 2006, Bishkek, Kyrgyzstan.

20. Author interview with Topchubek Turgunaliev, the leader of Erkin Kyrgyzstan, December 15, 2006, Bishkek, Kyrgyzstan.

21. I pattern this simplified presentation of the selectorate model after William Roberts Clark, Matt Golder, and Sona Nadenichke Golder's presentation in their *Principles of Comparative Politics,* 1st edition (Washington, D.C.: CQ Press, 2008), 339–410.

22. I pattern this scenario on Mesquita and colleagues, "Political Institutions, Policy Choice, and the Survival of Leaders," especially the discussion on pages 569–70.

23. Total Kazakh government revenue in 2007 was $5.1 billion, while total Kyrgyz revenues that year were $254 million, according to World Bank World Development Indicators.

24. I am grateful to the historian Stephen Kotkin for encouraging me toward this new research agenda.

25. Michael Lewin Ross, "Does Oil Hinder Democracy?" *World Politics* 53, no. 3 (2001): 332–34.

26. Barrington Moore, *Social Origins of Dictatorship and Democracy* (Boston: Beacon Press, 1993), 418; and Alexis de Tocqueville, *Democracy in America*, translated by Henry Reeve (New York: D. Appleton and Company, 1904), 598.

27. Anja Franke, Andrea Gawrich, and Gurban Alakbarov, "Kazakhstan and Azerbaijan as Post-Soviet Rentier States: Resource Incomes and Autocracy as a Double 'Curse' in Post-Soviet Regimes," *Europe-Asia Studies* 61, no. 1 (2009): 109–40, 134.

28. Theresa Sabonis-Helf, "The Rise of the Post-Soviet Petro-States: Energy Exports and Domestic Governance in Turkmenistan and Kazakhstan," in *In the Tracks of Tamerlane: Central Asia's Path to the Twenty-first Century,* edited by Daniel L. Burghart and Sabonis-Helf (Washington, D.C.: National Defense University, 2004), 181.

29. Pauline Jones Luong and Erika Weinthal, "Prelude to the Resource Curse: Explaining Oil and Gas Development Strategies in the Soviet Successor States and Beyond," *Comparative Political Studies* 34, no. 4 (May 1, 2001): 367–99, 387.

30. The poverty data for Kyrgyzstan and Kazakhstan are from 2001; the poverty data for Uzbekistan are from 2000. The World Bank's World Development Indicators are available online at http://data.worldbank.org/indicator.

31. According to World Bank data, the ratio of Kazakh to Kyrgyz government revenue ranges from a low of nine to one (1999) to a high of twenty-nine to one (2006). Unfortunately, comparable Uzbek government revenue data are not available. A reasonable conclusion is that Uzbekistan's gas, cotton, and gold industries yield government revenues greater than those available in resource-poor Kyrgyzstan but less than those of hydrocarbon-rich Kazakhstan.

32. Jeffrey S. Kopstein and David A. Reilly, "Geographic Diffusion and the Transformation of the Postcommunist World," *World Politics* 53 (2000): 1–37, 35.

33. Mehdi Parvizi Amineh and Henk Houweling, "The U.S. and the E.U. in CEA," in *Central Eurasia in Global Politics: Conflict, Security, and Development*, edited by Mehdi Parvizi Amineh and Henk Houweling (Boston: Brill, 2005), 230.

34. Ibid.

35. U.S. Department of State, Central Asia/South Caucasus, U.S. Subcommittee of the Senate Foreign Relations Committee, "U.S. Official Says Central Asia Developments Promising but Mixed," Office of International Information Programs, U.S. Department of State, Washington, D.C., 2002.

36. George A. Krol, Eric McGlinchey, Yevgeny Zhovtis, Erlan Idrissov, Benjamin Cardin, Alcee Hastings, Christopher Smith, and Eni Faleomavaega, *Approaching the OSCE Chairmanship: Kazakhstan 2010* (Washington, D.C.: Commission on Security and Cooperation in Europe, 2009). The congressional hearing is available online at http://csce.gov.

37. "Address of H. E. Dr. Marat Tazhin, Minister of Foreign Affairs of the Republic of Kazakhstan, at the OSCE Ministerial Meeting," Madrid, November 29, 2007, available online at http://en.government.kz/documents/publication/page09.

38. Krol and colleagues, *Approaching the OSCE Chairmanship: Kazakhstan 2010.*

39. Alexander Cooley, "U.S. Bases and Democratization in Central Asia," *Orbis* 52, no. 1 (Winter 2008): 65–90, 89.

40. Clifford J. Levy, "Strategic Issues, Not Abuses, Are U.S. Focus in Kyrgyzstan," *New York Times*, July 23, 2009.

41. Richard Boucher, "Intent to Designate as Foreign Terrorist Organization the Islamic Movement of Uzbekistan," press statement, U.S. Department of State, September 18, 2000.

42. Author interview with U.S. Department of State official, May 2009. The journalist Steve Coll has also noted the beginning of the covert Predator program in Uzbekistan in 2000. See Coll, *Ghost Wars: The Secret History of the CIA, Afghanistan, and bin Laden, from the Soviet Invasion to September 10, 2001* (New York: Penguin, 2005), 531.

43. "USA's Rumsfeld Thanks Uzbekistan for 'Stalwart Support' in War on Terror," *BBC Monitoring International Reports*, February 24, 2004. Although post-Andijan U.S. funding to Uzbekistan fell precipitously from 2006 to 2008, this funding is now on the rise as Washington has returned to Uzbekistan in the hopes of establishing a new and reliable north-south supply corridor to Afghanistan.

44. This observation is based on 2008 World Trade Organization statistics found online at http://stat.wto.org.

45. "Uzbek Leader Arrives in China, a Rare Supporter Amid International Criticism of Crackdown," Associated Press, May 25, 2005.

46. The 2009 comments of this U.S. defense official are not for attribution. U.S. payments for the Manas air base in Kyrgyzstan rose from $17.4 million in 2008 to $60 million in 2009. Rod Blagojevich was the governor of Illinois from 2003 to 2009. In January 2009 the Illinois legislature found him guilty of corruption and voted him out of office.

47. Bernard Lewis, "The Roots of Muslim Rage," *Atlantic* 266, no. 3 (September 1990): 47–60, 60.

48. Bernard Lewis, *What Went Wrong? Western Impact and Middle Eastern Response* (New York: Oxford University Press, 2002), 4.

49. Clifford Geertz, "Which Way to Mecca?" *New York Review of Books* 50, no. 10 (June 12, 2003): 27–30.

50. Edward W. Said, "The Clash of Ignorance," *Nation* (October 22, 2001): 11–13, 12.

51. Geertz, "Which Way to Mecca?"

52. Ali A. Mazrui, "Islam and the United States: Streams of Convergence, Strands of Divergence," *Third World Quarterly* 25, no. 5 (2004): 793–820, 814.

53. David S. Landes and Richard A. Landes, "Girl Power," *New Republic* 225, no. 15 (October 8, 2001): 20.

54. Ibid.

55. Ahmed Rashid, "The New Struggle in Central Asia," *World Policy Journal* 17, no. 4 (Winter 2000): 33–45, 33.

56. Samuel P. Huntington, "The Clash of Civilizations?" *Foreign Affairs* 72, no. 3 (Summer 1993): 22–49, 40.

57. Ronald Inglehart and Pippa Norris, "The True Clash of Civilizations," *Foreign Policy*, no. 135 (April 2003): 62–70, 66.

58. World Values Survey 2000, Official Data File v.7. World Values Survey Association, Aggregate File Producer: ASEP/JDS, Madrid, available online at http://www.worldvaluessurvey.org.

59. See also Eric McGlinchey, "Islamic Leaders in Uzbekistan," *Asia Policy* 1, no. 6 (January 2006): 123–44; and Eric McGlinchey, "Islamic Revivalism and State Failure in Kyrgyzstan," *Problems of Post-Communism* 56, no. 3 (June 2009): 16–28.

60. The focus on "religious attendance" rather than mosque attendance is intentional. As coauthors Dale F. Eickelman and James P. Piscatori have noted, religious practice is "subject to constant modification and change," depending on who practices Islam and where Islam is practiced. In Central Asia, for example, while the mosque is very much the domain of Muslim men, Central Asian women regularly partake in birth, wedding, and funeral ceremonies that are deeply shaped by Islamic beliefs. See Dale F. Eickelman and James P. Piscatori, *Muslim Politics* (Princeton: Princeton University Press, 2004), 17.

61. Douglas Northrop, *Veiled Empire: Gender and Power in Stalinist Central Asia*, 1st edition (Ithaca: Cornell University Press, 2004), 347.

62. John H. Herz, "The Problem of Successorship in Dictatorial Régimes; A Study in Comparative Law and Institutions," *Journal of Politics* 14, no. 1 (February 1952): 19–40, 28.

63. Alvin Rabushka and Kenneth Shepsle, *Politics in Plural Societies: A Theory of Democratic Instability* (Columbus, Ohio: Charles E. Merrill Publishing Company, 1972), 80–81.

64. Francine Hirsch, "Toward an Empire of Nations: Border Making and the Formation of Soviet National Identities," *Russian Review* 59, no. 2 (April 2000): 201–26, 214.

65. Rabushka and Shepsle, *Politics in Plural Societies,* 80–81; and Martha Brill Olcott, *Kazakhstan: Unfulfilled Promise* (New York: Carnegie Endowment for International Peace, 2002), 64.

66. Olcott, *Kazakhstan,* 65. The political scientist Edward Schatz similarly sees "elite efforts at ethnic nation building" in Kazakhstan. See Edward Schatz, "The Politics of Multiple Identities: Lineage and Ethnicity in Kazakhstan," *Europe-Asia Studies* 52, no. 4 (2000): 489–506, 489.

67. Kathleen Collins, *Clan Politics and Regime Transition in Central Asia* (Cambridge: Cambridge University Press, 2006), 17.

68. Ibid., 339.

69. Edward Schatz, *Modern Clan Politics: The Power of "Blood" in Kazakhstan and Beyond* (Seattle: University of Washington Press, 2004), 167, 162.

70. Collins, *Clan Politics and Regime Transition in Central Asia*, 303.

71. Ibid.

72. Both surveys were commissioned by USAID and conducted by the Almaty-based Central Asian polling agency in Brif in June 1999. The 1,219 Kazakh survey respondents are from Almaty (335), Karaganda (165), Shymkent (127), Pavlodar (103), Ust-Kamenogorsk (96), Semipalatinsk

(96), Astana (82), Aktubinsk (75), Uralsk (70), and Petropavlovsk (70). The 1,200 Kyrgyz survey respondents are from Bishkek (600) and Osh (600).

73. Nursultan Abishuly Nazarbaev, "Ideinaia konsolidatsia obshestva—kak uslovie progressa Kazakhstana," *Kizil-ordinkie vesti*, no. 126 (October 21, 1993); quoted in Vitalii Khlopin, "Eliti Kazakhstana: Natsional'nye kachestva ili natsionalisticheskie kolichestva?" *Navigator*, January 30, 2001.

74. Collins, *Clan Politics and Regime Transition in Central Asia*, 58.

75. Pauline Jones Luong, *Institutional Change and Political Continuity in Post-Soviet Central Asia: Power, Perceptions, and Pacts*, 1st edition (Cambridge: Cambridge University Press, 2002), 271.

76. Ibid., 108.

77. Ibid., 121.

78. Ibid., 136.

79. Herz, "Problem of Successorship in Dictatorial Régimes," 30.

80. Joel S. Migdal, *Strong Societies and Weak States: State-Society Relations and State Capabilities in the Third World* (Princeton: Princeton University Press, 1988), 209.

81. Tamir Moustafa, *The Struggle for Constitutional Power: Law, Politics, and Economic Development in Egypt* (Cambridge: Cambridge University Press, 2007), 179.

82. Holger Albrecht, "Authoritarian Opposition and the Politics of Challenge in Egypt," in *Debating Arab Authoritarianism: Dynamics and Durability in Nondemocratic Regimes*, edited by Oliver Schlumberger (Stanford: Stanford University Press), 59–74.

83. Moustafa, *Struggle for Constitutional Power*, 175.

84. Albert O. Hirschman, *Exit, Voice, and Loyalty: Responses to Decline in Firms, Organizations, and States* (Cambridge: Harvard University Press, 1970). Mancur Olson, *Logic of Collective Action: Public Goods and the Theory of Groups* (Cambridge: Harvard University Press, 1971).

2. The Soviet Origins of Post-Soviet Autocratic Variation

1. For a compelling discussion of the challenges of infinite regress, see Robert C. Lieberman, "Ideas, Institutions, and Political Order: Explaining Political Change," *American Political Science Review* 96, no. 4 (December 2002): 697–712.

2. Paul Pierson, "Big, Slow-Moving, and . . . Invisible: Macrosocial Processes in the Study of Comparative Politics," in *Comparative Historical Analysis in the Social Sciences*, edited by James Mahoney and Dietrich Rueschemeyer (New York: Cambridge University Press, 2003), 177–207, 179.

3. Manash Kabashevich Kozybaev, *Kazakhstan na rubezhe vekov: Razmyshleniia i poiski* (Almaty: Ghylym, 2000), 109; and Dzhumadil Sapalovich Baktygulov and Zhyrgal Kanaevna Mombekova, *Istoriia Kyrgyzov i Kyrgyzstana s drevneishikh vremen do nashikh dnei* (Bishkek: Kyrgyzstan: Mektep, 1999), 171.

4. Kozybaev, *Kazakhstan na rubezhe vekov*, 110; for more on conflicts between the Kazakhs, Jungars, and Kalmyks, see Martha Brill Olcott, *The Kazakhs* (Stanford: Hoover Institution Press at Stanford University, 1987), 25–31.

5. Adeeb Khalid, *Islam after Communism* (Berkeley: University of California Press, 2007), 40.

6. Alexander Burnes, "The Importance of Bukhara in Great Game Politics," in *Islamic Central Asia: An Anthology of Historical Sources*, edited by Scott Cameron Levi and Ron Sela (Bloomington: Indiana University Press, 2010), 281–87, 287.

7. Richard A. Pierce, *Russian Central Asia, 1867–1917: A Study in Colonial Rule* (Berkeley: University of California Press, 1960), 68.

8. Ibid., 75.

9. Baktygulov and Mombekova have noted, for example, that Russian bureaucrats in Kyrgyzstan were often co-opted by local networks of corruption. For more information on

this situation in Kyrgyzstan, see Baktygulov and Mombekova, *Istoriia Kyrgyzov i Kyrgyzstana s drevneishikh vremen do nashikh dnei*, 200.

10. Ibid.

11. For more on these land appropriations and the riots they sparked, see Kozybaev, *Kazakhstan na rubezhe vekov*, 150–66.

12. Turar K. Koichuev, Vladimir M. Ploskikh, and Vladimir P. Mokrynin, *Kyrgyzy i ikh predki: Netraditsionnyi vzgliad na istoriiu i sovremennost'* (Bishkek: Glav. red. Kyrgyzskoi Entsiklopedii, 1994), 54.

13. Kozybaev, *Kazakhstan na rubezhe vekov*, 188.

14. Vladimir I. Lenin, "The Question of Nationalities," in *The Lenin Anthology*, edited by Robert C. Tucker (New York: W. W. Norton, 1975), 721. Lenin, "Iz pervonachal'nogo nabroska statii 'ocherednye sadachi sovetskoi vlasti," dictated March 28, 1918; Soch. (4th edition), V. 27. pages 180–82, as quoted in *Lenin o natsional'nom i natsional'no-kolonial'nom voprose* (Moscow: Gospolitizdat, 1956), 470–72, as quoted in Gregory J. Massell, *The Surrogate Proletariat: Moslem Women and Revolutionary Strategies in Soviet Central Asia, 1919–1929* (Princeton: Princeton University Press, 1974), 46.

15. Francine Hirsch, "Toward an Empire of Nations: Border-Making and the Formation of Soviet National Identities," *Russian Review* 59, no. 2 (April 2000): 201–26.

16. Ibid., 215.

17. Vladimir I. Lenin, "Imperialism, the Highest Stage of Capitalism," in Tucker, *The Lenin Anthology* (New York: W. W. Norton, 1975), 268.

18. Lenin, "Question of Nationalities," 721.

19. Massell, *Surrogate Proletariat*, 54.

20. Koichuev, Ploskikh, and Mokrynin, *Kyrgyzy i ikh predki*, 72.

21. Nursultan Nazarbaev, *Nursultan Nazarbaev: Bez pravykh i levykh* (Moscow: Molodaia Gvardiia, 1991), 179.

22. Stephen F. Cohen, *Bukharin and the Bolshevik Revolution: A Political Biography, 1888–1938* (New York: A. A. Knopf, 1973), 315.

23. Olcott, *Kazakhs*, 162.

24. Robert C. Tucker, *Stalin in Power: The Revolution from Above, 1928–1941* (New York: W. W. Norton & Company, 1992), 45.

25. Ibid.

26. The term *hujum* has multiple meanings in several languages. Massell writes: "It denoted, especially in the military sense, 'all-out attack,' 'sweeping advance,' 'assault,' 'storm,' in all three main languages of Central Asia's cultural heritage: Turkic, Arabic, and Persian" (see Massell, *Surrogate Proletariat*, 229).

27. Douglas Northrop, *Veiled Empire: Gender and Power in Stalinist Central Asia*, 1st edition (Ithaca: Cornell University Press, 2004), 13.

28. Massell, *Surrogate Proletariat*, xxii–xxiii.

29. Northrop, *Veiled Empire*, 84.

30. Massell, *Surrogate Proletariat*, xxii–xxiii.

31. Ibid., 317.

32. Northrop, *Veiled Empire*, 225.

33. Northrop concludes, for example: "Stalin's powerful government had set itself a task at which it was all but bound to fail." The scholar Shoshana Keller has reached a similar conclusion, finding that "although the Soviets achieved significant changes in women's status, particularly among the educated classes, in the end they failed to stamp out any of the traditional practices against which they had campaigned so diligently." See Northrop, *Veiled Empire*, 313; Shoshana Keller, "Women's Liberation and Islam in Soviet Uzbekistan, 1926–1941," in *Bodies in Contact: Rethinking Colonial Encounters in World History*, edited by Tony Ballantyne and Antoinette Burton (Durham, N.C.: Duke University Press, 2005), 322.

34. Northrop, *Veiled Empire*, 142.

35. Ibid., 146–47.

36. U.S. State Department, "2005 Country Report on Human Rights Practices in Uzbekistan," Washington, D.C.

37. Northrop, *Veiled Empire*, 223. The Zhenotdel was the Communist Party's Women's Department.

38. A. Ar-na, "Ot 'nastupleniia' k sistematicheskoi rabote (k obsledovaniiu raboty v Srednei Azii)," *Kommunistka* 1 (1928): 62–63, quoted in Massell, *Surrogate Proletariat*, 310.

39. Kozybaev, *Kazakhstan na rubezhe vekov*, 20.

40. Koichuev, Ploskikh, and Mokrynin, *Kyrgyzy i ikh predki*, 75.

41. Michael Rywkin, *Moscow's Muslim Challenge: Soviet Central Asia*, revised edition (Armonk, N.Y.: M. E. Sharpe, 1990), 108.

42. Ibid.

43. Olcott, *Kazakhs*, 154.

44. Koichuev, Ploskikh, and Mokrynin, *Kyrgyzy i ikh predki*, 72–73. Several members of this Group of Thirty are now, in the post-Soviet search for national roots, esteemed as the founding fathers of the Kyrgyz nation. Abdykerim Sydykov, Ishenali Arabaev, and Yusup Abdrakhmanov, in particular, are credited with pressing Moscow into agreeing to the formation of the Kara-Kyrgyz autonomous oblast in 1924. See, for example, Askar Akaev, "Vozhrozhdeniie Kyrgyzskoi gosudarstvennosti," speech given at the conference "Kyrgyzskiia gosudarstvennost' v XX stoletii," Kyrgyz National University, Bishkek, Kyrgyzstan, December 24, 2001.

45. Northrop, *Veiled Empire*, 239.

46. The 2009 U.S. State Department report on human rights in Uzbekistan notes: "Family members reported several deaths in custody of prisoners who were serving sentences on charges related to religious extremism. In each such case family members reported that the body of the prisoner showed signs of beating or other abuse, but authorities pressured them to bury the body before a medical professional could examine it." See U.S. Department of State, Bureau of Democracy, Human Rights, and Labor, "2009 Human Rights Report: Uzbekistan," available online at http://www.state.gov/g/drl/rls/hrrpt/2009/sca/136096.htm. My own conclusions draw from discussions with the family members of deceased prisoners.

47. The sample size in all three surveys is one thousand.

48. David Collier and Steven Levitsky, "Research Note: Democracy with Adjectives: Conceptual Innovation in Comparative Research," *World Politics* 49, no. 3 (1997): 430–51, 451.

49. Adam Przeworski, Michael E. Alvarez, Jose Antonio Cheibub, and Fernando Limongi, *Democracy and Development: Political Institutions and Well-being in the World, 1950–1990*, 1st edition (Cambridge: Cambridge University Press, 2000), 27.

50. Linda Cook, *The Soviet Social Contract and Why It Failed: Welfare Policy and Workers' Politics from Brezhnev to Yeltsin* (Cambridge: Harvard University Press, 1993).

51. Stephen Kotkin, *Magnetic Mountain: Stalinism as a Civilization* (Berkeley: University of California Press, 1997), 358.

52. Khrushchev explains the thinking that went behind his 1956 so-called Secret Speech and his rejection of Stalinist methods of terror in his memoirs. See especially Nikita S. Khrushchev, "Ot XIX k XX sezdu KPSS," in *Vospominaniia: Izbrannye fragmenty* (Moscow: Vagrius, 1997), 285–99.

53. Curiously, given Khrushchev's belief in the superiority of all things Soviet, much of the design for the Virgin Lands was not domestic in origin, but rather came from Khrushchev's study of American agro business. See, for example, Roy A. Medvedev and Zhores A. Medvedev, *Khrushchev: The Years in Power* (New York: W. W. Norton, 1978), 102.

54. Khrushchev cannot be faulted for the weather. With regards to cadre policy, however, Khrushchev (fortunately for Central Asia) proved naïve. He believed his comrades would rally to the cause and eagerly travel to Central Asia to open the Virgin Lands: "I am convinced we will receive a warm response and will be able to raise hundreds of thousands of people [for the task]. Remember there was the time when people were forced to live not only in tents but in trenches as well, sacrificing their lives. Despite the trying conditions of the first years of the war, the people mobilized and were able to overcome all difficulties. Opening of the Virgin Lands, knowing that they are enriching their country . . . will give people the same sort of moral satisfaction"; see Khrushchev, *Vospominaniia*, 413. As the historian Martin McCauley has noted, however, many equally became quickly disillusioned and left. Statistics are difficult to find, but McCauley notes by way of example that in 1964, "49,800 mechanisers arrived but 51,200 departed." See Martin

McCauley, *Khrushchev and the Development of Soviet Agriculture: The Virgin Land Programme, 1953–1964* (New York: Holmes & Meier Publishers, 1976), 179.

55. For the Malenkov-Khrushchev bread and guns debate, see George W. Breslauer, *Khrushchev and Brezhnev as Leaders: Building Authority in Soviet Politics* (London: George Allen and Unwin, 1982), 23–38.

56. Khrushchev believes Shaiakhmetov's opposition was further motivated by a fear of a massive Slavic inmigration into Kazakhstan: "That Secretary [Shaiakhmetov] understood that the Kazakhs alone could not increase the grain harvest. . . . He understood—and no one hid this fact—that volunteers would have to be brought in for opening the Virgin Lands. We were certain that we could find the numbers and he certainly did not want that because then the Kazakh percentage of the population would decline even further"; see Khrushchev, *Vospominaniia*, 411.

57. Shaiakhmetov, Stalin's appointee and the first Kazakh to hold the position of first secretary in Kazakhstan, was replaced by Ponomarenko in 1954. Ponomarenko was replaced by Brezhnev in 1955. After Brezhnev was promoted to Moscow in 1956, Ivan Iakovlev served as first secretary until 1957. Iakovlev was replaced by Nikolai Beliaev, who was in turn replaced by Dinmukhamed Kunaev in 1959. In what would ultimately prove a boon to his career under Brezhnev, Kunaev was dismissed by an unsatisfied Khrushchev in 1962 and replaced with Iusopov. Except for the case of Brezhnev, the reason for the frequent leadership changes was the failure of the Virgin Lands campaign to meet the production goals laid out by Khrushchev.

58. See "Postanovleniie TsK KPSS o rabote partiinoi organizatsii Kyrgyzii po vyipolneniyu zadanii semiletnego plana v oblasti promyishlennosti, stroitel'stva i sel'skogo khozyistva," in *Kommunisticheskaia partiia Sovetskogo Soiuza v rezolutsiiakh i resheniiakh, 1959–1965*, April 9, 1963, page 405.

59. Koichuev, Ploskikh, and Mokrynin, *Kyrgyzy i ikh predki*, 82.

60. James C. Scott, *Seeing Like a State: How Certain Schemes to Improve the Human Condition Have Failed* (New Haven: Yale University Press, 1999), 5.

61. Quoted in Breslauer, *Khrushchev and Brezhnev as Leaders*, 156.

62. Unless otherwise noted, all translations are mine. Dinmukhamed Kunaev, *Dinmukhamed Kunaev: Ot Stalina do Gorbacheva* (Almaty: Sanat, 1994), 172. The Central Asian first secretaries, for their part, never challenged that their colleagues, the second secretaries, would be Russian.

63. Leonid I. Brezhnev, *The Virgin Lands* (Moscow: Progress Publishers, 1978), 18–19.

64. Brezhnev's speech before the Seventh Congress of the Kazakhstan Communist Party, quoted in Brezhnev, *Virgin Lands*, 19.

65. Arkady Sakhnin, "USSR Deputy Prosecutor General Reports that the Prosecutor's Office Has Resumed Its Investigation of the Nasriddinova Case," *Pravda*, November 2, 1988, 6, as translated in the *Current Digest of the Post Soviet Press*, November 30, 1988, 16.

66. Ibid.

67. Georgy Ovcharenko and Andrei Chernenko, "Interview in the USSR Ministry of Internal Affairs' Investigative Detention Center," *Pravda*, July 17, 1988, as translated in the *Current Digest of the Post-Soviet Press* 40, no. 29 (August 17, 1988): 26–27.

68. Ibid.

69. Ibid.

70. A. Tokombayev, "Our Moral Values: Only Friendship Does Good," *Pravda*, May 19, 1987, translated in *Current Digest of the Post-Soviet Press* 39, no. 20 (June 17, 1987): 22.

71. Grigory Dildyayev and Tleuzhan Yesilbayev, "Looking the Truth in the Eye," *Pravda*, March 16, 1987, 2, translated in *Current Digest of the Post-Soviet Press* 39, no. 11 (April 15, 1987): 14.

72. David Remnick, *Lenin's Tomb: The Last Days of the Soviet Empire* (New York: Vintage, 1994), 187. Remnick presents an entertaining analysis of Brezhnev's dealings with the Central Asian "dons." See, in particular, ibid., 186–90.

73. Stability in cadres was not absolute. For example, oblast first secretaries would occasionally be dismissed. Even in these rare cases, however, these first secretaries were often transferred to new oblasts rather than being dropped from the party altogether. Masaliev, for example, describes this practice in his February 28, 1986, speech to the Twenty-seventh CPSU Congress. See "Speech by First Secretary of the Communist Party of Kirgizia [CPKi] Absamat

M. Masaliev to 27th CPSU Congress," in *Perestroika in the Soviet Republics: Documents on the National Question*, edited by Charles F. Furtado Jr. and Andrea Chandler (Boulder, Colo.: Westview Press, 1992), 525. See also, Olcott, *Kazakhs*, 234.

74. Manash K. Kozybaev, *Kazakhskaia Sovetskaia entsiklopediia* (Alma-Ata: Kazakhstan 1981), 343.

75. Kaip O. Otorbaev and Aidarkan M. Moldokulov, *Ekonomika Kirgizii—sostavnaia chast' narodnokhoziaistvennogo kompleksa SSSR* (Frunze, Kyrgyzstan: Ilim, 1977), 138. Likely some of the explanation for these impressive investment figures is the active lobbying of the center by the Central Asian leadership. Thus, as Eugene Huskey has written of the Kyrgyz first secretary: "Usubaliev used every public platform, whether in Moscow or Frunze, to remind the centre of Kyrgyzstan's faithful delivery of goods to the country and the republic's reciprocal need for new projects and scarce supplies. . . . Usubaliev achieved notoriety in the 1980s for the avalanche of telegrams he directed to central ministries." See Eugene Huskey, "The Rise of Contested Politics in Central Asia: Elections in Kyrgyzstan, 1989–90," *Europe-Asia Studies* 47, no. 5 (July 1995): 813–33, 816.

76. Bert van Selm, *The Economics of Soviet Break-up* (New York: Routledge, 1997), 132.

77. Olcott, *Kazakhs*, 244.

78. Koichuev, Ploskikh, and Mokrynin, *Kyrgyzy i ikh predki*, 85.

79. Mary McAuley, "Party Recruitment and the Nationalities in the USSR: A Study in Centre-Republican Relationships," *British Journal of Political Science* 10, no. 4 (October 1980): 461–87, 466.

80. James Critchlow, *Nationalism in Uzbekistan: A Soviet Republic's Road to Sovereignty* (Boulder, Colo.: Westview Press, 1991), 142.

81. Olcott, *Kazakhs*, 243. Huskey has similarly noted the opportunities available for Slavs under Usubaliev's rule: "By exploiting the opportunities for personal gain, Slavic officials became political insiders rather than outsiders, thereby enhancing the autonomy of indigenous political elites." See Huskey, "Rise of Contested Politics in Central Asia," 816.

82. Korkin, born in Chelyabinsk, Russia, began his career in the construction and building industry in Karaganda, Kazakhstan, in 1949. Miroshkin, born in Saratov, Russia, began his career with Kazakhoil in Western Kazakhstan in 1951. See Daniiar R. Ashimbaer, *Kto est' kto v Kazakhstane* (Almaty, Kazakhstan: Credo, 1999), 293, 347.

83. Huskey, "Rise of Contested Politics in Central Asia," 816.

84. Tel'man Gdlian and Nicholai Ivanov, *Kremlevskoe delo* (Rostov-Na-Donu: Izd-vo "AO Kniga," 1994), 21.

85. Stephen Kotkin, *Armageddon Averted: The Soviet Collapse, 1970–2000* (New York: Oxford University Press, 2001), 16.

86. Robert C. Allen, "The Rise and Decline of the Soviet Economy," *Canadian Journal of Economics / Revue canadienne d'Economique* 34, no. 4 (November 2001): 862.

87. Kotkin, *Armageddon Averted*, 15.

88. "The 21st Congress of the Uzbekistan Communist Party: Report of the Uzbekistan Communist Party Central Committee to the 21st Congress of the Uzbekistan Communist Party, by Comrade I. B. Usmankhodzhayev, First Secretary of the Uzbekistan Communist Party Central Committee," translated in *Current Digest of the Post-Soviet Press* 38, no. 6 (March 12, 1986): 11–14.

89. "Speech by Comrade A. M. Masaliyev, First Secretary of the Kirgiz Communist Party Central Committee," translated in *Current Digest of the Post-Soviet Press* 38, no. 11 (April 16, 1986), 12–13. Usabiliev has since been rehabilitated. In November 2009, during a celebration of the former first secretary's ninetieth birthday, President Bakiev handed Usubaliev the keys to a new four-wheel drive Mitsubishi Pajero and established a twenty-thousand-dollar "presidential reserve fund to strengthen his [Usubaliev's] health." See "Kyrgyz President Gives Car to Soviet-Era Communist Leader," *AKIpress.com*, November 7, 2009.

90. "Speech by Comrade N. A. Nazarbayev, Chairman of the Kazakh Republic Council of Ministers," translated in *Current Digest of the Post-Soviet Press* 38, no. 15 (May 14, 1986): 12–13.

91. I. Yermachenko, "Economic Barometer: Dangerous Game over the Oil Wells," *Izvestia*, February 12, 1986.

92. Mikhail Sergeevich Gorbachev, *On My Country and the World* (New York: Columbia University Press, 2000), 26.

93. "Speech by Comrade N. A. Nazarbayev, Chairman of the Kazakh Republic Council of Ministers."

94. Gorbachev, *On My Country and the World*, 86.

95. Nazarbaev, *Nursultan Nazarbaev*, 24.

96. Zhanylzhan Kh. Dzhunusova, *Respublika Kazakhstan: Prezident, instituty demokratii* (Almaty: Zheti zharghy, 1996), 18.

97. Nazarbaev, *Nursultan Nazarbaev*, 94.

98. Nazarbaev wrote: "I thought they would dismiss me from my [party] work. I was not particularly worried though. I would not be done for, I would just return to the factory." Quoted in Dzhunusova, *Respublika Kazakhstan*, 22.

99. Nazarbaev, *Nursultan Nazarbaev*, 98.

100. Dinmukhamed Kunaev, *Ot Stalina do Gorbacheva: V aspekte istorii Kazakhstana* (Alma-Ata: Sanat, 1994), 277.

101. Nazarbaev, *Nursultan Nazarbaev*, 164.

102. Ibid., 150.

103. Ibid., 180.

104. Gorbachev, *On My Country and the World*, 6.

105. Dmitri Vasil'evich Valovoii, *Kremlevski tupik i Nazarbaev: Ocherki-razmyshlenia* (Moscow: Molodaia gvardia, 1993), 80. Apparently Nazarbaev was so shocked by Kunaev's claim that he was forced to spend the night under observation in a Moscow hospital.

106. I am grateful to Stephen Kotkin for sharing this information from his interviews with Ligachev.

107. Valovoii, *Kremlevski tupik i Nazarbaev*, 85.

108. "The Riots in Uzbekistan," *BBC Summary of World Broadcasts*, June 7, 1989.

109. Adylbek Kaipbergenov, "Still More Questions on the Events in Fergana Province," *Pravda*, June 28, 1989.

110. Ibid.

111. D. Makarov, "Chem vyshe kreslo, tem dal'she ot liudei. Islam Karimov: 'Tverdyi' poriadok pri polnoi ekonomicheskoi svobode," *Argumenty i fakty*, April 11, 1991.

112. A. Ganelin, "The Investigation Isn't Over," *Komsomolskaia pravda*, March 15, 1988.

113. Viktor Loshak, "We've Run Up against a Mafia," *Moskovskie novosti*, April 3, 1988.

114. Michael Dobbs, "Brezhnev Kin Jailed for Twelve Years," *Washington Post*, December 31, 1988.

115. "Sentences Announced in Churbanov Trial," *BBC Summary of World Broadcasts*, January 3, 1989.

116. Vladimir Itkin, "In the USSR Supreme Court: The Indictment Is Brought," *Izvestia*, September 10, 1988.

117. "Gorbachev's Visit to Uzbekistan: Meetings with Collective Farmers," *BBC Summary of World Broadcasts*, April 11, 1988.

118. "Gorbachev's Visit to Uzbekistan: Meetings with Collective Farmers," *BBC Summary of World Broadcasts*, April 11, 1988.

119. Svante E. Cornell, *Small Nations and Great Powers* (New York: Routledge, 2001), 182.

120. Critchlow, *Nationalism in Uzbekistan*, 72.

121. Curiously, the political scientist Donald Carlisle sees Karimov's gravitation to Rashidov as "totally unexpected" given that Karimov was an "outsider to the party apparatus." My reading of Uzbek history departs significantly from Carlisle's. Karimov, far from an outsider, began his apprenticeship in the Uzbek apparatus in the 1960s. Granted, much of this apprenticeship occurred within the economic ministries. Nevertheless, to advance from economic analyst to minister of finance surely required that Karimov be a familiar and trusted figure in the Uzbek Communist Party. For Carlisle's analysis, see Donald Carlisle, "Uzbekistan and the Uzbeks," *Problems of Communism* 40, no. 5 (September 1991): 23–44, 36.

122. Mikhail Berger, "We Have to Make Our Own Way: A Conversation with Islam Karimov, President of Uzbekistan," *Izvestia*, January 28, 1991.

123. Ibid.
124. "On the CPSU Central Committee's Draft Platform for the 28th Party Congress. M. S. Gorbachev's Report at the Plenary Session of the CPSU Central Committee on Feb. 5, 1990," translated in *Current Digest of the Post-Soviet Press* 42, no. 6 (March 14, 1990).
125. Gorbachev, *On My Country and the World*, 22.
126. John B. Dunlop, *The Rise of Russia and the Fall of the Soviet Empire* (Princeton: Princeton University Press, 1995), 92.
127. Talant Razakov, *Oshkie sobytiia: Na materialakh KGB* (Bishkek: Renaissance, 1993), 42.
128. Ibid.
129. Ibid., 46.
130. Ibid., 77, 101.
131. Abdygany Erkebaev, *1990 god: Prikhod k vlasti A. Akaeva* (Bishkek: Izd. Dom Kyrgyzstan, 1997), 23.
132. Ibid., 32.
133. Ibid., 51.
134. Ibid., 61–63.
135. Member of parliament I. T. Aitmatov, quoted in ibid., 65.
136. Ibid., 68.
137. Ibid., 71.

3. Kyrgyz Chaos

1.Yurii Razguliev, "Tri poteryannyikh goda: Iubilei, o kotorom Askar Akaev predpochel by ne vspominat," *Pravda*, November 10, 1993, 2.
2. Ibid.
3. "President Akayev Discusses Situation in Kyrgyzstan," *Utro* (television program, Ostankino Channel 1), as reprinted in *BBC Summary of World Broadcasts* (December 3, 1992), Part 1, "The USSR"; "Kyrgyzstan"; SU/1554/B/1.
4. Ibid.
5. Nominally the Brezhnev-era constitution was recognized as still existing. In reality, though, there was no formal document that delineated the powers of the president and the Supreme Soviet. Indeed, the position of the "president" had no constitutional basis in the Brezhnev constitution.
6. Erkin leader Topchubek Turgunaliev, quoted in Gillian Tett, "Moderate Re-elected in Soviet Republic," *Financial Times*, October 14, 1991, 2.
7. See, for example, Zamira Z. Sydykova, "Premir-ministr ne gospod' bog," *Res publica*, September 26, 1992, 1.
8. For a Kyrgyz account of the president's gold scandal, see Zamira Sydykova, *Za kulisami demokratii po-kyrgyzski* (Bishkek: Res Publica, 1997), 42–47. For an English-language account of the Kyrgyz gold scandal, see Leyla Boulton, "The Soviet Insider, the Gold, and Kyrgyzstan's Political Innocents," *Financial Times,* January 28, 1994, 4.
9. Boulton, "Soviet Insider, the Gold, and Kyrgyzstan's Political Innocents."
10. On Zhomagol Saadanbekov, see Kabai Karabekov, "Kak izvestnyi Kyrgyzskii pisatel' privatiziroval izvestnuiu gostinitsu," *Izvestia*, July 9, 1994, 1. On Bekamat Osmonov, see Igor Rotar, "Volneniia v Dzhal-Abade: 'Tadzhikskii Variant' v Kyrgyzstane?" *Nezavisimaiia gazeta*, October 28, 1992, 1. The Osmonov case was considerably complicated by long-standing tensions between the north and the south in Kyrgyzstan. Akaev by no means was a fan of the Jalal Abad akim, whom some saw as posing a potential threat to the president's own position. At the same time, Akaev did his best to co-opt Osmonov so as to neutralize the southern leader's possible opposition. Tellingly, after corruption allegations forced Osmonov to submit his resignation, he was quickly reappointed as the deputy akim of neighboring Osh oblast. For more on Osmonov, see Georgii Sitnyanskii, "Kyrgyziia: Natsional'nyie problemi, vnutrennie i vneshniie," *Tsentral'naia*

aziia i kavkaz, no. 15 (1988). On Tologon Kasymbekov, see Karabekov, "Kak izvestnyi Kyrgyzskii pisatel' privatiziroval izvestnuyu gostinitsu," 2.

   11. Quoted in Sadyrbek Dzhigitekov, "Politika v litsakh," *Res publica*, March 4, 1994, 1.

   12. For more on executive-parliamentary debates over language law, see Albert Bogdanov, "Kyrgyz Parliament Fails to Pass Amendment on Language," *Itar-Tass*, December 9, 1992.

   13. For more on the legislative-executive land conflict, see Kamil Bayalinov, "Akaev v menshestve," *Komsomolskaia pravda*, June 27, 1991, 1; and Otto Latsis, "Zemel'naia reforma, Kyrgyzskyi variant," *Izvestia*, May 27, 1992, 2.

   14. Before the adoption of the new constitution in 1993, the Brezhnev-era constitution was recognized as still existing. But again, there was no official document that defined the powers of the president and the Supreme Soviet. There was no constitutional basis for the position of the "president" in the Brezhnev constitution.

   15. Refer to Article 58, *Constitution of the Kyrgyz Republic*, May 5, 1993.

   16. For an excellent discussion of Kyrgyz electoral design, see Pauline Jones Luong, *Institutional Change and Political Continuity in Post-Soviet Central Asia: Power, Perceptions, and Pacts*, 1st edition (Cambridge: Cambridge University Press, 2002), 156–88.

   17. Tursunbai Bakir uulu, quoted in Sydykova, *Za kulisami*, 27. Although Bakir uulu was not elected to parliament until 1995, he and his newly formed Erkin party became one of the most vocal proponents of parliamentary power in the immediate post-Soviet years. As was the case with Russia's many political groupings in the first years of independence, so too did Kyrgyz politics quickly divide into a dizzying array of parties. For those seeking a detailed analysis of the leading personalities and parties of Kyrgyzstan's brief period of substantive political pluralism, helpful accounts are "Demokratiy v litsakh," *Res publica*, December 8, 1992, 1; and Sydykova's chapter, "Kak slovo demokrat stalo rugatel'nyim," in Sydykova, *Za kulisami*, 20–33.

   18. "Speech by the President of Kyrgyzstan, Askar Akaev," *Kremlin International News Broadcast*, International Press Club, Hotel Radisson Slavyanskaya, August 3, 1993.

   19. Three competing drafts were submitted—one by members of the party Erkin-Kyrgyzstan, one by members of the party Ata-Meken, and one by Akaev's administration. See Sydykova, *Za kulisami*, 26.

   20. *Slovo Kyrgyzstana*, August 14, 1992, as reprinted in "Former Party Functionaries Launch Attack on Akayev," *BBC Summary of World Broadcasts*, August 19, 1992, Part 1 "The USSR"; "Kyrgyzstan"; SU/1463/B/1.

   21. Igor Rotar, "Ugroza parlamentskogo-prezidentskogo krizisa: Povtoritsiia li rossiyskiy tsenariy?" *Nezavisimaia gazeta*, April 17, 1993, 3.

   22. Strobe Talbott, remarks before the U.S. House of Representatives, "Hearing of the House Foreign Affairs Committee: U.S. Aid to the Republics of the Former Soviet Union," Federal News Service, September 21, 1993.

   23. Not all back issues for these papers are easily accessible. I found several gaps in the National Archives' collections of *Res publica* and *Svobodnye gori* (gaps from when the papers were actually in press, not simply from when the papers were forcibly closed by the government). The chaotic archives of the Kyrgyz Academy of Science were able to fill some of these holes. I am also grateful to Sadirbek Dzhigitekov for his aid in helping me obtain several back issues of *Res publica* I could find nowhere else.

   24. Martha Brill Olcott, *Kazakhstan: Unfulfilled Promise* (New York: Carnegie Endowment for International Peace, 2002), 104.

   25. Sydykova, *Za kulisami*, 31. Turganaliev and Sydykova were imprisoned for libel against the president. Tursunbai Bakir uulu's brother was arrested, conveniently during the 1996 presidential election, for drug possession.

   26. Sydykova, *Za kulisami*, 70; author's discussions with Tolekan Ismailova, chairman of the Kyrgyz NGO Civil Society Against Corruption and Reagan-Fascell Democracy Fellow, during the November 15–16, 2002, Stanford University Workshop on Regime Transitions.

   27. For this quote and a list of the deputies, see "Obrashcheniia deputatov Zhagorku Kanesha k narodu Kyrgyzstana, prezidentu Kyrgyzskoi Respubliki Askaru Akaevu, Zhogorku Kaneshu Kyrgyzskoi Respubliki," *Vesti issyk kulya*, September 6, 1994, 1–2.

   28. Refer to the presidential decree "Ukaz prezidenta KR ot 5 sentiabria 1994 goda N UP-226

'Ob obespechenii politicheskoi stabil'nosti v Kyrgyzskoi Respublike i neotlozhnykh merakh sotsial'no-ekonomicheskogo kharaktera,'" September 5, 1994.

29. See President William J. Clinton, Office of the Press Secretary, "Press Conference by President Clinton and President Hosni Mubarak of Egypt," October 25, 1993, available online at the National Archives and Records Administration, Clinton Presidential Materials Project, http://clinton.archives.gov. Yeltsin's actions found support among academics as well. Anders Aslund, for example, reflecting on Russia's 1993 parliamentary-executive crisis, has written that not to dismiss the Communist-dominated Russian parliament was to in effect "accept hyperinflation." Aslund proceeds to note that "after the parliament had been dissolved, the most important reform wave since early 1992 erupted." See Anders Aslund, *How Russia Became a Market Economy* (Washington, D.C.: Brookings Institution Press, 1995), 56.

30. Askar Akaev, "Sprosit' i vyislushat' narod—Obrascheniie prezidenta Kyrgyzskoi Respubliki k narodu po povodu referenduma 22 oktyabrya 1994 goda," *Vesti issyk-kulia*, October 4, 1994, 1.

31. Pauline Jones Luong interview with Timurbek Kenenbaev, December 13, 1994, in Luong, *Institutional Change and Political Continuity in Post-Soviet Central Asia*, 185.

32. See the 1993 Constitution of the Kyrgyz Republic.

33. Ibid.

34. Akaev, "Sprosit' i vyislushat' narod."

35. Tsentral'naiia izbiratel'naiia komissiia po provedeniiu referenduma i vyboram v Kyrgyzskoi Respublike, "Spravochniie materiali o khode podgotovki i provedenii vyiborov deputatov dvukhpalatnogo parlamenta Zhogorku Kenesha Kyrgyzskoi Respubliki," Kyrgyz Central Elections Commission, Bishkek, 1995.

36. Ibid.

37. Almanbet Matubraimov, "Triumvirat dolzhen vzaimodeistvovat," *Ekho Osha*, February 15, 1996, 2.

38. Ibid.

39. Both Beknazarov and Kadyrbekov were jailed in 2002, although they were released after mass public protests.

40. European Bank for Reconstruction and Development, "Strategy for the Kyrgyz Republic," October 7, 2002, 4.

41. Askar Akaev, "Obrascheniia Prezidenta Kyrgyzskoi Respubliki k narodu po povodu referenduma 10 February 1996," *Ekho Osha*, January 6, 1996, 1.

42. Refer to the law Zakon Kyrgyzskoi Respubliki o vnesenii izmenenii i dopolnenii v konstitsiiu Kyrgyzskoi Respubliki, February 16, 1996.

43. Akaev, "Obrascheniia Prezidenta Kyrgyzskoi Respubliki."

44. World Bank Operations Evaluation Department, "Kyrgyz Republic Country Assistance Evaluation," World Bank, Washington, D.C., November 12, 2002, 5.

45. Ibid.

46. Ibid. The World Bank had disbursed $122 million under the Rehabilitation and Privatization and Enterprise Adjustment Credits. See ibid., annex table 6.

47. Asian Development Bank, "Special Evaluation Study on Advisory and Operational Technical Assistance in Kazakhstan and the Kyrgyz Republic," Manila, Philippines, December 1999, 13.

48. The UNDP disbursed $12.5 million in external assistance between 1994 and 2000. See Organization for Economic Cooperation and Development (OECD), Development Assistance Committee, *Geographical Distribution of Financial Flows to Aid Recipients 1999* (Paris: OECD, 1999), and OECD, Development Assistance Committee, *Geographical Distribution of Financial Flows to Aid Recipients 2002* (Paris: OECD, 2002).

49. United Nations Development Program (UNDP), "The UN Resident Coordinator Report for 1999," UNDP.

50. Author interview with senior Akaev administration official and Temirbek Koshoev, Presidential Administration Building (Dom Pravitel'stvo), November 1999, Bishkek, Kyrgyzstan.

51. See UNDP, "UN Resident Coordinator Report for 1999" for Kyrgyzstan.

52. United Nations Development Programme, *Government of the Kyrgyz Republic and UNDP:*

Political and Administrative Local Governance Programme, Decentralization Component Annual Report (Bishkek: UNDP, 2001), 10. Nonetheless, that an NGO should have such prime realty struck me as odd, particularly an NGO that ostensibly was to serve the interests of *local* rather than central governance. Some of the confusion may stem from the UN resident coordinator's loose use of the term NGO—the office for the Congress of Local Communities is in Kyrgyzstan's "White House," the presidential administration building.

53. Author interview with Koshoev. Dykimbaev is the director of the apparatus of the Congress of Local Communities, the main liaison organization for the UNDP's decentralization project. Koshoev was, at the time of the interview, UNDP program manager and vice president of the Congress of Local Communities. Koshoev reported directly to the Kyrgyz secretary of state. Koshoev's office was two floors below Akaev's.

54. "USAID FY 1999 Congressional Presentation: Kyrgyzstan," available online at http://www.usaid.gov/pubs/cp99/eni/kg.htm.

55. Ibid.

56. Alexander Tuzov and Makhmadzhan Khamidov, "Three Kyrgyz University Heads Sacked," *Vecherniy Bishkek*, April 8, 1998.

57. Chandra Mattingly, "Student Recalls Encouragement, Lessons," *Dearborn County Register*, April 1, 2005.

58. Talanbek Sakishev, "Sotsopros: Idem ne tuda i ne s temi," *Vecherniy Bishkek*, August 2, 1999.

59. As quoted in Alexander Tuzov, "V dalekuiu-blizkuiu Indiiu," *Vecherniy Bishkek*, February 21, 2000.

60. "Tochka v 'kakangeite,'" *Vecherniy Bishkek*, January 23, 2001.

61. Peggy Simpson, "IWMF: International Women's Media Foundation—Fifteen Years of Courage: Zamira Sydykova," available online at http://www.iwmf.org/article.aspx?id=389&c=carticles.

62. Zamira Sydykova, "Kyrgyzstan: Opposition Newspaper Published after Three-Month Hiatus," *Res publica*, May 4, 2002.

63. "Kommentarii press-sekretarya Prezidenta Kyrgyzskoi Respubliki K. Imanalieva k rasporyazheniyu Prezidenta A. Akaeva ot 15 Yanvarya 1997 goda 'O Sharapove,'" *Vesti issyk-kulia*, January 21, 1997, 1.

64. Ibid.

65. Author interview with Narynbek Alymkulov, professor of government at Bishkek State University, June 19, 2003, Bishkek, Kyrgyzstan.

66. Author interview with Alexander Zlatkin, the executive director of ST.art Ltd Printing House, June 18, 2003, Bishkek, Kyrgyzstan.

67. Author interview with Edil Baisalov, director of the Coalition of NGOs, June 19, 2003, Bishkek, Kyrgyzstan.

68. Tsentr ekstremal'noi zhurnalistiki Soyuza zhurnalistov Rossii, *Opasnaya professiya: Yezhenedel'nyy byulleten' sobytiy v sredstvakh massovoy informatsii stran SNG* (Moscow, December 9, 2002).

69. "O politicheskikh svobodakh grazhdan: Iz doklada Ombudsmena KR za 2003 god," *Moya stolitsa*, January 25, 2005.

70. Tsentr ekstremal'noi zhurnalistiki Soiuza zhurnalistov Rossii, *Opasnaia professiia*.

71. Arkady Dubnov, "V Kirgizii golodaiut deputaty. Prezident Akaev nabludaet," *Vremia novostei*, January 23, 2002.

72. David Stern, "Kyrgyz President Admits Relative Sells to U.S. Base," *Financial Times*, July 22, 2002.

73. Ibid.

74. Author correspondence with David Stern, April 26, 2010.

75. Author interview with Tolekan Ismailova, June 19, 2003, Bishkek, Kyrgyzstan.

76. David Cloud, "Pentagon's Fuel Deal Is Lesson in Risks of Graft-Prone Regions," November 14, 2005, available online at http://query.nytimes.com/gst/fullpage.html?res=9E07E4DC103EF 936A25752C1A9639C8B63&sec=&spon=&pagewanted=print; and Aram Rostom, "A Crooked

Alliance in the War on Terror?," October 30, 2006, available online at http://www.msnbc.msn. com/id/15448018/ns/nightly_news-lisa_myers_and_the_nbc_news_investigative_unit/page/2/.

77. Alexander Cooley, "U.S. Bases and Democratization in Central Asia," *Orbis* 52, no. 1 (Winter 2008): 74.

78. Rina Prizhivoit, "'Prezident izdal ukaz vsekh otmyt' v poslednyi raz," *Moya stolitsa Novosti*, February 8, 2005.

79. Roza Otunbaeva, "Will There Be a Tulip Revolution in Kyrgyzstan? Who Is Next after Ukraine?" Moscow Carnegie Center, February 11, 2005.

80. Ibid.

81. Ibid.

82. Ibid.

83. For an excellent discussion of the initially local nature of these 2005 protests, see Scott Radnitz, "What Really Happened in Kyrgyzstan?" *Journal of Democracy* 17, no. 2 (April 2006): 132–46.

84. "Opposition Plans to Take Control of Half of Kyrgyzstan," *Interfax*, March 22, 2005.

85. Ibid.

86. "Probe into Akayev Property," *RIA Novosti*, April 1, 2005.

87. Ibid.

88. Cloud, "Pentagon's Fuel Deal Is Lesson."

89. Ibid.

90. FBI report, as quoted in Cloud, "Pentagon's Fuel Deal Is Lesson." I have submitted a Freedom of Information Act (FOIA) request for this report (FBI file number 272A-WF-232920).

91. "Kyrgyzstan's Ex-Chief Prosecutor Makes Statement after Dismissal," *Kabar*, September 20, 2005.

92. "Kyrgyz Government Refuses to Restore British Gold Company's License," *AKIpress.com*, December 7, 2005.

93. Peter Klinger, "Kyrgyz President Rebukes Blair as Oxus Intervention Backfires," *Times*, February 3, 2006; and Lawrence Williams, "Global Gold in Deal with Kazakh Investment Group over Jerooy," *Mineweb*, August 21, 2007, available online at http://www.mineweb.com/mineweb/ view/mineweb/en/page34?oid=25741&sn=Detail.

94. International Crisis Group, "Kyrgyzstan: A Faltering State," International Crisis Group, December 16, 2005, 7.

95. Author discussions with Alisher Saipov, June 2007. See also Institute for Public Policy, *Kyrgyzstan Brief*, no. 2 (December 2005–January 2006): 19, for more information on the Bakiev family's interest in Kant Cement. See Bruce Pannier, "Kyrgyzstan: Pyramid TV Employees Question Source of Takeover Attempt," *Radio Free Europe / Radio Liberty*, December 14, 2005; "Kyrgyz Private TV Claims Authorities Behind Arson," *AKIpress.com*, October 2, 2006; and "Kyrgyz Leader Says TV Company's Case Should Be Resolved by Court," *Kabar*, December 12, 2005, for more on the Bakiev family's interest in the Pyramid TV station. See "Dispute over Ownership of Hotel Pinara Bishkek," *Asia Pulse*, March 13, 2005, for more on the Bakiev family's interest in the Hotel Pinar.

96. Gulnoza Saidazimova, "Kyrgyzstan: Economic Reforms Seem Stalled," *Radio Free Europe / Radio Liberty*, May 25, 2006.

97. "President Rebukes Envoy over Fiscal Claims to USA over Airbase," *AKIpress.com*, December 6, 2005.

98. Ibid.

99. Ibid.

100. Andrew E. Kramer, "Fuel Sales to U.S. at Issue in Kyrgyzstan," *New York Times*, April 11, 2010, available online at http://www.nytimes.com/2010/04/12/world/asia/12manas.html.

101. Ibid. For the Washington law firm identification, see Scott Horton, "Crisis in Kyrgyzstan: Fuel, Contractors, and Revolution along the Afghan Supply Chain," Congressional Hearing, U.S. House of Representatives Committee on Oversight and Government Reform, Subcommittee on National Security and Foreign Affairs, April 22, 2010.

102. U.S. Department of Defense Intelligence Information Report (IIR) 6 955 0176 05, May

19, 2005. Content made available to author by Department of Defense employee who asked not to be identified, May 5, 2010.

103. Author discussions with U.S. Department of Defense employee, May 5, 2010. Name withheld by mutual agreement.

104. Kramer, "Fuel Sales to U.S. at Issue in Kyrgyzstan."

105. Kazy Sultanov, "Pouring Kerosene into Kyrgyz Revolution," *Kommersant Online*, May 4, 2010.

106. Ibid.

107. Andrew E. Kramer, "Kyrgyzstan Opens an Inquiry into Fuel Sales to a U.S. Base," *New York Times*, May 5, 2010.

108. Author interview with Gegham Sarkisyan, NDI country director; Kevin Gash, NDI parliamentary program manager; and Matthew Blevins, NDI civic program manager, December 13, 2006, Bishkek, Kyrgyzstan.

109. Author interview with Edil Baisalov, December 13, 2006, Bishkek, Kyrgyzstan.

110. Author interview with Melis Eshimkanov, December 14, 2006, Bishkek, Kyrgyzstan.

111. Author interview with Kubatbek Baibalov, December 21, 2006, Bishkek, Kyrgyzstan.

112. Author interview with Roza Otunbaeva, December 15, 2006, Bishkek, Kyrgyzstan.

113. Ibid.

114. Quoted in Bek Orozaliev, "Constitutional Revolution," *Kommersant Online*, November 3, 2006.

115. Quoted in ibid.

116. Quoted in ibid.

117. "President Bakiev Names Chair of Advisory Board of Development Fund," *AKIpress. com*, November 6, 2009.

118. "General Prosecutor Files Suit against Edil Baisalov," *Times of Central Asia*, December 7, 2007.

119. "Kyrgyz Ministry Defends Arrest of 4 Opposition Activists," Central Asia General Newswire, January 17, 2009.

120. Freedom House, "Freedom in the World—Kyrgyzstan (2007)," available online at http://www.freedomhouse.org/inc/content/pubs/fiw/inc_country_detail.cfm?year =2007&country=7210&pf.

121. "Reporters Sans Frontières—Letter to Kyrgyz Authorities about Wave of Violence Against Journalists," April 6, 2007, available online at http://en.rsf.org/kyrgyzstan-letter-to-kyrgyz-authorities-about-06-04-2007,21627.html.

122. Jipara Abdrakhmanova, "Kyrgyz Journalists: Better Protection Calls," Institute for War and Peace Reporting, April 29, 2007.

123. Author interviews with Cholpon Ata merchant and Hizb ut-Tahrir activist, Erlan (last name withheld by mutual agreement), May 21, 2007, Bishkek. Author interview with Abdymalik and Sabira Akmatbaev, parents of slain member of parliament Ryspek Akmatbaev, June 2, 2007, Cholpon Ata.

124. Author interviews with Ak Terek villagers and Hizb ut-Tahrir activists (names withheld by mutual agreement), June 3, 2007, Ak Terek, Kyrgyzstan.

125. Author interview with Sadykzhan Kamalov, May 26, 2007, Osh, Kyrgyzstan.

126. Author interview with Abdulla Usupov, June 8, 2007, Bishkek, Kyrgyzstan.

127. Author interview with Zhantoro Satybaldiev, December 19, 2006, Osh, Kyrgyzstan.

128. "Zhantoro Satybaldiev: Reshenie o svoei otstavke eto muzhestvennyi postupok poriadochnogo pravitel'stva Kyrgyzstana," *24.kg*, December 12, 2006.

129. "United Opposition Announces Meetings in yhe Kyrgyz Regions," *AKIpress.com*, March 31, 2010.

130. Ibid.

131. "Kyrgyz Premier Criticizes Regional Protests," Kyrgyz Television 1, April 6, 2010, Bishkek, Kyrgyzstan.

132. Medina Maratova, "Protest Moods Increasing in Kyrgyzstan," *Delovaya nedelya* (Almaty), March 19, 2010.

133. Otunbaeva, quoted in Ilya Azar, "Bakiyev Turned Out to Be a Greater Monster Than Akayev," *Gazeta.ru*, March 25, 2010.

134. Bakiev, quoted in Bruce Pannier and Andy Heil, "Kyrgyz President Pooh-Poohs Western-Style Democracy," *Radio Free Europe / Radio Liberty*, March 24, 2010.

135. At least eighty protestors died during clashes with Bakiev's security forces on April 7, 2010.

136. "Kyrgyz Communist Leader Calls His Detention 'Political Provocation,'" Interfax Central Asia General Newswire, May 12, 2010.

137. Albert O. Hirschman, *Exit, Voice, and Loyalty: Responses to Decline in Firms, Organizations, and States* (Cambridge: Harvard University Press, 1970).

4. Uzbek Violence

The author thanks *Asia Policy* and *Europe-Asia Studies* for their permission to reprint and adapt portions of the following two articles: Eric McGlinchey, "Islamic Leaders in Uzbekistan," *Asia Policy* 1, no. 1 (January 2006): 123–44; and Eric M. McGlinchey, "Searching for Kamalot: Political Patronage and Youth Politics in Uzbekistan," *Europe-Asia Studies* 61, no. 7 (2009): 1,137–50, 1,137.

1. Dmitry Zaks, "Karimov Wins Re-election in Farcical Vote," Agence France Presse, January 9, 2010.

2. Before achieving this post in January 2010, Karimova was Uzbekistan's ambassador to the United Nations in Geneva.

3. "Uzbekistan: Sting Stung amid Media Swarm," *Eurasianet.org*, February 24, 2010, available online at http://www.eurasianet.org/print/59116; and Tom Harper, "Sting Plays Concert for Daughter of 'Boil Your Enemies' Dictator," *Daily Mail Online*, February 21, 2010.

4. For a video of the Iglesias-Karimova performance, see http://www.youtube.com/watch?v=BRPsFOf5LXc&feature=player_embedded#!.

5. Grant Podelco, "It's Gulnara's World. We Only Live in It," *Radio Free Europe / Radio Liberty*, December 18, 2009.

6. "Sources Claim Powerful Uzbek Conglomerate Shut Down," *Radio Free Europe / Radio Liberty*, May 14, 2010; "Les 300 plus riches de Suisse," *Bilan*, December 4, 2009, 108.

7. "Les 300 plus riches de Suisse."

8. The Karimov government, citing Umarov's poor health, released the former oppositionist in November 2009. Umarov currently resides with his family in Germantown, Tennessee.

9. A *mahalla* is a state-controlled neighborhood committee.

10. Author interview with Abdulmajid qori, head imam of Quqon city, November 18, 2004, Quqon, Uzbekistan; author interview with Ismail Hajji Raikhanov, head imam of Qarshi, November 24, 2004, Qarshi, Uzbekistan.

11. Author interview with Saidakbar Agzamkhodjaev, dean of the Tashkent Islamic University history department, July 6, 2005, Tashkent, Uzbekistan.

12. Author interviews with students at Tashkent Islamic University, August and November 2004, Tashkent, Uzbekistan. Names withheld by mutual agreement.

13. Author interview with Agzamkhodjaev.

14. See Article 9, "Religious Schools," from the 1998 Law on Freedom of Conscience and Religious Organizations, available online at http://www.pravo.uz.

15. Author focus groups conducted in August 2004 in Andijan and November 2004 in Quqon.

16. Ahmed Rashid, "They're Only Sleeping: Why Militant Islamicists in Central Asia Aren't Going to Go Away," *New Yorker*, January 14, 2002.

17. Adeeb Khalid, *Islam after Communism: Religion and Politics in Central Asia* (Berkeley: University of California Press, 2007), 140.

18. Kremlin International News Broadcast, "Interview with Mufti Mukhammad-Yusuf

Mukhammad-Sedik, Head of the Central Asian Theological Moslem Board," *Federal Information Systems Corporation*, January 9, 1992.

19. Daniel Sneider, "Violence Shakes Soviet Republic," *Christian Science Monitor*, December 11, 1990.

20. "Namangan Calm," *BBC Summary of World Broadcasts*, December 7, 1990.

21. I. Chantseva, "The Koran Is No Obstacle to Politics," *Kuranty*, October 26, 1991.

22. "Muslim Rallies in Uzbekistan," *BBC Summary of World Broadcasts*, October 2, 1991.

23. "Uzbek President Reportedly Orders Arrest of Muslim Opposition Leaders," *Nezavisimaya gazeta*, March 21, 1992.

24. Ibid.

25. Clifford Bond, as quoted in "U.S. Representative Benjamin Gilman (R-N.Y.) Holds Hearing on U.S. Policy in Central Asia," Federal Document Clearing House (FDCH) Political Transcripts, June 6, 2001.

26. U.S. Department of State, Bureau for Democracy, Human Rights, and Labor, "Annual Report on International Religious Freedom for 1999: Uzbekistan," September 9, 1999, available online at http://www.state.gov/www/global/human_rights/irf/irf_rpt/1999/irf_uzbekist99.html.

27. "Islam Karimov: Nikto ne Smozhet Svernut' Nas s Izbrannogo puti," *Narodnoe slovo* (Tashkent), May 18, 2005.

28. International Crisis Group, "Uzbekistan: The Andijon Uprising," *Asia Briefing*, no. 38 (May 25, 2005).

29. Author interview with Andijan refugee, May 26, 2007, Osh, Kyrgyzstan. Name withheld by mutual agreement.

30. U.S. Department of State, Bureau for Democracy, Human Rights, and Labor, "2009 Human Rights Report: Uzbekistan," March 11, 2010, available online at http://www.state.gov/g/drl/rls/hrrpt/2009/sca/136096.htm.

31. Author discussions with Alisher Saipov, June 2007, Osh, Kyrgyzstan.

32. As quoted in "Verkhovnyi sud Kyrgyzsta naostavil v sile reshenie Oshskogo oblastnogo suda po delu ob ubystve zhurnalista Alishera Saipova," *24.kg*, December 9, 2009.

33. Author interview with Andijan refugee, May 26, 2007, Osh, Kyrgyzstan. Name withheld by mutual agreement.

34. Shirin Akiner, "Violence in Andijan, 13 May 2005: An Independent Assessment," *CACI Silk Road Paper*, July 2005, 30.

35. Ibid., 45.

36. Ibid., 25.

37. The explanation as to why Quqon has more independent imams than other regions is not immediately clear. I hope to answer this question in future research.

38. See, for example, Quintan Wiktorowicz, ed., *Islamic Activism: A Social Movement Theory Approach* (Bloomington: Indiana University Press, 2004); William B. Quandt, *Between Ballots and Bullets: Algeria's Transition from Authoritarian Rule* (Washington, D.C.: Brookings Institution Press, 1998); and Gilles Kepel, *Jihad: The Trail of Political Islam* (Cambridge: Harvard University Press, 2002).

39. The name of Uzbekistan's current mufti, Abdurashid Bahromov, was also frequently mentioned but never in a positive light.

40. For more on the collapse of the Muslim Spiritual Board, see Bakhtiyar Babajanov, "Sredneaziatskoe dukhovnoe upravlenie musul'man: Predystoriia i posledstviia raspada," in *Mnogomernye granitsi Tsentral'noi Azii* (The multidimensional borders of Central Asia), edited by Martha Brill Olcott and Aleksei Malashenko (Moscow: Carnegie Endowment for International Peace, 2000), 55–69.

41. Ibid.

42. Interfax, "Leader of Central Asian Muslims Condemns Turanjonzoda Involvement in Conflict, January 27, 1993," reprinted in *BBC Summary of World Broadcasts*, January 29, 1993.

43. Ibid.

44. "Uzbekistan Muslims Demonstrate against Communist Leadership," Russian television program, September 22, 1991, in *BBC Summary of World Broadcasts*, September 24, 1991.

45. Kremlin International News Broadcast, "Interview with Mufti Mukhammad-Yusuf Mukhammad-Sedik."

46. "Uzbek Students Withdrawn from Turkey," *Hurriyet*, August 25, 1997.

47. Author interview with Muhammad Sodik, former mufti, August 17, 2004, Tashkent.

48. Alexei Malashenko, "Islam in Central Asia," in *Central Asian Security: The New International Conflict*, edited by Roy Allison and Lena Jonson (Washington, D.C.: Brookings Institution Press, 2001), 52.

49. Author interview with Sodik.

50. "Visit to Uzbekistan of Exiled Mufti," *Eurasianet.org*, January 2000.

51. Yury Mashin, "Uzbekistan poetapno idet k demokratii (Uzhe mozhno smotret' telivizor)," *Kommersant Online*, February 1, 2000, 9.

52. Sodik has weekly radio shows on the Uzbek station Narooz and on the Uzbek-language broadcasts of the BBC and Radio Freedom (author's interview with Sodik). The Sodik quotations are from Charles Recknagel and Zamira Eshanova, "U.S.: 11 September—Muslims Debate Fundamentalism in Wake of Attacks (Part 5)," *Radio Free Europe / Radio Liberty*, September 6, 2002.

53. See Article 9 of Uzbekistan's 1998 Law on Freedom of Conscience and Religious Organizations.

54. Recknagel and Eshanova, "Muslims Debate Fundamentalism in Wake of Attacks."

55. Galima Bukharbaeva, "Byvshii mufti Uzbekistana—o religioznoi zhizni v strane," Institute for War and Peace Reporting (IWPR), November 8, 2002.

56. Ibid.

57. Author interview with Sodik.

58. Joel S. Migdal, *Strong Societies and Weak States: State-Society Relations and State Capabilities in the Third World* (Princeton: Princeton University Press, 1998), 223.

59. Author interviews with Imam Klichev's supporters, August and November 2004, Qarshi. Names withheld by mutual agreement.

60. Three cordons of Uzbek and American troops secure the Khanabad base.

61. Author focus group, August 2004, and author discussions with human rights activists. Qarshi. .

62. Ismail Raikhanov described the Muslim Spiritual Board's prepared notes for Friday prayer as a "great help. . . . They draw from multiple sources and scholarly works. . . . I would not be able to write such a sermon alone." Author interview with Ismail Raikhanov, Qarshi's head imam, November 24, 2004, Qarshi.

63. Klichev attended the Kitab madrassa, a hundred kilometers northeast of Qarshi.

64. Author interviews with students at Tashkent Islamic University, August and November 2004, Tashkent. Names withheld by mutual agreement.

65. Author interview with Rakhmatulla qori Obidov, prominent Tashkent imam, November 17, 2004, Tashkent.

66. Ahmed Rashid, "Asking for Holy War," *Far Eastern Economic Review* (November 9, 2000): 28–29.

67. Author interview with Qarshi human rights activists, November 2004, Qarshi. Names withheld by mutual agreement.

68. Douglass C. North, *Institutions, Institutional Change and Economic Performance* (Cambridge: Cambridge University Press, 1990); Sven Steinmo, Kathleen Thelen, and Frank Longstreth, *Structuring Politics: Historical Institutionalism in Comparative Analysis* (Cambridge: Cambridge University Press, 1992); Timur Kuran, "Now out of Never: The Element of Surprise in the East European Revolution of 1989," *World Politics* 44, no. 1 (1991): 7–48; Samuel P. Huntington, "The Clash of Civilizations?" *Foreign Affairs* 72, no. 3 (1993): 22–49; and Paul Pierson, "Increasing Returns, Path Dependence, and the Study of Politics," *American Political Science Review* 94, no. 2 (2000): 251–67.

69. Kuran, "Now out of Never."

70. The Helsinki Final Act, signed by U.S. President Gerald Ford and Soviet General Secretary Leonid Brezhnev, as well as the executives of thirty-three other members of the Conference on Security and Co-operation in Europe (CSCE), was attractive to Moscow in

that it codified the sovereign rights of Eastern bloc states. At the same time, it was attractive to Washington because the act committed all signatories to respect human rights.

71. Anthony Lewis, "Echoes of Helsinki," *New York Times*, August 2, 1976.

72. Daniel Charles Thomas, *The Helsinki Effect: International Norms, Human Rights, and the Demise of Communism* (Princeton: Princeton University Press, 2001), 23.

73. John A. Hall, "Ideas and the Social Sciences," in *Ideas and Foreign Policy: Beliefs, Institutions, and Political Change*, edited by Judith Goldstein and Robert Owen Keohane (Ithaca: Cornell University Press, 1993), 52.

74. Judith Goldstein and Robert Owen Keohane, eds., *Ideas and Foreign Policy: Beliefs, Institutions, and Political Change* (Ithaca: Cornell University Press, 1993), 26–27.

75. David I. Kertzer, *Politics and Symbols: The Italian Communist Party and the Fall of Communism* (New Haven: Yale University Press, 1996), x.

76. Alison Brysk, "'Hearts and Minds': Bringing Symbolic Politics Back In," *Polity* 27, no. 4 (Summer 1995): 559–85, 564.

77. Calculations based on the *United Nations World Population Prospects, The 2008 Revision*; the full population data set is available online at http://esa.un.org/unpp/.

78. In the 1990s I studied the development of post-Soviet Uzbek bazaars, and in the 2000s I have focused on the emergence of local Islamic associations and elites.

79. Uzbek Television Second Channel, Yoshlar, "Uzbek President's Daughter Sings in Patriotic Chorus," January 7, 2006, *BBC Monitoring of International Reports*. For more on Kelazhak Ovozi, see the organization's Web site at http://www.kelajakovozi.uz.

80. "Journalism Contest Announced for News Agencies, Printed, and Online Media," *UzReport.com*, August 19, 2008.

81. Ibid.

82. "Uzbekistan Founds Military Sports Camp for Difficult Children," *Narodnoe slovo*, July 24, 2003.

83. "Young Uzbeks Skate against Drugs," *Ishonch*, September 23, 2003.

84. "Marafontsy napravalis' v Bukharu," *Narodnoe slovo*, December 1, 2005, 1.

85. "Young Andijon Athletes Compete to Condemn Terror," *Huquq*, June 28, 2006.

86. "2008 the Year of Youth in Uzbekistan," *UzReport.com*, January 31, 2008.

87. Vladislav Novintskyi, "V Uzbekistane sozdaetsia obschestvennaia obrazovatel'naia informatsionnaia set 'Ziyonet,'" *Narodnoe slovo*, October 1, 2005, 2.

88. "Ferghana Implements 'Values, Customs, Traditions, and Youth' Project," *Times of Central Asia*, March 28, 2008.

89. "'Do You Know the Law' Nationwide Contest Ends in Jizzakh Region," *UzReport.com*, May 17, 2007.

90. "Fourth International Education and Career Exhibition Opens in Uzbek Capital," *UzReport.com*, February 19, 2009; and "Uzbek Youth Movement Leader Says Its Ranks Increasing," *BBC Monitoring Central Asia Unit Supplied by BBC Worldwide Monitoring*, February 2, 2006.

91. "Uzbek Body Mulls Prevention of Religious Extremism among Minors," *Turkiston*, December 23, 2006.

92. "The First Stage of Charity Campaign Held in Tashkent," *Times of Central Asia*, July 24, 2008.

93. "Youth of Uzbekistan Interested in Cooperation with Azerbaijan Coevals," *Times of Central Asia*, July 21, 2005.

94. Anvar Karimov, "'Kamolot' dolzhen stat' mostom mezhdu molodezh'iu i gosudarstvom," *Narodnoe slovo*, March 16, 2001, 1.

95. Calculations based on the *United Nations World Population Prospects, the 2008 Revision*; see the UNPP database at http://esa.un.org/UNPP.

96. "Uzbek Youth Movement Leader Says Its Ranks Increasing," February 2, 2006, *BBC Monitoring International Reports*.

97. Yegor Sharai, "Vospityvaia patriotov, intellektualov, biznesmenov," *Narodnoe slovo*, August 3, 2005, 1.

98. Said Shukurov, "Proyavlenie patriotizma i lubvyi k otchizne," *Narodnoye slovo*, July 12, 2005, 2.

99. Although the International Monetary Fund has encouraged the Karimov government to liberalize the domestic pricing of cotton, Uzbekistan's cotton farmers receive only a fraction of the international market price for their crop. For more on how the Karimov government extracts rents from the cotton industry, see International Crisis Group, "The Curse of Cotton: Central Asia's Destructive Monoculture," February 28, 2005.

100. Maurizio Guadagni, Martin Raiser, Anna Crole-Rees, and Dilshod Khidirov, "Cotton Taxation in Uzbekistan: Opportunities for Reform," World Bank, Environmentally and Socially Sustainable Development Unit for Europe and Central Asia (ECSSD) Working Paper No. 41, August 26, 2005, 1.

101. Ibid., 3.

102. U.S. General Accounting Office, "Central and Southwest Asian Countries: Trends in U.S. Assistance and Key Economic, Governance, and Demographic Characteristics," May 2003, 20.

103. Ewen MacAskil, "Ex-envoy to Face Discipline Charges, Says FO," *Guardian*, October 22, 2004, 19.

104. U.S. Department of State, Bureau of European and Eurasian Affairs, "U.S. Assistance to Uzbekistan—Fiscal Year 2002," December 9, 2002.

105. For a detailed discussion of intergroup competition and the politics of political survival, see Migdal, *Strong Societies and Weak States*.

106. Uzbek Television Second Channel, "Uzbek President Slams Andijon Governor over Corruption," *BBC Monitoring International Reports*, May 25, 2004.

107. For a more extensive treatment of the Andijan events, see Eric McGlinchey, "Autocrats, Islamists, and the Rise of Radicalism in Central Asia," *Current History* (October 2005): 336–42.

108. "President Karimov Sacks Regional Governor: 'Nepotism, Cronyism, Bribery' Rife," *Uzbek Radio Second Program*, March 23, 2000.

109. "Uzbek Leader Warns of Perils of Mismanagement," *Uzbek Television First Channel*, October 16, 2004.

110. "Uzbek Leader Sacks Regional, District Governors," *Uzbek Television First Channel*, December 16, 2008.

111. "Uzbek Chief Prosecutor Points to Corruption Crack-Down," *Narodnoe slovo*, April 22, 2005.

112. Author interviews with Tulkun Karaev, Qarshi, and activists in Quqon, November 2004. Names withheld by mutual agreement. See also "Some 500 Female Traders Stage Protest in Uzbek East," September 9, 2004.

113. "Uzbekistan Possibly on Way to 'Velvet Revolution,'" AFX News, May 17, 2005.

114. Valerie J. Bunce and Sharon L. Wolchik, "Youth and Electoral Revolutions in Slovakia, Serbia, and Georgia," *SAIS Review* 26, no. 2 (2006): 56–57.

115. Dr. Dot (Dorothy Stein) is an American massage therapist whose February 2009 week in Georgia attending to President Saakashvili's aches and pains attracted considerable attention in Georgia and abroad. See, for example, Robert Mackey, "A President, His Masseuse, and Her Blog," *New York Times*, April 8, 2009.

116. Lucan A. Way, "Kuchma's Failed Authoritarianism," *Journal of Democracy* 16, no. 2 (April 2005): 131–45, 144.

117. Migdal, *Strong Societies and Weak States*, 4, 32.

118. Lisa Wedeen, "Conceptualizing Culture: Possibilities for Political Science," *American Political Science Review* 96, no. 4 (December 2002): 713–28, 723.

5. Kazakh Dynasty

1. George A. Krol, *Approaching the OSCE Chairmanship: Kazakhstan 2010* (Washington, D.C.: Commission on Security and Cooperation in Europe, 2009).

2. See the Web site of the OSCE at http://www.osce.org.

3. See the introduction for a more extended treatment of these rankings.

4. "Nazarbaev on the Reform Process and the Future of the Republic—Presidential Address," *BBC Summary of World Broadcasts*, October 26, 1992.

5. "Parliament Approves Constitution after Energetic Debate," *Kazakh Radio* (Almaty), June 6, 1992.

6. Tatyana Kvyatkovskaya, "Skirmish for Power: The Kazakhstan Version," *Kazakhstanskaia pravda*, January 21, 1993.

7. As quoted in Leonid Bershidsky, "Kazakh Parliament: It's a Farce but No Joke," *Moscow News*, February 4, 1995.

8. Author interview with Petr Svoik, Kazakh journalist, political activist, cochair of the political party Azamat, September 2000, Almaty, Kazakhstan.

9. Azhdar Kurtov, "Partii Kazakhstana i osobennosti razvitiia politicheskogo protsessa v respublike," in *Kazakhstan: Realii i perspektivy*, edited by Eugenii M. Kozhokin (Moscow: Rossikii institute strategicheskikh issledovanii, 1995), 205.

10. Ibid.

11. Vladimir Ardayev, "President of Kazakhstan Announces Return to State Planning," *Izvestia*, January 26, 1993.

12. Ibid.

13. Refer to "Kodeks Respubliki Kazakhstan ot 9 Dekabria 1993 goda o vyborakh v Respublike Kazakhstan" (this is a Kazakh election law).

14. Kviatkovskaia, curiously, is the same person who penned the January 1993 *Kazakhstanskaia pravda* article that described the cataclysmic struggle between Abdildin and Nazarbaev.

15. Vladimir Ardaev, "Kak grazhdanka Kviatkovskaia parlament svalila," *Izvestia,* March 14, 1995. See also "Pochemu parlament priznan nelegitimnyim," *Industrial'naiia Karaganda*, March 15, 1995, 1.

16. Gennadii Bocharov, "Prezident Nazarbaev nastroen reshitel'no," *Izvestia,* April 18, 1994.

17. Ibid. The Kazakh parliament in its next iteration was divided into two houses.

18. "Kazak Opposition Leader Seeks Protection for Family after Beating," Associated Press, December 8, 1997.

19. In May 2003, Ablyazov repented and pledged to Nazarbaev that he would stay out of politics. The Kazakh president, not one to hold a grudge, pardoned his former energy minister, and in May 2005, Ablyazov once again emerged as a major player, assuming chairmanship of Kazakhstan's largest bank, TuranAlem. Ablyazov and TuranAlem, Nazarbaev likely thought, were a good fit. In December 2004, TuranAlem along with Kazakhstan's other leading banks, Halyk and Kazkomertsbank, "pledged to be loyal to the president" and not to fund members of the political opposition. It appears that Ablyazov, however, has once again run afoul of the Kazakh president. In February 2009, Nazarbaev nationalized TuranAlem (now known as BTA) and Ablyazov, fearing the worst, fled to Europe. Ablyazov has subsequently been charged with embezzling one billion dollars of BTA assets. For more on the Ablyazov case, see "Kazakh Banks Pledge to Be Loyal to President, Not to Fund Any Political Groups," Associated Press, December 3, 2004; and Joanna Lillis, "Kazakhstan: Banking Sector Hit by Allegations of Politically Motivated Manipulation," *Eurasianet.org*, March 25, 2009.

20. Kazhegeldin's offense was his participation with the unregistered nongovernmental organization For Free Elections. "Kazakh Supreme Court Bars Kazhegeldin from Presidential Race," *Interfax-Kazakhstan* (Astana), November 24, 1998.

21. "Address of H. E. Dr. Marat Tazhin, Minister of Foreign Affairs of the Republic of Kazakhstan, at the OSCE Ministerial Meeting," November 29, 2007, available online at http:// en.government.kz/documents/publication/page09.

22. Adam Przeworski, Michael E. Alvarez, Jose Antonio Cheibub, and Fernando Limongi, *Democracy and Development: Political Institutions and Well-being in the World, 1950–1990*, 1st edition (Cambridge: Cambridge University Press, 2000), 27.

23. Ibid., 27.

24. Natalia Todorova, "Nashe vremia pirshlo," *Kazakhstanskaia pravda*, September 8, 2005.

25. Joe Becker and Don Van Natta, "After Mining Deal, Financier Donated to Clinton," *New York Times*, January 31, 2008.

26. Lower Gini scores correspond with greater income equality. As a point of comparison, the U.S. Gini index in 1999 was forty-one, a score that indicates there is greater income inequality in the United States than in the Central Asian countries studied here. Data are available from the World Bank's World Development Indicators; see http://data.worldbank.org.

27. Kiren Aziz Chaudhry, "Economic Liberalization and the Lineages of the Rentier State," *Comparative Politics* 27, no. 1 (October 1994): 1–25, 18.

28. Author interview with Roza Akylbekova, director of the Kazakh International Bureau for Human Rights Information and Education Center, July 15, 2003, Almaty, Kazakhstan.

29. Author interview with Democratic Choice of Kazakhstan activist, July 15, 2003, Almaty, Kazakhstan. Name withheld by mutual agreement.

30. Author interview with Petr Svoik, Kazakh human rights lawyer, October 10, 2000, Almaty, Kazakhstan.

31. Author interview with Ermukhamet Ertisbaev, Nazarbaev adviser, July 17, 2003, Almaty, Kazakhstan.

32. For a discussion of enduring regional identities in Kazakhstan, see Pauline Jones Luong, *Institutional Change and Political Continuity in Post-Soviet Central Asia: Power, Perceptions, and Pacts*, 1st edition (Cambridge: Cambridge University Press, 2002); for a discussion of enduring clan identities, see Edward Schatz, *Modern Clan Politics: The Power of "Blood" in Kazakhstan and Beyond* (Seattle: University of Washington Press, 2004); and Kathleen Collins, *Clan Politics and Regime Transition in Central Asia* (Cambridge: Cambridge University Press, 2006).

33. World Bank, "Kazakhstan Country Brief 2010," April 2010, available online at http://www.worldbank.org.kz/WBSITE/EXTERNAL/COUNTRIES/ECAEXT/KAZAKHSTANEXTN/0,,contentMDK:20629270~menuPK:361877~pagePK:141137~piPK:141127~theSitePK:361869,00.html.

34. See, for example, "O Respublikanskom Biudzhete na 2010–2012 Godi," December 7, 2009, available online at http://www.minjust.kz:81/doc/show/id/1125/.

35. As quoted in Venla Sipila, "Kazakh Budget Revenues Slightly below Target in 2008," *Global Insight*, February 9, 2009.

36. "Kazakhstan Macroeconomic Review," *IntelliNews*, March 19, 2010.

37. Terry Lynn Karl, *The Paradox of Plenty: Oil Booms and Petro States* (Berkeley: University of California Press, 1997), 104.

38. Ibid., 163.

39. Hasani Gittens, "Kazakhstan: Borat, Come Home," *New York Post*, October 20, 2006.

40. Viktoria Panfilova, "Rakhat Aliev—interview pered arestom," *Nezavisimaya gazeta*, June 1, 2007.

41. "KNB Head Shabdarbayev on Aliyev Scandal, National Security Concerns," *Interfax-Kazakhstan*, April 29, 2008.

42. Krol and colleagues, *Approaching the OSCE Chairmanship: Kazakhstan 2010*.

43. Vladimir Osipov, "Garant stabil'nosti i uspeshnogo razvitiia," *Kazakhstanskaia pravda* (Astana), May 6, 2010.

44. "Kazakh Leader's New Status to Ensure Stability, Adviser Says," *Interfax-Kazakhstan*, May 14, 2010.

45. For excellent discussions of how uncertainty generates identity-based politics, see Henry E. Hale, *The Foundations of Ethnic Politics: Separatism of States and Nations in Eurasia and the World* (Cambridge: Cambridge University Press, 2008); and Daniel N. Posner, *Institutions and Ethnic Politics in Africa* (Cambridge: Cambridge University Press, 2005).

Bibliography

Abdrakhmanova, Jipara. "Kyrgyz Journalists: Better Protection Calls." Institute for War and Peace Reporting. April 29, 2007.
"Address of H. E. Dr. Marat Tazhin, Minister of Foreign Affairs of the Republic of Kazakhstan, at the OSCE Ministerial Meeting." Madrid. November 29, 2007.
Akiner, Shirin. "Violence in Andijan, 13 May 2005: An Independent Assessment." *CACI Silk Road Paper* (July 2005).
Albrecht, Holger. "Authoritarian Opposition and the Politics of Challenge in Egypt." In *Debating Arab Authoritarianism: Dynamics and Durability in Nondemocratic Regimes,* edited by Oliver Schlumberger, 59–74. Stanford: Stanford University Press.
Allen, Robert C. "The Rise and Decline of the Soviet Economy." *Canadian Journal of Economics / Revue canadienne d'Economique* 34, no. 4 (November 2001): 859–81.
Amineh, Mehdi Parvizi, and Henk Houweling. "The U.S. and the EU in CEA." In *Central Eurasia in Global Politics: Conflict, Security, and Development,* edited by Mehdi Parvizi Amineh and Henk Houweling, 207–34. Boston: Brill, 2005.
Anderson, John. "Creating a Framework for Civil Society in Kyrgyzstan." *Europe-Asia Studies* 52, no. 1 (2000): 77–93.
———. *Kyrgyzstan: Central Asia's Island of Democracy?* New York: Taylor & Francis, 1999.
Anderson, Lisa. "The State in the Middle East and North Africa." *Comparative Politics* 20, no. 1 (October 1987): 1–18.
Antelava, Natalia. "Kazakhs Pave Way for President for Life." *BBC News* (Almaty). May 21, 2007.
Ashakeeva, Gulaiym. "Interview: Up to Kyrgyz to Decide How to Build Their Democracy, Obama Adviser Says." *Radio Free Europe / Radio Liberty.* May 6, 2010.
Azar, Ilya. "Bakiyev Turned out to Be a Greater Monster Than Akayev." *Gazeta.ru.* March 25, 2010.
Baktygulov, Dzhumadil Sapalovich. *Istoriia Kyrgyzov i Kyrgyzstana s drevneishikh vremen do nashikh dnei.* Bishkek: Mektep, 1999.
Baran, Zeyno. "Building a Democracy in Uzebekistan [*sic*]." Testimony of Zeyno Baran, director, International Security and Energy Programs, the Nixon Center. Hearing of the Committee on House International Relations Subcommittee on the Middle East and Central Asia. Delivered June 15, 2004. Text from *Federal Document Clearing House Congressional Testimony.*

Bates, Robert. "Contra Contractarianism: Some Reflections on the New Institutionalism." *Politics and Society* 16, no. 2 (1988): 387–401.

Becker, Joe, and Don Van Natta. "After Mining Deal, Financier Donated to Clinton." *New York Times.* January 31, 2008.

Berg, Andrea, and Anna Kreikemeyer, eds. *Realities of Transformation: Democratization Policies in Central Asia Revisited.* 1st edition. Baden-Baden: Nomos, 2006.

Berger, Mikhail. "We Have to Make Our Own Way: A Conversation with Islam Karimov, President of Uzbekistan." *Izvestia.* January 28, 1991.

Bershidsky, Leonid. "Kazakh Parliament: It's a Farce but No Joke." *Moscow News.* February 4, 1995.

Bratton, Michael, and Nicholas Van de Walle. "Neopatrimonial Regimes and Political Transitions in Africa." *World Politics* 46, no. 4 (July 1994): 453–89.

Brysk, Alison. "'Hearts and Minds': Bringing Symbolic Politics Back In." *Polity* 27, no. 4 (Summer 1995): 559–85.

Bunce, Valerie. *Subversive Institutions.* Cambridge: Cambridge University Press, 1999.

———, and Sharon L. Wolchik. "Youth and Electoral Revolutions in Slovakia, Serbia, and Georgia." *SAIS Review* 26, no. 2 (2006): 55–65.

Carlisle, Donald S. "Uzbekistan and the Uzbeks." *Problems of Communism* 40, no. 5 (September 1991): 23.

Carothers, Thomas. *Aiding Democracy Abroad.* Washington, D.C.: Carnegie Endowment for International Peace, 1999.

———. "The End of the Transition Paradigm." *Journal of Democracy* 13, no. 1 (2002): 5–21.

———. "Political Party Aid." Paper prepared for the Swedish International Development Agency. October 2004.

"Central Asia: Chinese Investment Welcome, to a Point." Oxford Analytica Daily Brief Service. September 15, 2009, 1.

Central Asia/South Caucasus Subcommittee of the U.S. Senate Foreign Relations Committee. *U.S. Official Says Central Asia Developments Promising but Mixed.* Office of International Information Programs, U.S. Department of State, 2002.

Chantseva, I. "The Koran Is No Obstacle to Politics." *Kuranty.* October 26, 1991.

Chaudhry, Kiren Aziz. "Economic Liberalization and the Lineages of the Rentier State." *Comparative Politics* 27, no. 1 (October 1994): 1–25.

Chehabi, Houchang E., and Juan José Linz. *Sultanistic Regimes.* Baltimore: Johns Hopkins University Press, 1998.

Chroust, Peter. "Neo-Nazis and Taliban On-Line: Anti-Modern Political Movements and Modern Media." *Democratization* 7, no. 1 (Spring 2000): 102–18.

Clark, William Roberts, Matt Golder, and Sona Nadenichek Golder. *Principles of Comparative Politics.* 1st edition. Washington, D.C.: CQ Press, 2008.

Cloud, David. "Pentagon's Fuel Deal Is Lesson in Risks of Graft-Prone Regions." *New York Times.* November 14, 2005.

Coburn, Tom. *Coburn Amendment 2631—Prohibits the National Science Foundation from Wasting Federal Research Funding on Political Science Projects.* 111th Congress. 2009.

Cohen, Stephen F. *Bukharin and the Bolshevik Revolution: A Political Biography, 1888–1938.* New York: Knopf, 1973.

Coll, Steve. *Ghost Wars: The Secret History of the CIA, Afghanistan, and Bin Laden, from the Soviet Invasion to September 10, 2001.* New York: Penguin, 2004.

Collier, David, and Steven. Levitsky. "Research Note: Democracy with Adjectives: Conceptual Innovation in Comparative Research." *World Politics* 49, no. 3 (1997): 430–51.

Collins, Kathleen. *Clan Politics and Regime Transition in Central Asia.* Cambridge: Cambridge University Press, 2006.

———. "The Logic of Clan Politics Evidence from the Central Asian Trajectories." *World Politics* 56, no. 2 (2004): 224–61.

Cooley, Alexander. "Principles in the Pipeline: Managing Transatlantic Values and Interests in Central Asia." *International Affairs* 84, no. 6 (Ocober 2008): 1,173–88.

———. "U.S. Bases and Democratization in Central Asia." *Orbis* 52, no. 1 (Winter 2008): 65–90.

Cornell, Svante E. *Small Nations and Great Powers.* London: Routledge, 2001.

Critchlow, James. *Nationalism in Uzbekistan: A Soviet Republic's Road to Sovereignty.* Boulder: Westview Press, 1991.
Dildyayev, Grigory, and Tleuzhan Yesilbayev. "Looking the Truth in the Eye." *Pravda.* March 16, 1987.
Dobbs, Michael. "Brezhnev Kin Jailed for Twelve Years." *Washington Post.* December 31, 1988.
"'Do You Know the Law' Nationwide Contest Ends in Jizzakh Region." *UzReport.com.* May 17, 2007.
Dubnov, Arkady. "V Kirgizii golodaiut deputati. Prezident Akaev nablyudaet." *Vremia novosti.* January 23, 2002.
Dunlop, John B. *The Rise of Russia and the Fall of the Soviet Empire.* Princeton: Princeton University Press, 1995.
Dzhunusova, Zhanylzhan Kh. *Respublika Kazakhstan: Prezident, instituty demokratii.* Almaty: Zheti zharghy, 1996.
Eickelman, Dale F., ed. *Russia's Muslim Frontiers: New Directions in Cross-cultural Analysis.* Bloomington: Indiana University Press, 1993.
Erkebaev, Abdygany. *1990 God—Prikhod k vlasti A. Akaeva.* Bishkek: Kyrgyzstan, 1997.
Evans, Peter B. *Embedded Autonomy.* Princeton: Princeton University Press, 1995.
"Excerpts from Remarks by Gorbachev before Central Committee of Party." *New York Times.* February 6, 1990.
Faizullaev, Dzhakhongir. "Uzbekistan-Kyrgyziia: Politiko-ekonomicheskie posledstviya territorial'nikh problem." *Aziia i Afrika segodnia* (July 2005): 9–14.
"Ferghana Implements 'Values, Customs, Traditions and Youth' Project." *Times of Central Asia.* March 28, 2008.
"The First Stage of Charity Campaign Held in Tashkent." *Times of Central Asia.* July 24, 2008.
"Five-hour Power Outage a Day Planned in Kyrgyzstan from 1 October." *AKIpress.com.* September 29, 2009.
Foggo, Daniel. "Royal's &#163." *Sunday Times.* July 27, 2008.
"Fourth International Education and Career Exhibition Opens in Uzbek Capital." *UzReport.com.* February 19, 2009.
Franke, Anja, Andrea Gawrich, and Gurban Alakbarov. "Kazakhstan and Azerbaijan as Post-Soviet Rentier States: Resource Incomes and Autocracy as a Double 'Curse' in Post-Soviet Regimes." *Europe-Asia Studies* 61, no. 1 (2009): 109–40.
Ganelin, A. "The Investigation Isn't Over." *Komsomolskaia pravda.* March 15, 1988.
Garrett, R. Kelly. "Protest in an Information Society: A Review of Literature on Social Movements and New ICTs." *Information, Communication, and Society* 9, no. 2 (April 2006): 202–24.
Gdlian, Tel'man, and Nicholai Ivanov. *Kremlevskoe delo.* Rostov-Na-Donu: Izd-vo "AO Kniga", 1994.
Geertz, Clifford. "Which Way to Mecca?" *New York Review of Books* 50, no. 10 (June 12, 2003): 27–30.
"General Prosecutor Files Suit against Edil Baisalov." *Times of Central Asia.* December 7, 2007.
Gittens, Hasani. "Kazakhstan: Borat, Come Home." *New York Post.* October 20, 2006.
Gleason, Gregory. "Fealty and Loyalty: Informal Authority Structures in Soviet Asia." *Soviet Studies* 43, no. 4 (1991): 613–28.
Gorbachev, Mikhail Sergeevich. *On My Country and the World.* New York: Columbia University Press, 2000.
"Gorbachev's Visit to Uzbekistan: Meetings with Collective Farmers." *BBC Summary of World Broadcasts.* April 11, 1988.
Grabot, Andre. "3,500 Demonstrate against Kazakh President." *Agence France Presse.* December 8, 1996.
Guadagni, Maurizio, Martin Raiser, Anna Crole-Rees, and Dilshod Khidirov. "Cotton Taxation in Uzbekistan: Opportunities for Reform." Environmentally and Socially Sustainable Development Unit for Europe and Central Asia (ECSSD) Working Papers. World Bank. August 26, 2005.
Gunn, T. Jeremy. "Shaping an Islamic Identity: Religion, Islamism, and the State in Central Asia." *Sociology of Religion* 64, no. 3 (Autumn 2003): 389–410.

Haggard, Stephan, and Robert R. Kaufman. *The Political Economy of Democratic Transitions.* Princeton: Princeton University Press, 1995.

Hagopian, Frances. "Review: After Regime Change: Authoritarian Legacies, Political Representation, and the Democratic Future of South America." *World Politics* 45, no. 3 (April 1993): 464–500.

Harper, Tom. "Sting Plays Concert for Daughter of 'Boil Your Enemies' Dictator." *Daily Mail— Mail Online.* February 21, 2010.

Herz, John H. "The Problem of Successorship in Dictatorial Régimes: A Study in Comparative Law and Institutions." *Journal of Politics* 14, no. 1 (February 1952): 19–40.

Hill, David T., and Krishna Sen. "The Internet in Indonesia's New Democracy." *Democratization* 7, no. 1 (Spring 2000): 119–36.

Hirsch, Francine. "Toward an Empire of Nations: Border-Making and the Formation of Soviet National Identities." *Russian Review* 59, no. 2 (April 2000): 201–26.

Hirschman, Albert O. *Exit, Voice, and Loyalty: Responses to Decline in Firms, Organizations, and States.* Cambridge: Harvard University Press, 1970.

Huntington, Samuel P. "The Clash of Civilizations?" *Foreign Affairs* 72, no. 3 (1993): 22–49.

Huskey, Eugene. "The Rise of Contested Politics in Central Asia: Elections in Kyrgyzstan, 1989–90." *Europe-Asia Studies* 47, no. 5 (July 1995): 813–33.

Ilkhamov, Alisher. "Neopatrimonialism, Interest Groups, and Patronage Networks: The Impasses of the Governance System in Uzbekistan." *Central Asian Survey* 26, no. 1 (March 2007): 65–84.

Inglehart, Ronald, and Pippa Norris. "The True Clash of Civilizations." *Foreign Policy*, no. 135 (April 2003): 62–70.

"Intent to Designate as Foreign Terrorist Organization the Islamic Movement of Uzbekistan." U.S. Department of State, September 18, 2000.

International Crisis Group. "Kyrgyzstan: A Faltering State." December 16, 2005.

———. "Uzbekistan: The Andijon Uprising." *Asia Briefing* no. 38 (May 25, 2005).

"International Youth Film Festival 'Creative Flight' Starts." *UzReport.com.* May 14, 2008.

"Interview with Mufti Mukhammad-Yusuf Mukhammad-Sedik, Head of the Central Asian Theological Moslem Board." *Kremlin International News Broadcast.* January 19, 1992.

"In the Chiller: Uzbekistan." *Economist.* July 15, 2006.

Ipek, Pinar. "The Role of Oil and Gas in Kazakhstan's Foreign Policy: Looking East or West?" *Europe-Asia Studies* 59, no. 7 (November 2007): 179–99.

"Iranian Radio Reports 'Mass Arrests' in Uzbek South Following Terror Attacks." *Voice of the Islamic Republic of Iran* (Mashhad). April 7, 2004.

Itkin, Vladimir. "In the USSR Supreme Court: The Indictment is Brought." *Izvestia.* September 10, 1988.

Johnston, David. "Kazakh Mastermind, or New Ugly American?." *New York Times.* December 17, 2000.

"Journalism Contest Announced for News Agencies, Printed and Online Media." *UzReport.com.* August 19, 2008.

Kaipbergenov, Adylbek. "Still More Questions on the Events in Fregana Province." *Pravda.* June 28, 1989.

Kalathil, Shanthi, and Taylor C. Boas. *Open Networks, Closed Regimes: The Impact of the Internet on Authoritarian Rule.* Washington, D.C.: Carnegie Endowment for International Peace, 2003.

Karimov, Anvar. "'Kamolot' dolzhen stat' mostom mezhdu molodezh'iu i gosudarstvom." *Narodnoe slovo.* March 16, 2001.

Karl, Terry Lynn. *The Paradox of Plenty: Oil Booms and Petro States.* Berkeley: University of California Press, 1997.

Kaufmann, Daniel, Aart Kraay, and Massimo Mastruzzi. "Governance Matters VII: Aggregate and Individual Governance Indicators 1996–2007." *World Bank Policy Research Working Paper*, No. 4654 (June 2008): 1–105.

"Kazakh Banks Pledge to Be Loyal to President, Not to Fund Any Political Groups." Associated Press. December 3, 2004.

"The Kazakh Government Is Lacking Funds to Raise Wages of Social Workers and State Officials on January 1." Kazakhstan General Newswire. October 19, 2009.

"Kazakh Leader's New Status to Ensure Stability, Adviser Says." *Interfax-Kazakhstan.* May 14, 2010.

"Kazakh MPs Outraged by Salary of National Company Head." Kazakh Television First Channel. September 27, 2006.

"Kazakh Supreme Court Bars Kazhegeldin from Presidential Race." *Interfax-Kazakhstan* (Astana). November 24, 1998.

"Kazakhstan Macroeconomic Review." *IntelliNews.* March 19, 2010.

"Kazak Opposition Leader Seeks Protection for Family after Beating." Associated Press. December 8, 1997.

Keller, Shoshana. *To Moscow, Not Mecca: The Soviet Campaign against Islam in Central Asia, 1917– 1941.* Westport: Praeger Publishers, 2001.

———. "Women's Liberation and Islam in Soviet Uzbekistan, 1926–1941." In *Bodies in Contact: Rethinking Colonial Encounters in World History.* Durham, N.C.: Duke University Press, 2005.

Kertzer, David I. *Politics and Symbols: The Italian Communist Party and the Fall of Communism.* New Haven: Yale University Press, 1996.

Kharlamov, Vasilii. "Ochen' Vygodnoe Ustranenie." *Nezavisimaya gazeta.* February 27, 2006.

Kimmage, Daniel. "Uzbekistan: One Witness's Testimony Forces Courtroom Collision." *Radio Free Europe / Radio Liberty.* October 23, 2005.

Klinger, Peter. "Kyrgyz President Rebukes Blair as Oxus Intervention Backfires." *Times.* February 3, 2006.

Knack, Stephen. "Does Foreign Aid Promote Democracy?." *International Studies Quarterly* 48, no. 1 (March 2004): 251–66.

"KNB Head Shabdarbayev on Aliyev Scandal, National Security Concerns." *Interfax-Kazakhstan.* April 29, 2008.

Kohli, Atul, and Vivienne Shue. "Contention and Accommodation in the Third World." In *State Power and Social Forces: Domination and Transformation in the Third World,* edited by Joel Samuel Migdal, Atul Kohli, and Vivienne Shue, 293–326. New York: Cambridge University Press, 1994.

Koichuev, Turar K., and Vladimir M. Ploskikh. *Kyrgyzy i ikh predki: Netraditsionnyi vzgliad na istoriiu i sovremennost'.* Bishkek: Glav. red. Kyrgyzskoi Entsiklopedii, 1994.

Kopstein, Jeffrey S., and David A. Reilly. "Geographic Diffusion and the Transformation of the Postcommunist World." *World Politics* 53 (2000): 1–37.

Kotkin, Stephen. *Magnetic Mountain: Stalinism as a Civilization.* Berkeley: University of California Press, 1997.

———. "A World War among Professors." *New York Times.* September 7, 2002.

Kozybaev, Manash Kabashevich. *Kazakhstan na rubezhe vekov: Razmyshleniia i poiski.* Almaty: Ghylym, 2000.

Kramer, Andrew E. "Fuel Sales to U.S. at Issue in Kyrgyzstan." *New York Times.* April 11, 2010.

———. "Kyrgyzstan Opens an Inquiry into Fuel Sales to a U.S. Base." *New York Times.* May 5, 2010.

Krol, George A., Eric McGlinchey, Yevgeny Zhovtis, Erlan Idrissov, Benjamin Cardin, Alcee Hastings, Christopher Smith, and Eni Faleomavaega. *Approaching the OSCE Chairmanship: Kazakhstan 2010.* Washington, D.C.: Commission on Security and Cooperation in Europe, 2009.

"Kulibayev to Chair Boards of Directors in Three National Companies." *Kazakh Oil & Gas Weekly.* May 25, 2009.

Kunaev, D. *Ot Stalina do Gorbacheva: V aspekte istorii Kazakhstana.* Alma-Ata: Sanat, 1994.

Kvyatkovskaia, Tatyana. "Skirmish for Power: The Kazakhstan Version." *Kazakhstanskaia Pravda.* January 21, 1993.

"Kyrgyz Government Refuses to Restore British Gold Company's Licence." *AKIpress.com.* December 7, 2005.

"Kyrgyz Ministry Defends Arrest of 4 Opposition Activists." Central Asia General Newswire. January 17, 2009.

"Kyrgyz Premier Criticizes Regional Protests." Kyrgyz Television 1 (Bishkek), April 6, 2010.

"Kyrgyz President Gives Car to Soviet-Era Communist Leader." *AKIpress.com.* November 7, 2009.

"Kyrgyz Teachers Sue Government over Debt for Long Service." Kyrgyz Channel 5 TV / BBC Monitoring. February 6, 2008.

"Kyrgyzstan: Economic Reforms Seem Stalled." *Times of Central Asia.* June 1, 2006.

"Kyrgyzstan's Ex-Chief Prosecutor Makes Statement after Dismissal." *Kabar.* September 20, 2005.

Legvold, Robert. "National Identity and Globalization: Youth, State, and Society in Post-Soviet Eurasia." *Foreign Affairs* 87, no. 5 (September 2008): 178–79.

Lenin, Vladimir I. "Imperialism, the Highest Stage of Capitalism." In *The Lenin Anthology,* edited by Robert C. Tucker, 204–74. New York: W. W. Norton, 1975.

———. "The Question of Nationalities." In Tucker, *Lenin Anthology,* 719–24. New York: W. W. Norton, 1975.

"Les 300 plus riches de Suisse." *Bilan.* December 4, 2009.

Levy, Clifford J. "Strategic Issues, Not Abuses, Are U.S. Focus in Kyrgyzstan." *New York Times.* July 23, 2009.

Levy, Geoffrey, and Richard Kay. "The Duke, the Dame, and the Dictator." *Daily Mail.* March 14, 2009.

Lewis, Anthony. "Echoes of Helsinki." *New York Times.* August 2, 1976.

Lewis, Bernard. "The Roots of Muslim Rage." *Atlantic* 266, no. 3 (September 1990): 47–60.

———. *What Went Wrong? Western Impact and Middle Eastern Response.* New York: Oxford University Press, 2002.

Lieberman, Robert C. "Ideas, Institutions, and Political Order: Explaining Political Change." *American Political Science Review* 96, no. 4 (December 2002): 697–712.

Lillis, Joanna. "Kazakhstan: Banking Sector Hit by Allegations of Politically Motivated Manipulation." *Eurasianet.org.* March 25, 2009.

Loshak, Viktor. "We've Run Up against a Mafia." *Movskovskie novosti.* April 3, 1988.

Lubin, Nancy. "Uzbekistan: The Challenges Ahead." *Middle East Journal* 43, no. 4 (Autumn 1989): 619–34.

Luong, Pauline Jones. *Institutional Change and Political Continuity in Post-Soviet Central Asia: Power, Perceptions, and Pacts.* 1st edition. Cambridge: Cambridge University Press, 2002.

———, and Erika Weinthal. "Prelude to the Resource Curse: Explaining Oil and Gas Development Strategies in the Soviet Successor States and Beyond." *Comparative Political Studies* 34, no. 4 (May 1, 2001): 367–99.

Mackey, Robert. "A President, His Masseuse, and Her Blog." *New York Times.* April 8, 2009.

Mahoney, James, and Dietrich Rueschemeyer. *Comparative Historical Analysis in the Social Sciences.* Cambridge: Cambridge University Press, 2003.

Makarov, D. "Chem vyshe kreslo, tem dal'she ot liudei. Islam Karimov: 'Tverdyi' poriadok pri polnoi ekonomicheskoi svobode." *Argumenty i fakty.* April 11, 1991.

Malashenko, Alexei. "Islam versus Communism." In *Russia's Muslim Frontiers,* edited by Dale F. Eickelman, 63–78. Bloomington: Indiana University Press, 1993.

"Manas Air Base—Home." Available online at http://www.manas.afcent.af.mil/.

"Marafontsy napravalis' v Bukharu." *Narodnoe slovo.* December 1, 2005.

Maratova, Medina. "Protest Moods Increasing in Kyrgyzstan." *Delovaya nedelia* (Almaty). March 19, 2010.

March, Andrew F. "From Leninism to Karimovism: Hegemony, Ideology, and Authoritarian Legitimation." *Post-Soviet Affairs* 19, no. 4 (December 2003): 307–36.

Massell, Gregory J. *The Surrogate Proletariat: Moslem Women and Revolutionary Strategies in Soviet Central Asia, 1919–1929.* Princeton: Princeton University Press, 1974.

Mattes, Robert, and Michael Bratton. "Learning about Democracy in Africa: Awareness, Performance, and Experience." *American Journal of Political Science* 51, no. 1 (January 2007): 192–217.

Mattingly, Chandra. "Student Recalls Encouragement, Lessons." *Dearborn County Register.* April 1, 2005.

Matveeva, Anna. "Democratization, Legitimacy, and Political Change in Central Asia." *International Affairs* (Royal Institute of International Affairs 1944–) 75, no. 1 (January 1999): 23–44.

Mazrui, Ali A. "Islam and the United States: Streams of Convergence, Strands of Divergence." *Third World Quarterly* 25, no. 5 (2004): 793–820.

McAuley, Mary. "Party Recruitment and the Nationalities in the USSR: A Study in Centre-Republican Relationships." *British Journal of Political Science* 10, no. 4 (October 1980): 461–87.

McGlinchey, Eric. "Autocrats, Islamists, and the Rise of Radicalism in Central Asia." *Current History* (October 2005): 336–42.

———. "Exploring Regime Instability and Ethnic Violence in Kyrgyzstan," *Asia Policy* 12 (July 2011).

———. "Islamic Leaders in Uzbekistan." *Asia Policy* 1, no. 1 (January 2006): 123–44.

———. "Islamic Revivalism and State Failure in Kyrgyzstan." *Problems of Post-Communism* 56, no. 3 (May 2009): 16–28.

———. "Running in Circles in Kyrgyzstan." *New York Times.* April 10, 2010.

———. "Searching for Kamalot: Political Patronage and Youth Politics in Uzbekistan." *Europe-Asia Studies* 61, no. 7 (2009): 1,137–50.

———, and Ed Crane. "A Study of Political Party Assistance in Eastern Europe and Eurasia." US-AID. June 2007.

"Meeting on Human Trafficking Held in Uzbek East." *UzReport.com.* September 15, 2008.

Mesquita, Bruce Bueno de, James D. Morrow, Randolph M. Siverson, and Alastair Smith. "Political Institutions, Policy Choice, and the Survival of Leaders." *British Journal of Political Science* 32, no. 4 (October 2002): 559–90.

Mesquita, Bruce Bueno de, Alastair Smith, Randolph M. Siverson, and James D. Morrow. *The Logic of Political Survival.* Cambridge: MIT Press, 2005.

Migdal, Joel S. *Strong Societies and Weak States: State-Society Relations and State Capabilities in the Third World.* Princeton: Princeton University Press, 1988.

Moore, Barrington. *Social Origins of Dictatorship and Democracy.* Boston: Beacon Press, 1993.

Morse, Edward L., and James Richard. "The Battle for Energy Dominance." *Foreign Affairs* (April 2002): 16–31.

Moustafa, Tamir. *The Struggle for Constitutional Power: Law, Politics, and Economic Development in Egypt.* Cambridge: Cambridge University Press, 2007.

"Muslim Rallies in Uzbekistan." *BBC Summary of World Broadcasts.* October 2, 1991.

"Namangan Calm." *BBC Summary of World Broadcasts.* December 7, 1990.

National Science Foundation, Directorate for Social, Behavioral, and Economic Sciences (SES), "nsf.gov—SES—Funding—Political Science—US National Science Foundation (NSF)." Available online at http://www.nsf.gov/funding/pgm_summ.jsp?pims_id=5418&org=SES.

Nazarbaev, Nursultan. *Nursultan Nazarbaev: Bez pravykh i levykh.* Moscow: Molodaia Gvardiia, 1991.

"Nazarbaev on the Reform Process and the Future of the Republic—Presidential Address." *BBC Summary of World Broadcasts.* October 26, 1992.

Northrop, Douglas. *Veiled Empire: Gender and Power in Stalinist Central Asia.* 1st edition. Ithaca: Cornell University Press, 2004.

Novintskyi, Vladislav. "V Uzbekistane sozdaetsia obschestvennaia obrazovatel'naia informatsionnaya set 'ziyonet'." *Narodnoe slovo.* October 1, 2005.

"O politicheskikh svobodakh grazhdan: Iz doklada Ombudsmena KR za 2003 god." *Moya stolitsa.* January 25, 2005.

"O Respublikanskom Byudzhete na 2010–2012 Godi." Kazakh Ministry of Justice. December 7, 2009. Available online at http://www.minjust.kz:81/doc/show/id/1125/.

Olcott, Martha Brill. *Central Asia's Second Chance.* New York: Carnegie Endowment for International Peace, 2005.

———. *The Kazakhs.* Stanford: Hoover Institution Press at Stanford University, 1987.

———. *Kazakhstan: Unfulfilled Promise.* New York: Carnegie Endowment for International Peace, 2002.

Oliker, Olga. "Two Years after Andijan: Assessing the Past and Thinking towards the Future." Rand Corporation. 2007. Available online at https://www.rand.org/pubs/testimonies/CT282/.

Olson, Mancur. *Logic of Collective Action: Public Goods and the Theory of Groups.* Cambridge: Harvard University Press, 1971.

"On the CPSU Central Committee's Draft Platform for the 28th Party Congress. M. S. Gorbachev's Report at the Plenary Session of the CPSU Central Committee on Feb. 5, 1990." *Current Digest of the Post-Soviet Press.* March 14, 1990.

OpenNet Initiative. "Country Profile: Kazakhstan." May 10, 2007. Available online at http://opennet.net/research/profiles/kazakhstan.

———. "Country Profile: Kyrgyzstan." May 10, 2007. Available online at http://opennet.net/research/profiles/kyrgyzstan.

———. "Country Profile: Uzbekistan." May 9, 2007. Available online at http://opennet.net/research/profiles/uzbekistan.

"Opposition Plans to Take Control of Half of Kyrgyzstan." *Interfax.com.* March 22, 2005.

Orozaliev, Bek. "Constitutional Revolution." *Kommersant Online.* November 3, 2006.

Osipov, Vladimir. "Garant stabil'nosti i uspeshnogo razvitiia." *Kazakhstanskaia pravda* (Astana). May 6, 2010.

Ostrom, Elinor. *Governing the Commons: The Evolution of Institutions for Collective Action.* Cambridge: Cambridge University Press, 1990.

Otunbaeva, Roza. "Will There Be a Tulip Revolution in Kyrgyzstan? Who Is Next after Ukraine?" Moscow Carnegie Center. February 11, 2005.

Ovcharenko, Georgi, and Andrei Chernenko. "Interview in the USSR Ministry of Internal Affairs' Investigative Detention Center." *Pravda.* July 17, 1988.

"Over 100bn Dollars of Direct Investment Attracted to Kazakhstan." *Kazinform* (Astana). May 25, 2010.

Panfilova, Viktoria. "Rakhat Aliev—interview pered arestom." *Nezavisimaya gazeta.* June 1, 2007.

Pannier, Bruce, and Andy Heil. "Kyrgyz President Pooh-Poohs Western-style Democracy." *Radio Free Europe / Radio Liberty.* March 24, 2010.

"Parliament Approves Constitution after Energetic Debate." *Kazakh Radio* (Alma-Ata). June 6, 1992.

Peceny, Mark, Caroline C. Beer, and Shannon Sanchez-Terry. "Dictatorial Peace?" *American Political Science Review* 96, no. 1 (March 2002): 15–26.

Pierce, Richard A. *Russian Central Asia, 1867–1917: A Study in Colonial Rule.* Berkeley: University of California Press, 1960.

Pierson, Paul. "Big, Slow-Moving, and . . . Invisible: Macrosocial Processes in the Study of Comparative Politics." In *Comparative Historical Analysis in the Social Sciences,* edited by James Mahoney and Dietrich Rueschemeyer, 177–207. New York: Cambridge University Press, 2003.

Podelco, Grant. "It's Gulnara's World. We Only Live in It." *Radio Free Europe / Radio Liberty.* December 18, 2009.

Pomfret, Richard. "Kazakhstan's Economy since Independence: Does the Oil Boom Offer a Second Chance for Sustainable Development?" *Europe-Asia Studies* 57, no. 6 (2005): 859–76.

"President Bakiev Names Chair of Advisory Board of Development Fund." *AKIpress.com.* November 6, 2009.

"President Karimov Sacks Regional Governor: 'Nepotism, Cronyism, Bribery' Rife." *Uzbek Radio Second Program.* March 23, 2000.

"President Rebukes Envoy over Fiscal Claims to USA over Airbase." *AKIpress.com.* December 6, 2005.

Prizhivoit, Rina. "Prezident izdal ukaz vsekh otmyt' v poslednyi raz." *Moya stolitsa novosti.* February 8, 2005.

"Probe into Akayev Property." *RIA novosti.* April 1, 2005.

"Pro-governmental Youth Organization Elects New Leader." *Times of Central Asia.* November 30, 2006.

Przeworski, Adam, Michael E. Alvarez, Jose Antonio Cheibub, and Fernando Limongi. *Democracy and Development: Political Institutions and Well-being in the World, 1950–1990.* 1st edition. Cambridge: Cambridge University Press, 2000.

Rabushka, Alvin, and Kenneth Shepsle. *Politics in Plural Societies: A Theory of Democratic Instability.* Columbus, Ohio: Charles E. Merrill Publishing Company, 1972.

Radnitz, Scott. "What Really Happened in Kyrgyzstan?" *Journal of Democracy* 17, no. 2 (April 2006): 132–46.

Rashid, Ahmed. "The New Struggle in Central Asia." *World Policy Journal* 17, no. 4 (Winter 2000): 33–45.

———. "They're Only Sleeping: Why Militant Islamicists in Central Asia Aren't Going to Go Away." *New Yorker.* January 14, 2002.

Razakov, Talant. *Oshkie sobytiia: Na materialakh KGB.* Biskek: Renaissance, 1993.

Remmer, Karen L. "Neopatrimonialism: The Politics of Military Rule in Chile, 1973–1987." *Comparative Politics* 21, no. 2 (January 1989): 149–70.

Reno, William. "Congo: From State Collapse to 'Absolutism,' to State Failure." *Third World Quarterly* 27, no. 1 (2006): 43–56.

"Reporters Sans Frontières—Letter to Kyrgyz Authorities about Wave of Violence against Journalists," *Reporters without Borders for Press Freedom.* April 6, 2007. Available online at http://en.rsf.org/kyrgyzstan-letter-to-kyrgyz-authorities-about-06-04-2007,21627.html.

"The Riots in Uzbekistan." *BBC Summary of World Broadcasts.* June 7, 1989.

Romanovskii, Mikhail. "Oppozitsiia obviniaet Nazarbaeva v korruptsii." *Nezavisimaia gazeta.* June 21, 2002.

Ross, Michael L. "The Political Economy of the Resource Curse." *World Politics* 51, no. 2 (1999): 297–322.

Ross, Michael Lewin. "Does Oil Hinder Democracy?" *World Politics* 53, no. 3 (2001): 325–61.

Rostom, Aram. "A Crooked Alliance in the War on Terror?" *NBC News.* October 30, 2006. Available online at http://www.msnbc.msn.com/id/15448018/ns/nightly_news-lisa_myers_and_the_nbc_news_investigative_unit/page/2/.

Ruffin, M. Holt, and Daniel Clarke Waugh, eds. *Civil Society in Central Asia.* Seattle: University of Washington Press, 1999.

Rywkin, Michael. *Moscow's Muslim Challenge: Soviet Central Asia.* Revised edition. Armonk, N.Y.: M. E. Sharpe, 1990.

Sabonis-Helf, Theresa. "The Rise of the Post-Soviet Petro-States: Energy Exports and Domestic Governance in Turkmenistan and Kazakhstan." In *In the Tracks of Tamerlane: Central Asia's Path to the Twenty-first Century,* edited by Daniel L. Burghart and Theresa Sabonis-Helf. Washington, D.C.: National Defense University, 2004.

Saidazimova, Gulnoza. "Kyrgyzstan: Economic Reforms Seem Stalled." *Radio Free Europe / Radio Liberty.* May 25, 2006.

Sakhnin, Arkady. "USSR Deputy Prosecutor General Reports that the Prosecutor's Office Has Resumed Its Investigation of the Nasriddinova case." *Pravda.* November 2, 1988, 6.

Sakishev, Talanbek. "Sotsopros: Idem ne tuda i ne s temi." *Vecherniy Bishkek.* August 2, 1999.

Sartori, Giovanni. "Concept Misformation in Comparative Politics." *American Political Science Review* 64, no. 4 (December 1970): 1,033–53.

Schatz, Edward. *Modern Clan Politics: The Power of "Blood" in Kazakhstan and Beyond.* Seattle: University of Washington Press, 2004.

———. "The Politics of Multiple Identities: Lineage and Ethnicity in Kazakhstan." *Europe-Asia Studies* 52, no. 4 (2000): 489–506.

Schlumberger, Oliver. *Debating Arab Authoritarianism: Dynamics and Durability in Nondemocratic Regimes.* Stanford: Stanford University Press, 2007.

Schlyter, Birgit N., ed. *Prospects for Democracy in Central Asia: Papers Read at a Conference in Istanbul, 1–3 June 2003, and Additional Chapters.* Istanbul: Swedish Research Institute in Istanbul, 2005.

Scott, James C. *Seeing Like a State: How Certain Schemes to Improve the Human Condition Have Failed.* New Haven: Yale University Press, 1999.

Selm, Bert van. *The Economics of Soviet Break-Up.* New York: Routledge, 1997.

"Sentences Announced in Churbanov Trial." *BBC Summary of World Broadcasts.* January 3, 1989.

Sergeeva, Irina, and Aleksandr Ustinov. "SamrukKazyne ne grozit optimizatsiia." *Respublika* (Almaty). February 13, 2009.

Shambayati, Hootan. "The Rentier State, Interest Groups, and the Paradox of Autonomy: State and Business in Turkey and Iran." *Comparative Politics* 26, no. 3 (April 1994): 307–31.

Sharai, Yegor. "Vospityvaia patriotov, intellektualov, biznesmenov." *Narodnoe slovo.* August 3, 2005.

Shukurov, S. "Proyavlenie patriotizma i lubvyi k otchizne." *Narodnoe slovo.* July 12, 2005.

Simpson, Peggy. "IWMF: International Women's Media Foundation—Fifteen Years of Courage: Zamira Sydykova." Available online at http://www.iwmf.org/article.aspx?id=389&c=carticles.

Sipila, Venla. "Kazakh Budget Revenues Slightly below Target in 2008." *IHS Global Insight.com.* February 9, 2009.

———. "Kazakh President Pledges Frugal Spending as GDP Growth Slows in 2007." *IHS Global Insight.com.* February 7, 2008.

Sneider, Daniel. "Violence Shakes Soviet Republic." *Christian Science Monitor.* December 11, 1990.

"Some 500 Female Traders Stage Protest in Uzbek East." *Muslimuzbekistan.com.* September 9, 2004.

Spechler, Martin C. "Authoritarian Politics and Economic Reform in Uzbekistan: Past, Present and Prospects." *Central Asian Survey* 26, no. 2 (June 2007): 185–202.

"Speech by Comrade A. M. Masaliyev, First Secretary of the Kirgiz Communist Party Central Committee." *Current Digest of the Post-Soviet Press* 38, no. 11 (April 16, 1986): 12–13.

"Speech by Comrade N. A. Nazarbayev, Chairman of the Kazakh Republic Council of Ministers." *Current Digest of the Post-Soviet Press* 38, no. 15 (May 14, 1986): 12–13.

Stern, David. "Kyrgyz President Admits Relative Sells to U.S. Base." *Financial Times.* July 22, 2002.

Stevens, Daniel. "Political Society and Civil Society in Uzbekistan—Never the Twain Shall Meet?" *Central Asian Survey* 26, no. 1 (March 2007): 49–64.

Sultanov, Kazy. "Pouring Kerosene into Kyrgyz Revolution." *Kommersant Online.* May 4, 2010.

Sydykova, Zamira. "Kyrgyzstan: Opposition Newspaper Published after Three-month Hiatus." *Res publica.* May 4, 2002.

Thomas, Daniel Charles. *The Helsinki Effect: International Norms, Human Rights, and the Demise of Communism.* Princeton: Princeton University Press, 2001.

Tocqueville, Alexis de. *Democracy in America.* Translated by Henry Reeve. New York: D. Appleton and Company, 1904.

Todorova, Natalia. "Nashe vremia pirshlo." *Kazakhstanskaia pravda.* September 8, 2005.

Tokombayev, A. "Our Moral Values: Only Friendship Does Good." *Pravda.* May 19, 1987.

Tsentr ekstremal'noi zhurnalistiki Soiuza zhurnalistov Rossii. "Opasnaia professiia: Yezhenedel'nyi byulleten' sobytii v sredstvakh massovoi informatsii stran SNG." December 9, 2002.

Tucker, Robert C. *Stalin in Power: The Revolutin from Above, 1928–1941.* New York: W. W. Norton & Company, 1992.

Tuzov, A. "V dalekuyu-blizkuyu Indiyu." *Vecherniy Bishkek.* February 21, 2000.

———, and M. Khamidov. "Three Kyrgyz University Heads Sacked." *Vecherniy Bishkek.* April 8, 1998.

Tvorogova, Yekaterina. "Net vyibora." *Delovaya nedelya.* August 2, 2002.

"The Twenty-first Congress of the Uzbekistan Communist Party: Report of the Uzbekistan Communist Party Central Committee to the Twenty-first Congress of the Uzbekistan Communist Party, by Comrade I. B. Usmankhodzhayev, First Secretary of the Uzbekistan Communist Party Central Committee." *Current Digest of the Post-Soviet Press* 38, no. 6 (March 12, 1986).

"2005 Country Report on Human Rights Practices in Uzbekistan." U.S. Department of State. Available online at http://www.state.gov/y/drl/rls/hrrpt/2005/61684.htm.

"2008 the Year of Youth in Uzbekistan." *UzReport.com.* January 31, 2008.

"2009 Human Rights Report: Uzbekistan." U.S. Department of State. March 11, 2010. Available online at http://www.state.gov/g/drl/rls/hrrpt/2009/sca/136096.htm.

United Nations Population Division. "World Population Prospects: The 2008 Revision Population Database." Available online at http://esa.un.org/unpp/index.asp.

"United Opposition Announces Meetings in the Kyrgyz Regions." *AKIpress.com.* March 31, 2010.

United States Agency for International Development (USAID). "USAID FY 1999 Congressional Presentation: Kyrgyzstan." Available online at http://www.usaid.gov/pubs/cp99/eni/kg.htm.

Urumbaev, Makhmadzhan. "Svyatye otsi v setyax politikov?" *Vecherniy Bishkek.* February 15, 2005.

"USA's Rumsfeld Thanks Uzbekistan for 'Stalwart Support' in War on Terror." *BBC Monitoring International Reports.* February 24, 2004.

U.S. Department of State, Bureau of Democracy, Human Rights, and Labor. "2009 Human Rights

Report: Kazakhstan." *2009 Country Reports on Human Rights Practices.* March 11, 2010. Available online at http://www.state.gov/g/drl/rls/hrrpt/2009/sca/136088.htm.

U.S. Department of State, Bureau of European and Eurasian Affairs. *U.S. Assistance to Uzbekistan—Fiscal Year 2002.* Washington, D.C.: U.S. Department of State, 2002.

U.S. Department of State, Bureau of South and Central Asian Affairs. "Background Note: Kazakhstan." U.S. Department of State. April 20, 2009.

U.S. General Accounting Office (GAO). *Central and Southwest Asian Countries: Trends in U.S. Assistance and Key Economic, Governance, and Demographic Characteristics.* Washington, D.C.: GAO, 2003.

"Uzbek Body Mulls Prevention of Religious Extremism among Minors." *Turkiston.* December 23, 2006.

"Uzbek Chief Prosecutor Points to Corruption Crack-Down." *Narodnoe slovo.* April 22, 2005.

"Uzbek Human Rights Defender Sentenced." Associated Press Online. May 8, 2007.

"Uzbek Leader Arrives in China, a Rare Supporter amid International Criticism of Crackdown." Associated Press. May 25, 2005.

"Uzbek Leader Sacks Regional, District Governors." Uzbek Television First Channel. December 16, 2008.

"Uzbek Leader Warns of Perils of Mismanagement." Uzbek Television First Channel. October 16, 2004.

"Uzbek President Reportedly Orders Arrest of Muslim Opposition Leaders." *Nezavisimaya gazeta.* March 21, 1992.

"Uzbek President's Address Dedicated to 15th Anniversary of Constitution." *UzReport.com.* December 11, 2007.

"Uzbek President's Daughter Sings in Patriotic Chorus." *BBC Monitoring of International Reports.*

"Uzbek Youth Movement Leader Says Its Ranks Increasing." *BBC Monitoring Central Asia Unit, BBC Worldwide Monitoring.* February 2, 2006.

"Uzbekistan, China Establish U.S. $600 Mln JV to Produce Oil." *Asia Pulse.* June 3, 2005.

"Uzbekistan Founds Military Sports Camp for Difficult Children." *Narodnoe slovo.* July 24, 2003.

"Uzbekistan Possibly on Way to 'Velvet Revolution'—Exiled Opposition Leader." *AFX News.* May 17, 2005.

"Uzbekistan: Sting Stung amid Media Swarm." *Eurasianet.org.* February 24, 2010.

"Uzbekistan: Thousands Protest Trade Restrictions at Uzbek Market." *Radio Free Europe / Radio Liberty.* November 2, 2004.

"Uzbeks to Have Longer Weekend to Mark Id al-Adha." *UzReport.com.* December 2, 2008.

Valovoii, Dmitri Vasil'evich. *Kremlevski Tupik i Nazarbaev: Ocherki-Razmyshlenia.* Moscow: Molodaia gvardia, 1993.

"Verkhovnyy sud Kyrgyzsta naostavil v sile reshenie Oshskogo oblastnogo suda po delu ob ubiystve zhurnalista Alishera Saipova." *24.kg* (Bishkek). December 9, 2009.

"Visit to Uzbekistan of Exiled Mufti." *Eurasianet.org.* January 2000.

Way, Lucan. "Kuchma's Failed Authoritarianism." *Journal of Democracy* 16, no. 2 (April 2005): 131–45.

"'We Are the Children of Independent Country' Forum Inaugurated in Tashkent." *UzReport.com.* April 27, 2007.

Wedeen, Lisa. "Conceptualizing Culture: Possibilities for Political Science." *American Political Science Review* 96, no. 4 (December 2002): 713–28.

Williams, Lawrence. "Global Gold in Deal with Kazakh Investment Group over Jerooy." *Mineweb.* August 21, 2007. Available online at http://www.mineweb.com/mineweb/view/mineweb/en/page34?oid=25741&sn=Detail.

World Bank. "Kazakhstan Country Brief 2010." World Bank, April 2010. Available online at http://www.worldbank.org.kz.

Yermachenko, I. "Economic Barometer: Dangerous Game over the Oil Wells." *Izvestia.* February 12, 1986.

Yevlashkov, Dmitriy. "Head of Kyrgyz Interim Government Details Plans for Future." *Rossiyskaya gazeta.* April 23, 2010.

"Young Andijon Athletes Compete to Condemn Terror." *Huquq* (Uzbek newspaper). June 28, 2006.
"Young Painter's Expo Devoted to World Children's Day Launched in Andijan." *UzReport.com.* May 17, 2007.
"Young Uzbeks Skate against Drugs." *Ishonch* (Uzbek newspaper). September 23, 2003.
Youngs, Richard. "What Has Europe Been Doing?" *Journal of Democracy* 19, no. 2 (April 2008): 160–69.
"Youth of Uzbekistan Interested in Cooperation with Azerbaijan Coevals." *Times of Central Asia.* July 21, 2005.
Zaks, Dmitry. "Karimov Wins Re-election in Farcical Vote." Agence France Presse. January 9, 2010.
"Zeromax GmbH." May 17, 2010. (Website is now defunct.)
"Zhantoro Satybaldiev: Reshenie o svoei otstavke eto muzhestvennyi postupok poriadochnogo pravitel'stva Kyrgyzstana." *24.kg.* December 12, 2006.
Zheng, Yongnian, and Guoguang Wu. "Information Technology, Public Space, and Collective Action in China." *Comparative Political Studies* 38, no. 5 (June 2005): 507–36.

Index

Aalam Services, 98
Abdildin, Serikbolsyn, 149, 150
Abdrahmanov, Omurbek, 102
Abdrakhmanov, Yusup, 180n44
Abdrisiaev, Baktybek, 91
Ablyazov, Mukhtar, 150, 151, 195n19
ABN Amro, 101
Adolat (Justice) party, 76, 120, 128
Afanov, Ivan I., 61
Afghanistan, 5, 12, 33
airplane analogy, 10–11, 15–16, 19–22, 166.
    See also selectorate model
Aitmatov, Chingiz, 78, 91
Aitmuratov, Yerezhap, 63
Ak Terek, Kyrgyzstan, 106
Akaev, Aidar, 97–98
Akaev, Askar, x, 2, 7, 10, 12, 15, 20–21, 42, 45,
    78, 80–105, 109–10, 113, 166–67, 169
Akaeva, Bermet, 21
Akiner, Shirin, 123
Akmatbaev, Ryspek, 110
Akmatbaev, T., 91
Akun, Tursunbek, 23, 106
Akylbekova, Roza, 154
Alakbarov, Gurban, 30
Alash Orda, 53, 57
Alga Bakiev, 104–5
Alga Kyrgyzstan, 104

Aliev, Rakhat, 150, 158–59, 164; *Godfather-in-Law*, 3
Alma-Ata, Kazakhstan, 50, 67–69
Amanbaev, Dzhmgalbek, 78
American University of Central Asia, 12
Andijan, Uzbekistan, 125
Andijan protests, 3, 5, 15, 34, 56, 121–23,
    141–43
Andropov, Yuri, 64
Arabaev, Ishenali, 180n44
Ar-Namys party, 23, 99
Asaba party, 23
Assad, Hafez al-, 145
Asanaliev, G., 91
Ashirkulov, Misir, 99
Asian Development Bank, 93
Aslund, Anders, 186n29
assassinations. *See* murders and assaults
Ata Meken party, 23
Ata Zhurt (Homeland), 99
Atambaev, Almazbek, 33, 105, 107
authoritarianism, 17–47; clan identities and,
    41–44; economic resources and, 29–31,
    59–60; ethnic identities and, 40–41; lack
    of study of, 18; and leadership succession,
    39, 43, 158–64; model for understanding,
    19–29, 38–47, 51, 78–79, 135; and political
    opposition, 33; regional identities and,